# ALTERNATIVE, COUNTRY, HIP-HOP RAP, AND MORE

## MUSIC FROM THE 1980s TO TODAY

# POPULAR MUSIC
## THROUGH THE DECADES

# ALTERNATIVE, COUNTRY, HIP-HOP, RAP, AND MORE

## MUSIC FROM THE 1980s TO TODAY

### EDITED BY MICHAEL RAY

Britannica
Educational Publishing

IN ASSOCIATION WITH

ROSEN
EDUCATIONAL SERVICES

Published in 2013 by Britannica Educational Publishing
(a trademark of Encyclopædia Britannica, Inc.) in association with Rosen Educational Services, LLC

29 East 21st Street, New York, NY 10010.

Distributed exclusively by Rosen Educational Services.
For a listing of additional Britannica Educational Publishing titles, call toll free (800) 237-9932.

First Edition

Britannica Educational Publishing
J.E. Luebering: Senior Manager
Adam Augustyn: Assistant Manager
Marilyn L. Barton: Senior Coordinator, Production Control
Steven Bosco: Director, Editorial Technologies
Lisa S. Braucher: Senior Producer and Data Editor
Yvette Charboneau: Senior Copy Editor
Kathy Nakamura: Manager, Media Acquisition
Michael Ray: Assistant Editor, Geography and Popular Culture

Rosen Educational Services
Hope Lourie Killcoyne: Executive Editor
Nelson Sá: Art Director
Cindy Reiman: Photography Manager
Karen Huang: Photo Researcher
Brian Garvey: Designer, Cover Design
Introduction by Michael Ray

**Library of Congress Cataloging-in-Publication Data**

Alternative, country, hip-hop, rap, and more: music from the 1980s to today/edited by Michael Ray.
    p. cm.—(Popular music through the decades)
"In association with Britannica Educational Publishing, Rosen Educational Services."
Includes bibliographical references and index.
ISBN 978-1-61530-909-2 (library binding)
1. Popular music—1981-1990—History and criticism. 2. Popular music—1991–2000—History and criticism. 3. Popular music—2001–2010—History and criticism. I. Ray, Michael (Michael J.), 1973–
ML3470.A27 2013
781.640973'09048—dc23

                                                                                                    2012034012

*Manufactured in the United States of America*

**On the cover, p. iii:** American rapper and entrepreneur Jay-Z performing in New York City, November 9, 2011. *Michael Stewart/ Getty Images*

Pages 1, 31, 46, 76, 116, 137, 153, 174, 189, 205, 216, 229, 254, 274 Ethan Miller/Getty Images (Fender Stratocaster guitar), © iStockphoto.com/catrinka81 (treble clef graphic); interior background image © iStockphoto.com/hepatus; back cover © iStockphoto.com/Vladimir Jajin

# CONTENTS

59

83

96

## Chapter 5: Hip-Hop in the 21st Century 116

## Chapter 6: Club Sounds: Trip-Hop, House, Industrial, and Techno 137

## Chapter 7: Dance Pop 153

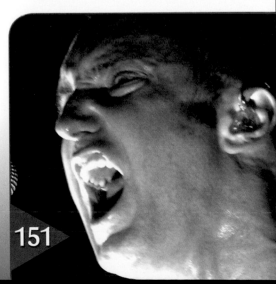

158

170

176

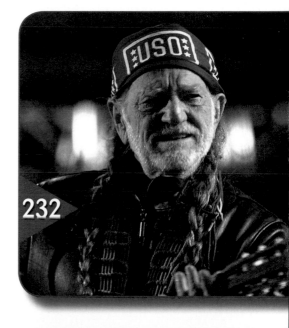

266

273

294

# Introduction

"And I am a Material Girl." Channeling her inner Marilyn Monroe, Madonna laid claim to that title in one of the most memorable videos of the 1980s. Indeed, over the span of her three-decade career, the singer has demonstrated a remarkable command of the visual aspect of rock. Her music videos are consistently arresting and often provocative, and her concert tours—featuring names such as "Blond Ambition" and "Girlie Show"— are high-energy, multimedia affairs. Given the influence that Madonna has asserted on global popular culture, it can be difficult to remember that "Material Girl" was the lead track on what was just her second album. But that album, which also produced the single "Like a Virgin," essentially established the Madonna brand, paving the way for her unparalleled stature in music. Lest there be any doubt about her intention to become one of the most powerful women in the entertainment industry, Madonna made her plans quite clear on *American Bandstand* in 1984. When host Dick Clark asked, "What are your dreams? What's left?" Madonna's response was, "To rule the world."

"Dearly beloved, we are gathered here today to get through this thing called life." And if we amass a truly impressive collection of names while we're at it, so much the better. Prince Rogers Nelson established himself as a music industry giant before spending the latter half of his career engaging in experimentation that met with varying degrees of popular and critical success. Like Madonna, his purple majesty recognized the power of imagery, appearing at the Brit Awards in 1995 with the word "slave" written on his face to protest an ongoing feud with his label, Warner Brothers. Once that relationship was severed, the artist formerly known as the Artist Formerly Known as Prince began exploring novel distribution methods for his material, but unlike a number of his contemporaries, he rejected the online model, stating that the Internet was "completely over."

"Miss Jackson if you're nasty." Almost two decades before her Super Bowl appearance added the phrase "wardrobe malfunction" to the popular lexicon, Janet Jackson was just beginning to emerge from the shadow of her elder siblings. With the assistance of former Prince associates Jimmy Jam and Terry Lewis, Jackson crafted a body of infectious dance hits that dominated radio and MTV playlists throughout the late 1980s. Her elaborately choreographed videos showcased dance skills that rivaled those of her moonwalking brother, and the confident sensuality that she displayed was a huge departure for those who knew her best as Penny on *Good Times*. In 1995 Michael and Janet Jackson recorded "Scream," a song that still holds the title of most expensive video ever made, at a time when Janet's pop cachet had arguably superceded her brother's. Michael's death in 2009 had a rehabilitative effect on his musical career, but by that time Janet had increasingly turned her attention to acting.

"I will follow." These are the first words heard on the opening track of *Boy*, U2's 1980 debut album. The irony is that the band proceeded to spend the remainder of its career breaking that promise. U2 routinely reinvented its sound, drawing on disparate influences to remain innovative without alienating its core audience, daring to depart from the script of what "the world's biggest band" is expected to do. Even that title was one that came in an unlikely way, with an abbreviated set that found them sandwiched between Bryan Adams and the Beach Boys in the Live Aid 1985 lineup. Originally scheduled to close with "Pride (In the Name of Love)," their biggest song at that point, the group instead played a 12-minute extended version of "Bad," a lesser-known album track that was never released as a single. Halfway through the song, lead singer Bono jumped from the stage to pull a young woman from the crowd (she later claimed that she was being crushed, and that Bono had saved her life) and his bandmates continued to play. Folk legend Joan Baez, who had opened the Philadelphia Live Aid concert hours earlier, described the scene that followed:

> She lands on her feet and is in his arms, and he dances with her. She is probably stage-struck and in shock, and her head is sweetly bent down, and for the next few seconds he is cradling her as they dance. I can't recall ever having seen anything like it in my life. It is an act, but it is not an act. It is a private moment, accepted by seventy thousand people. The dance is short, sensuous, and heartbreakingly tender.

The band initially thought that the set had been a bust, that they had missed an enormous opportunity in front of a global audience. Instead, the connection that Bono made

with that fan—with all the fans at Wembley that day—was felt around the world. U2's Live Aid set is now discussed with reverence as one of the most important moments in the history of rock.

"That's great, it starts with an earthquake…" The rumble that signaled college rock's emergence into the mainstream was centered on Athens, Georgia. Invoking the Beat spirit of Bob Dylan's classic "Subterranean Homesick Blues," R.E.M.'s "It's the End of the World as We Know It (and I Feel Fine)" was far from the group's most successful single. It did, however, capture much of the essence of the band—equal parts catchy and obscure, poppy and intellectual. Their blend of folk, punk, and classic guitar rock skirted the fringes of the new wave sound; by the time alternative rock exploded in the early 1990s, R.E.M. were regarded as the elder statesmen of the movement.

"We'll wade in the shine of the ever." One could argue that there is no such thing as a "typical" Pixies lyric. Ensconced between Kim Deal's melodic backing vocals and the sonic assault of Joey Santiago's guitar, lead singer Black Francis spun tales

*Madonna at the 1985 American Music Awards, several months after the release of her smash single, "Like a Virgin."* Julian Wasser/Getty Images

of mermaids, monkeys, and motorways as one of rock's most distinctive lyricists. Releasing four albums in rapid succession, the group amassed a worshipful following among college rock literati. However, the Pixies disbanded just as alternative rock—a genre for which they helped build the foundation—was breaking into the mainstream. Although the individual members achieved varying degrees of success with subsequent projects—Black Francis soloing it as Frank Black—the band's artistic legacy would continue to inspire long after the Pixies' demise.

"Here we are now, entertain us." Generation X found its voice when Kurt Cobain growled the now legendary chorus in the genre-defining "Smells Like Teen Spirit." Stripped of context, Cobain's lyric reeks of entitlement, but the jaded, ironic narrator of the song presents the request more as a dare than a demand. "Smells Like Teen Spirit" was an unlikely anthem; Cobain admitted to writing it in the style of the Pixies, and it does loosely follow the model of sometimes-nonsensical lyrics punctuated by a ferociously driving guitar. But few would confuse Nirvana's emerging grunge sound with the wall-of-sound, reimagined surf rock of the Pixies. While the latter soared to surreal heights, the former plumbed the angst-filled reaches of punk's darkest depths. Even the structure of the band was a rejection of the pop metal excesses that pervaded the airwaves in the late 1980s. Nirvana was a classic three-piece outfit—drums, guitar, and bass. Grunge's do-it-yourself ethic was apparent even in the group's appearance. The utilitarian flannel-and-jeans combination would spark a global fashion craze, and Cobain, reluctantly finding himself to be the spokesperson for a generation, rebelled against the rebellion that he had sparked. He entered a self-destructive spiral of drug abuse and took his own life, perceived by many to be a victim of his own success.

"But it's like that, and that's the way it is." As grunge resonated with the white, middle-class heirs to the baby boomer generation, Run-D.M.C. had long been documenting life on the streets of their native Queens. As the first rap act to reach a mainstream audience, the trio did much to inform the look and attitude of hip-hop culture in the decades to come. In some ways, Run-D.M.C. exemplified the notion of rap for rap's sake. Provocative without being openly militant, technologically innovative and lyrically adept, they advanced the art of rap and avoided the turf wars that would characterize the later gangsta era. So-called "sucker M.C.s" would find themselves ridiculed in verse, a conflict resolution method that seemed almost quaint when compared with the '90s East

Coast-West Coast feud. Thus, it was especially sad when Jam Master Jay, the group's turntablist, was killed in a shooting in a New York studio.

"And I got mad hits like I was Rod Carew." Although their race was initially something of a novelty, the Beastie Boys were not the only white rappers. Nor were they the only rappers to dig deep into the recesses of popular culture to uncover truly inspired rhymes (A Tribe Called Quest's "Scenario" is a virtual clinic in that particular endeavor). But the combination of those two factors, along with a host of other intangibles, allowed for the transformation of MCA, Ad-Rock, and Mike D from party rock pranksters into some of the most critically acclaimed and commercially successful artists in hip-hop. Their inspired use of samples earned them respect among their peers, and their fiercely creative videos won them wide exposure on MTV.

"Cause when you diss Dre, you diss yourself." In the world of rap, disrespect is not given. It is earned. And in the expletive-laden "Dre Day," Dr. Dre and Snoop Dogg (who later re-named himself Snoop Lion) unleash a truly dazzling litany of disrespect against Dre's former N.W.A. bandmate Eazy-E. The dispute began during the disintegration of N.W.A., when Dre's new management was trying to secure his release from his previous recording contract. Threats were made and bad blood festered between the entourages of both performers. Although this particular dispute did not result in a body count, it heralded violence to come.

"I wish I was special." The further one travels from a point of evolutionary origin, the more difficult it is to predict what characteristics might arise along that path. When one begins with "Creep," a straightforward modern rock song that is distinguished by the vocal power of singer Thom Yorke and a level of self-loathing that is unusual for the pop charts, it is nearly impossible to anticipate the virtuosity of *OK Computer* and later works. In a sea of British acts clamoring for late '90s success, Radiohead transcended its peers with wildly original work that incorporated elements of art rock and electronic music. Sometimes, wishes do come true.

"I hurt myself today, to see if I still feel." Trent Reznor penned those lines for *The Downward Spiral*, the second album from his musical namesake, Nine Inch Nails. The ballad "Hurt" was a departure from the industrial dance sound that typified his prior album, but the meditation on addiction and regret was a surprise radio hit. Even more surprising was its later interpretation by country music icon Johnny Cash. First exposed to the song by longtime collaborator Rick Rubin, Cash declared that "Hurt" was one of the most effective anti-drug abuse messages that he had ever heard. Cash covered the song as an acoustic track, and the result was a poignant meditation on mortality. The reverential treatment of his work by an artist of Cash's status deeply affected Reznor, and he cited the event as a turning point in both his personal life and his musical career.

"I'm not ready to make nice, I'm not ready to back down." As the line between modern country and pop became increasingly blurry, success in the latter genre was sometimes interpreted as a rejection of the former. The Dixie Chicks, however, did not turn their backs on country; in a very real way, country turned its back on them. After lead singer Natalie Maines made a statement that was critical of then-U.S. President George W. Bush, country stations exiled the group from their playlists, and many would not even accept paid advertising from the band. When a hastily crafted apology failed to shift the prevailing mood, the Dixie Chicks chose to play the hand that they had dealt themselves. They appeared in the documentary *Shut Up and Sing*, which examined the fallout that resulted from Maines's comment, and their later releases embraced a decidedly adult contemporary rock sound, trading fiddle and banjo for electric guitar.

"Screams from the haters got a nice ring to it, I guess every superhero need his theme music." In a Freudian interpretation of hip-hop, Kanye West would function as the genre's unfiltered id. From his public denunciation of George W. Bush's response to Hurricane Katrina to his memorable stage-rush at the MTV Video Music Awards, impulsivity seems to be simply an element of Kanye being Kanye. The immediacy of the social network Twitter gave West an outlet like no other, and his feed, which became the subject of both study and parody, covered a dizzying array of seemingly disconnected topics: ninjas, his dinner, the status of his antique fish tank, the nature of celebrity, and the Illuminati. But Kanye seemed to gain strength from his detractors, and that "theme music" propelled him to the top of the 21st century hip-hop scene.

"Love, love, love, I want your love." Infectious dance pop might not seem to be the most obvious outlet for an aspiring performance artist, but Stefani Joanne Angelina Germanotta is not exactly a slave to convention. Styling herself as Lada Gaga, she paired high-energy dance music with over-the-top fashion, unbridled sexuality, and elaborate choreography in a manner that drew numerous comparisons to an earlier "ambitious blonde." And like Madonna, Lady Gaga understood the role of the music video perhaps better than any performer of her generation; she virtually rebooted the medium for the YouTube era. Madonna's stated goal was to rule the world, and if there is a Queen of Pop, she is surely it. But in this case, where there is a Queen, there will always be a Lady in waiting.

"We're gonna rock, rock, rock, 'til broad daylight…" By the 21st century, rock was more than a half century removed from its country and rhythm-and-blues roots. Technical innovations such as the solid-body electric guitar, the synthesizer, and digital recording software had revolutionized rock both as an art form and as an industry. Each generation had rebelled against the one that came before it, while often recapitulating the sounds of generations that were earlier still. Trip-hop evoked the cool atmosphere of 1940s lounge music. Alternative was punk with better marketing. Hip-hop DJs directly sampled cuts from their funk forebears. Singer-songwriters put down their guitars in favor of two turntables and a microphone. Increasingly, artists defied easy "genrefication," and the definition of rock was more fluid than ever. From Bjork to Britney, from Bono to Bieber, performers of all stripes were eager to rock around the clock again.

Nothing makes a memory come alive like a song, and nothing makes that song more memorable than learning the story behind it. *Alternative, Country, Hip-Hop, Rap, and More: Music from the 1980s to Today* profiles the seminal groups and artists of the late 20th and early 21st century, offering deep and detailed profiles of the musicians who keep us humming.

# CHAPTER 1

# Video Killed the Radio Star: The Globalization of Rock

The post-punk regeneration of the DIY (do-it-yourself) attitude in rock paralleled the development of new means of global music marketing. The 1985 Live Aid event, in which live television broadcasts of charity concerts taking place on both sides of the Atlantic were shown worldwide, not only put on public display the rock establishment and its variety of sounds but also made clear television's potential as a marketing tool. MTV, the American cable company that had adopted the Top 40 radio format and made video clips as vital a promotional tool as singles, looked to satellite technology to spread its message: "One world, one music." And the most successful acts of the 1980s, Madonna and Michael Jackson (the latter of whose 1982 album, *Thriller*, became the best-selling album of all time by crossing rock's internal divides), were the first video acts, using MTV brilliantly to sell themselves as stars while being used, in turn, as global icons in the advertising strategies of companies such as Pepsi-Cola.

# MADONNA

Madonna (born Madonna Louise Ciccone, August 16, 1958, Bay City, Michigan, U.S.) achieved levels of power and control unprecedented for a woman in the entertainment industry. Born into a large Italian American family, she studied dance at the University of Michigan and with the Alvin Ailey American Dance Theater in New York City in the late 1970s before relocating briefly to Paris as a member of Patrick Hernandez's disco revue. Returning to New York City, she performed with a number of rock groups before signing with Sire Records. Her first hit, "Holiday" (1983), provided the blueprint for her later material—an upbeat dance-club sound with sharp production and an immediate appeal. Madonna's melodic pop incorporated catchy choruses and her lyrics concerned love, sex, and relationships—ranging from the breezy innocence of "True Blue" (1986) to the erotic fantasies of "Justify My Love" (1990) to the spirituality of later songs such as "Ray of Light" (1998). Criticized by some as being limited in range, her sweet, girlish voice nonetheless was well-suited to pop music.

Madonna was the first female artist to exploit fully the potential of the music video. She collaborated with top designers (Jean-Paul Gaultier), photographers (Steven Meisel and Herb Ritts), and directors (Mary Lambert and David Fincher), drawing inspiration from underground club culture or the avant-garde to create distinctive sexual and satirical images—from the knowing ingenue of "Like a Virgin" (1984) to the controversial red-dressed "sinner" who kisses a black saint in "Like a Prayer" (1989). By 1991 she had scored 21 Top Ten hits in the United States and sold some 70 million albums internationally, generating $1.2 billion in sales. Committed to controlling her image and career herself, Madonna became the head of Maverick, a subsidiary of Time-Warner created by the entertainment giant as part of a $60 million deal with the performer. Her success signaled a clear message of financial control to other women in the industry, but in terms of image she was a more ambivalent role model.

In 1992 Madonna took her role as a sexual siren to its full extent when she published *Sex*, a soft-core pornographic coffee-table book featuring her in a variety of "erotic" poses. She was criticized for being exploitative and overcalculating, and writer Norman Mailer said she had become "secretary to herself." Soon afterward Madonna temporarily withdrew from pop music to concentrate on a film career that had begun with a strong performance in *Desperately Seeking Susan* (1985), faltered with the flimsy *Shanghai Surprise* (1986)

Madonna performing in her last show of the "Sticky & Sweet" tour, Tel Aviv–Yafo, Sept. 2, 2009. Frank Micelotta—Live Nation/PRNewsFoto/AP Images

and *Dick Tracy* (1990), and recovered with *Truth or Dare* (1991, also known as *In Bed with Madonna*), a documentary of one of her tours. She scored massive success in 1996 with the starring role in the film musical *Evita*. That year she also gave birth to a daughter.

In 1998 Madonna released her first album of new material in four years, *Ray of Light*. A fusion of techno music and self-conscious lyrics, it was a commercial and critical success, earning the singer her first musical Grammy Awards (her previous win had been for a video).

# ROCK AND ROLL HALL OF FAME AND MUSEUM

In 1983 a group of leading figures in the music industry—including Atlantic Records cofounder Ahmet Ertegun and Jann Wenner, the publisher of *Rolling Stone* magazine—established the nonprofit Rock and Roll Hall of Fame Foundation. It was responsible for the creation of the museum and hall of fame, which began inducting honorees in 1986. After considering the bids of other American cities that had been pivotal to rock history (including New Orleans, Memphis, Chicago, San Francisco, and New York City), the foundation located the museum in Cleveland, where disc jockey Alan Freed had coined the term "rock and roll" in the 1950s and which had put together a package of public and private funding to aid in the facility's development.

Architect I.M. Pei designed the museum's 150,000-square-foot (14,000-square-metre) glass-dominated building, an angular assemblage of geometric forms set on the shore of Lake Erie. It opened to the public in 1995. In addition to the Hall of Fame, the facility includes a wide variety of frequently changing "permanent" exhibits that draw on the museum's extensive holdings of artifacts to examine rock music, its origins, and its influence through the prisms of genre, geography, fashion, and biography, as well as social, cultural, and political history. Typical artifacts include instruments used by famous musicians, stage clothing and props, drafts of song lyrics, correspondence, original album art, handbills, posters, and photographs. Many of the exhibits are highly interactive, and the sound of music is omnipresent. The museum also mounts major temporary exhibits, has a large research library and archives, offers educational outreach, and conducts conferences and symposia. Annex NYC, a branch of the museum that focused on New York City's contributions to rock culture, opened in Manhattan in November 2008 but closed a little more than a year later, when its financial viability was undermined by the struggling U.S. economy of the time.

Musicians become eligible for induction into the hall of fame 25 years after the release of their first recording. The foundation's nominating committee, made up of rock historians, selects nominees each year in the performer category, who are then voted upon by an international body of some 500 rock experts. Those nominees with the highest vote total (and more than 50 percent of the total vote) are inducted, five to seven performers being chosen each year. There is often tension between commercial success and reverence by critics in the selection process. Moreover, the committee has been criticized by some for its alleged music industry establishment bias. In addition to performers, categories of inductees include those who were early influences on rock, sidemen (supporting musicians), and nonperformers (e.g., producers, entrepreneurs, journalists, disc jockeys). The annual induction ceremony, held in New York City and featuring performances by inductees and prominent guests, culminates in an all-star jam session.

In 2009 the Rock and Roll Hall of Fame and Museum's 25th anniversary was celebrated with a two-day concert event in New York that featured some of rock's biggest names.

Rock and Roll Hall of Fame inductees are listed in the table in the Appendix.

Her experimentation in electronica continued with *Music* (2000). In 2005 she returned to her roots with *Confessions on a Dance Floor*. Despite a marriage in the 1980s to actor Sean Penn and another to English director Guy Ritchie (married 2000; divorced 2008), with whom she had a son, Madonna remained resolutely independent. (She also adopted a boy and a girl from Malawi.) That independent streak, however, did not prevent her from enlisting the biggest names in music to assist on specific projects. This fact was clear on *Hard Candy* (2008), a hip-hop infused effort with writing and vocal and production work by Justin Timberlake,

Timbaland, and Pharrell Williams of the hit-making duo the Neptunes. Just weeks after the release of *Hard Candy*, Madonna was inducted into the Rock and Roll Hall of Fame. With *MDNA* (2012), which featured cameos from women rappers M.I.A. and Nicki Minaj, Madonna continued to prove herself a shrewd assimilator of cutting-edge musical styles.

In addition to acting in movies—she also starred in the romantic comedy *The Next Best Thing* (2000) and in Ritchie's *Swept Away* (2002)—Madonna pursued work behind the camera. She cowrote and directed *Filth and Wisdom* (2008), a comedy about a trio of mismatched flatmates in London, as well as the drama *W.E.* (2011), which juxtaposed the historical romance between Wallis Simpson and King Edward VIII with the fictional story of a woman in the 1990s researching Simpson's life.

## PRINCE

Known variously as Prince, the Artist Formerly Known as Prince, and the Artist, this revolutionary performer began his life as Prince Rogers Nelson (born June 7, 1958, Minneapolis, Minnesota, U.S.). Like Stevie Wonder, he was a rare composer who could perform at a professional level on virtually all the instruments he required, and a considerable number of his recordings feature him in all the performing roles. Prince's recording career began with funk and soul marketed to a black audience; his early music also reflected the contemporary musical impact of disco. Later records incorporated a vast array of influences, including jazz, punk, heavy metal, the Beatles, and hip-hop, usually within an overall approach most informed by funky up-tempo styles and soulful ballads; the latter often featured his expressive falsetto singing.

Taking an early interest in music, Prince began playing the piano at age 7 and had mastered the guitar and drums by the time he joined his first band at age 14. With very few African American residents, his hometown, Minneapolis, was an unlikely site for the development of a major black star, but Prince even managed to lead other local musicians, most notably Jimmy Jam and Terry Lewis, to major success.

Mirrored by correspondingly intense music, Prince's lyrics often address sexuality and desire with frankness and imagination. Much of his work, in its lyrics and imagery, struggles with the constriction of social conventions and categories. As one of his biographers put it, "The whole thrust of Prince's art can be understood in terms of a desire to escape the social identities thrust upon him by simple virtue of his being small, black, and male."

Prince explored typographical oddities in his song titles and lyrics as another way of evading convention. In 1993 he announced that he had changed his name to a combination of the male and female gender signs.

There is also a strong religious impulse in some of his music, sometimes fused into a kind of sacred erotic experience that has roots in African American churches.

"Little Red Corvette" (1983) was Prince's first big crossover hit, gaining airplay on MTV at a time when virtually no black artists appeared on the influential new medium. *Purple Rain* (1984) made him one of the major stars of the 1980s and remains his biggest-selling album. Three of its singles were hits: the frenetic "Let's Go Crazy," the androgynous but vulnerable "When Doves Cry," and the anthemic title cut. Thereafter, he continued to produce inventive music of broad appeal; outside the United States he was particularly popular in Britain and the rest of Europe.

Throughout most of his career, Prince's prolific inventiveness as a songwriter clashed with his record company's policy of releasing only a single album each year. As a backlog of his completed but unreleased recordings piled up, he gave songs to other performers—some of whom recorded at and for Paisley Park, the studio and label he established in suburban Minneapolis—and even organized

Gender-blending symbol used by Prince in 1993. As there was no agreed-upon name or pronunciation for the symbol, many people took to calling him "the Artist Formerly Known as Prince."

ostensibly independent groups, such as the Time, to record his material. His 1996 album *Emancipation* celebrated the forthcoming end of his Warner Brothers contract, which enabled him to release as much music as he liked on his NPG label. Later he explored marketing his work on the Internet and through private

*Prince.* PRNewsFoto/42 West/AP Images

# ROCK IN THE TWIN CITIES

Buried by snow in winter, Minneapolis, the northernmost major city on the Mississippi River, is a long way from the fountainhead of modern popular music, the Mississippi delta—some 800 miles as the crow flies, a little farther if one takes Highway 61 or Ol' Man River itself. Yet some of the most significant early blues songs were recorded by Paramount, in neighbouring Wisconsin. Moreover, Bob Dylan wrote his early songs and dreamed of becoming a pop star during a short stint as a student at the University of Minnesota in Minneapolis.

It was not until the early 1980s, however, that Minneapolis emerged as a significant player in pop music. The city's first hit, "Funkytown" (1980), by Lipps Inc. on Casablanca Records, was one of disco's last high moments. It also was a kind of blueprint for musical success in Minneapolis in the 1980s: pop dance music electronically created by a one-man band (Steven Greenberg in this case). Prince would make much more of the approach.

Although Prince had moved to New York City in 1976, signed to Warner Brothers in 1978, and established his revolutionary working practices by 1980, it was not until his heyday in the mid-1980s that his impact was fully felt. Many of Prince's riffs and rhythms drew from funk's rich history—notably from James Brown and George Clinton—but what was entirely novel was the way he made his music alone in the studio, a development made possible by the rapid development of the microprocessor. While Europeans working in the same manner chose to emphasize the mechanical nature of computer-generated music, Prince grabbed the opportunity it offered for control. A formidable guitarist, he sometimes used a backing group, but his music was always essentially a solo creation, entirely envisaged and produced by Prince.

Removing himself from established industry centres, he opened his own studio in suburban Minneapolis in 1982 and by 1987 had his own label and recording complex, both named Paisley Park—as advertised in his 1985 single of the same name. From this isolated base, he helped rejuvenate pop music not only with his own records but also with songs and productions of other artists, particularly female singers such as Chaka Khan, Cyndi Lauper, and Sheena Easton. He also set the stage for the success of his various protégés, including Sheila E., Vanity 6, the Time (from which producers Jimmy Jam and Terry Lewis emerged), and Apollonia 6.

arrangements with retail chains as a means of circumventing the control of large record companies. In 1999, however, he released *Rave Un2 the Joy Fantastic* under the Arista label; a collaboration with Sheryl Crow, Chuck D, Ani DiFranco, and others, the album received mixed reviews and failed to find a large audience.

Prince (who, following the formal termination of his contract with Warner Brothers in 1999, stopped using the symbol as his name) was inducted into the Rock and Roll Hall of Fame in 2004. That year he also released *Musicology*, a comeback album that represented Prince's first appearance in the Billboard Top 10 list in almost a decade. He followed with the similarly well-received *3121* (2006), before experimenting with a novel distribution method for his next

album. In a deal with the *Daily Mail*, a British newspaper, millions of copies of *Planet Earth* (2007) were bundled with the paper's Sunday edition, weeks prior to the album's release in stores. The triple-album *LotusFlow3r* (2009), a collection of smooth ballads and guitar-driven retro-funk numbers, devoted an entire disc to the music of Prince protégé Bria Valente. For his 2010 release, the aptly named *20Ten*, Prince once again confounded music retailers by bundling the disc with print publications—namely, the German edition of *Rolling Stone* and the British tabloid *The Mirror*.

## JANET JACKSON

The youngest of nine siblings in Motown's famed Jackson family, Janet Jackson (born May 16, 1966, Gary,

*Janet Jackson and LL Cool J, 2008.* Live Nation/PRNewsFoto/AP Image

Indiana, U.S.) parlayed her family's success into an independent career that spanned recordings, television, and film. She appeared as a regular on the 1970s television comedy series *Good Times* and later as a teenager in the dance-oriented series *Fame*. Following an unremarkable recording debut in 1982 and a 1984 follow-up album, Jackson took control of her

# JAM AND LEWIS

Keyboard player Jimmy Jam (James Harris III) and bassist Terry Lewis played together in local Minneapolis bands while in high school, graduating to Flyte Tyme, which evolved into Prince's backing band, the Time, in 1981. When Jam and Lewis produced the SOS Band's hit "Just Be Good to Me" in 1983, they broke Prince's rule that no member of the Time do outside work, and he fired them. They then set up an alternative Minneapolis production powerhouse, Flyte Tyme studios, where they crafted hits for Force MDs, Patti Austin, and Cheryl Lynn. They also made a star of Alexander O'Neal, updating the romantic crooner formula that served Al Green so well in the 1970s (a smooth, soulful voice; stylish clothes; and sexy stage moves).

But Jam and Lewis made their biggest impact in the mid-1980s, after Janet Jackson came to them fresh from a broken marriage and eager for the kind of success her brother Michael Jackson had found. Recycling tracks that had been created for a former member of Atlantic Starr, Sharon Bryant, but were rejected by her label, Jam and Lewis gave Jackson a steel-hard sound and five Top Five singles that catapulted her to superstardom. The duo continued to collaborate successfully with Jackson after she switched labels from A&M to Virgin, and they also applied their magic touch to other acts, including Britain's Human League.

career, moved out on her own, and developed her own sound and influential style.

She reemerged in 1986 with her breakthrough record *Control*, which featured five singles that topped the rhythm-and-blues charts, including two Top Ten pop hits, "What Have You Done for Me Lately" and "Nasty." Her fierce independence struck a chord with the youth of the day, and Jackson rose to a level of stardom that rivaled that of Michael Jackson, the most famous of her brothers. Her collaborations with the production team of Jimmy Jam and Terry Lewis (based in Minneapolis, Minnesota) produced bold, beat-heavy, catchy songs that defined the punch and power of 1980s dance and pop music. Jackson returned in 1989 with her most diverse work, *Janet Jackson's Rhythm Nation 1814*. The album delivered seven pop Top Ten hit singles, including "Miss You Much," "Escapade," and "Love Will Never Do (Without You)."

Jackson continued to enjoy worldwide popularity and critical acclaim in the 1990s with the albums *janet.* (1993), *Design of a Decade* (1995), and *The Velvet Rope* (1997). Between the release of *All for You* (2001), which continued in the sensual vein of *janet.*, and *Damita Jo* (2004), Jackson was at the centre of a debate on decency standards on television, when a "wardrobe malfunction" (that some argued was accidental and others premeditated) caused a scandal during her live performance at halftime of the 2004 Super Bowl. Her later albums include *20 Y.O.* (2006) and *Discipline* (2008).

In addition to her music career, Jackson continued to act. In 1993 she made her film debut in *Poetic Justice*, which also starred Tupac Shakur. Her later movie credits include *Why Did I Get Married?* (2007) and its sequel, *Why Did I Get Married Too?* (2010), both written and directed by Tyler Perry. She also appeared in *For Colored Girls* (2010), Perry's adaptation of Ntozake Shange's 1975 theatre piece *For Colored Girls Who Have Considered Suicide/When the Rainbow Is Enuf.*

## WE GOT OUR MTV

The groundbreaking cable television network MTV debuted just after midnight on August 1, 1981, with the broadcast of "Video Killed the Radio Star" by the Buggles. Following the format of Top 40 radio, video disc jockeys (or "veejays") introduced videos and bantered about music news between clips. After an initial splash, the network struggled in its early years. The music video reservoir was still somewhat shallow, resulting in frequent repetition of clips, and cable television remained a luxury that had not quite found its market. MTV expanded its programming to include rhythm and blues artists, and the network took off. Singles such as "Billie Jean" and "Beat It" from Michael Jackson's *Thriller* (1982) not only showcased the strengths of the music video format but proved that exposure on MTV could propel artists to superstardom.

The network brought success to such newcomers as Madonna and new wave icons Duran Duran, who

The original MTV "veejays" (from left to right): Nina Blackwood, Mark Goodman (back), Alan Hunter (holding microphone), Martha Quinn, and J.J. Jackson. Mark Weiss/WireImage/Getty Images

used increasingly sophisticated techniques to make the visual elements of the video as important as the music. MTV also gave renewed life to veteran performers such as ZZ Top, Tina Turner, and Peter Gabriel, each of whom scored the biggest hits of their careers thanks to heavy rotation of their videos. By the mid-1980s, MTV had produced a noticeable effect on motion pictures, commercials, and television. It also changed the music industry; looking good (or at least interesting) on MTV became as

important as sounding good when it came to selling recordings.

In 1985 entertainment conglomerate Viacom Inc. purchased MTV Networks, the parent corporation of MTV, from Warner Communications Inc., and the shift in content was both dramatic and immediate. Instead of free-form playlists of music that covered a veejay's entire shift, videos were packaged into discrete blocks based on genre. This gave rise to specialty shows such as *120 Minutes* (alternative rock), *Headbangers Ball* (heavy metal), and *Yo! MTV Raps* (hip-hop). Before long, game shows, reality shows, animated cartoons, and soap operas began to appear in the MTV lineup, and the network shifted its focus from music to youth-oriented pop culture.

By the mid-1990s, the majority of MTV's daily schedule was devoted to programming that was not related to music. Its sister station VH1 had been broadcasting adult-oriented rock videos since 1985, and it soon filled the vacuum, with original content such as *Pop Up Video* and the documentary series *Behind the Music*. MTV Networks launched MTV2 in 1996, with the intention of recapturing the spirit that had led millions in the 1980s to demand, "I want my MTV." MTV2 started with the same free-form structure that characterized early MTV, but it soon shifted to genre-specific programs. By 2005 MTV2 had followed the same course as its parent network, with the bulk of its schedule consisting of reality shows, celebrity coverage, and comedies.

While music had a reduced presence on MTV, videos remained important to the network and its image. Beginning in 1984, MTV honoured achievement in the format with its annual Video Music Awards. *Total Request Live* (*TRL*), an hour-long interview and music video show, debuted in 1998 and anchored the weekday lineup. By the early 21st century, however, MTV increasingly sought to position itself as a destination for music on the Internet. Its Web site offered streaming video and audio content, and in 2007 it launched Rhapsody America, a joint venture with RealNetworks and Verizon Wireless, as a subscription-based alternative to Apple Inc.'s wildly popular iTunes service. Partly because of the popularity of viewing music videos on the Internet, *TRL* was cancelled in 2008.

## MUSIC VIDEO

The evolution of the music video began relatively early in the history of rock. Bands with the clout to swing it—the Beatles, first and foremost—had begun substituting filmed clips for in-person TV appearances in the late 1960s. Bands marginalized by conventional commercial outlets—punks, first and foremost—were among the first to recognize the form's usefulness as both sales pitch and agitprop a decade later. But music videos did not become ubiquitous until the advent of MTV (Music Television) in 1981 made them an all but indispensable adjunct to marketing a song. Their stylistic foundation came from the Beatles, too, via *A Hard Day's Night* and *Help!*—whose director, Richard Lester, freed song on film from even a vague subordination to plot or context, only to substitute silent-movie antics, the new function of which was to celebrate an attitude.

In 1975 the stir created by Queen's clip for "Bohemian Rhapsody" showed how video could augment if not outright define a song's qualities. In the late 1970s key videos by Devo and other new wave artists crystallized the nature of the form. By the MTV era, performance clips had been all but superseded by a conceptual approach that incorporated slick editing and stylistic dramatic situations.

Two of the form's preeminent auteurs peaked in the 1980s: Michael Jackson, who broke ground with "Beat It," "Billie Jean," and "Thriller" (all 1983), and Madonna, responsible in her prime for both one of the most acclaimed videos ever made ("Like a Prayer," 1989) and the most deliberately salacious ("Justify My Love," 1990). Yet in the right imaginative hands, video remained a richly expressive means of establishing (Nirvana's "Smells Like Teen Spirit," 1991), decoding (R.E.M.'s "Losing My Religion," 1991), or simply inventing (Fatboy Silm's "Weapon of Choice," 2001) a song's essential meaning. Good songs still help, of course; while MTV exposure helped sell many a mediocre tune, in the long run music still wins out often enough to seriously qualify if not disprove the gleeful prediction of the first clip

the network ever aired—the Buggles' "Video Killed the Radio Star."

In the 21st century, as the importance of airplay on MTV diminished and as more and more people watched music videos on the Internet (e.g., on YouTube and Myspace) and on the smaller screens of mobile devices (e.g., MP3 players and cellular phones), the approach taken by many music video makers began to change. The visual imagery employed became less complicated and less dense, though not less arresting, and "centre framing," which places images in the middle of the screen, became the norm. Although the occasional standout, such as Lady Gaga's "Bad Romance" (2009), hearkened back to the elaborate dance choreography of the "Thriller" era, bizarre or clever concepts proved crucial for capturing YouTube viewers. OK Go, which first broke into the mainstream with "Here It Goes Again" (2006), a video that translated band members on treadmills into a fluid modern dance, was one of the most successful artists to adopt this approach.

In what was perhaps a sign that the form had achieved critical maturity, music video directors began to acquire a degree of recognition in their own right. French technical wizard Michel Gondry pioneered the use of "bullet time" (a camera technique that became ubiquitous after its use in *The Matrix*), and his videos for the White Stripes, the Chemical Brothers, and Björk were strikingly innovative. Mark Romanek created wildly imagined worlds for Madonna and Nine Inch Nails, but he was perhaps best known for Johnny Cash's "Hurt," a somber reflection on the country legend as he neared the end of his life. Chris Cunningham's work was notable for the grotesque or shocking images that pervaded it, while Spike Jonze trafficked in humour and nostalgia. Both Gondry and Jonze embarked on feature film careers and, perhaps not coincidentally, each scored success with scripts from screenwriter Charlie Kaufman. Jonze helmed *Being John Malkovich* (1999) and *Adaptation* (2002), and Gondry directed and cowrote *Eternal Sunshine of the Spotless Mind* (2004), a film that earned Gondry and Kaufman an Academy Award for best original screenplay.

*Spike Jonze, 2003.* © AP Images

## SPIKE JONZE

American director and producer Spike Jonze (born Adam Spiegel, October 22, 1969, Rockville, Maryland, U.S.) grew up in Maryland and moved to Los Angeles in 1987 upon his graduation from high school. An ardent BMX biker, he soon became an assistant editor and later photographer for the independent biking magazine *Freestylin'*. Jonze was also involved in the alternative skateboarding scene, and his unique videos of skateboarders, most notably *Video Days*, led to his work on music videos.

In 1992 Jonze codirected the music video for "100%," a song by the influential noise band Sonic Youth. The video features footage of skateboarders in Los Angeles cut against clips of the band playing in an unimpressive living room. Jonze's music video for the Beastie Boys' "Sabotage" garnered notice in 1994. The video parodies popular police shows as the band members fight, slide, and needlessly set off explosives while wearing fake hairpieces. Jonze's quirky humour appeared again in the 1994 video for Weezer's "Buddy Holly," which features the band in 1950s attire performing as if in a scene from the American television show *Happy Days*. Jonze earned further accolades for his music video for Fatboy Slim's "Praise You" (1998), in which he portrayed a choreographer who leads a dance routine outside a California movie theatre. The 2001 video for Fatboy Slim's "Weapon of Choice" showcased Jonze's talent for long tracking shots and beautiful visual images with no explanation. It featured actor Christopher Walken tap-dancing in an empty hotel, often defying the laws of physics. In addition to music videos, Jonze also worked as a cinematographer for the short film *Bed, Bath and Beyond* (1996), which was cowritten by Sofia Coppola, whom Jonze married in 1998 (divorced 2003).

After directing the documentary short *Amarillo by Morning* (1998), Jonze helmed his first feature film, *Being John Malkovich* (1999). The surreal comedy, which was written by Charlie Kaufman, chronicles the series of bizarre events that occur after a puppeteer (played by John Cusack) discovers a portal into the mind of actor John Malkovich. The film was critically acclaimed and earned Jonze an Academy Award nomination for best director. In 1999 he also starred in his first major film role, portraying a U.S. soldier during the Persian Gulf War in *The Three Kings*.

Jonze next earned notice as the creator and executive producer of the television show *Jackass* (2000–02) and the subsequent films *Jackass: The Movie* (2002) and *Jackass: Number Two* (2006). The series consists of short videos of people, including skateboarder and cocreator Johnny Knoxville, performing dangerous stunts and unpleasant feats and often injuring themselves. While a huge commercial success, *Jackass* sparked controversy and criticism for its lack of taste and its potential encouragement of destructive action, especially among teenage boys.

In 2002 Jonze directed his second feature film, *Adaptation*, which was also written by Kaufman. The acclaimed dramedy centres on a screenwriter named Charlie Kaufman (Nicolas Cage) who has difficulty adapting a book about orchids into a movie. A parallel story line follows the book's author (Meryl Streep) and the orchid thief (Chris Cooper) she is profiling. Jonze's next movie, *Where the Wild Things Are* (2009), was an adaptation of Maurice Sendak's classic children's book.

## U2

By the end of the 1980s U2 had established itself not only as one of the world's most popular bands but also as one of the most innovative. The members are Bono (born Paul Hewson, May 10, 1960, Dublin, Ireland), the Edge (born David Evans, August 8, 1961, Barking, Essex [now in Greater London], England), Adam

*The Edge.* PRNewsFoto/Hard Rock International—Wire Image/AP Images

Clayton (born March 13, 1960, Oxford, Oxfordshire), and Larry Mullen, Jr. (born October 31, 1961, Dublin).

Though forged in the crucible of punk rock that swept Europe in the late 1970s, U2 instantly created a distinctive identity with its grandiose sound, a merger of the Edge's minimal, reverb-drenched guitar and Bono's quasi-operatic vocals. The band members were attending a Dublin secondary school when they began rehearsing, undeterred by their lack of technical expertise. The band's early records were characterized by an intense spirituality, and

*Album cover of* The Joshua Tree *(1987) by U2.* PRNewsFoto/Universal Music Enterprises/AP Images

they commented on social and political issues, such as the civil strife in Northern Ireland, with compassion and tenderness. The group became renowned for its inspirational live performances and was a word-of-mouth sensation long before it made much of an impact on the pop charts. But, with the multimillion-selling success of *The Joshua Tree* (1987) and the number one hits "With or Without You" and "I Still Haven't Found What I'm Looking For," U2 became pop stars. On *Rattle and Hum* (1988), a double album and documentary movie, the band explored American roots music—blues, country, gospel, and folk—with typical earnestness but were pilloried by some critics who found the project pompous.

U2 reinvented itself for the new decade, reemerging in 1991 with the album *Achtung Baby* and a sound heavily influenced by European experimental, electronic, and disco music. With this came a stage show that trafficked in irony and self-deprecating humour, qualities virtually absent from the band's music in the previous decade; the 1992 Zoo TV tour was one of the most technically ambitious and artistically accomplished large-scale rock spectacles ever staged. But, despite the flashier exterior, the band's lyrics remained obsessed with matters of the soul. The dehumanizing aspects of media and technology were a recurring theme on subsequent records, even as the band immersed itself in techno textures.

In 1997 the band rush-released the *Pop* album to fulfill obligations for a stadium tour and was greeted with its worst reviews since *Rattle and Hum*. Another reinvention was in store, but this time, rather than boldly pushing forward, the band sought to reassure fans by making music that referenced its 1980s roots. The aptly titled *All That You Can't Leave Behind* (2000) and *How to Dismantle an Atomic Bomb* (2004) were focused on riffs and songs rather than atmosphere and mystery, and they succeeded in reestablishing the quartet as a commercial force, though some might have wondered at what price. The band took five years before releasing its 12th studio album, *No Line on the Horizon* (2009). Longtime collaborators Brian Eno and Daniel Lanois played a bigger role in the production and songwriting, and the layered textures of the album's most experimental work crept back prominently in the mix.

The group supported the album with a world tour that stretched over the next two years. It was interrupted in May 2010, however, when Bono underwent emergency surgery after injuring his back during concert rehearsals in Germany.

In addition to actively touring, Bono and the Edge contributed the

21

# BONO

Bono was born of a Roman Catholic father and a Protestant mother (who died when he was 14). In Dublin in 1977, he and school friends David Evans (later "the Edge"), Larry Mullen, Jr., and Adam Clayton formed a band that would become U2. They shared a commitment not only to ambitious rock music but also to a deeply spiritual Christianity. Indeed, one of the few genuine threats to U2's extraordinary longevity (a collaboration—with the manager, Paul McGuinness—of more than 30 years) occurred extremely early in the band's life when three of its members, including Bono, considered joining a Christian fellowship. Throughout U2's career, religiosity has infused the group's songwriting and performance.

Led by vocalist Bono, U2 gained popularity on a global scale that few musicians have ever experienced. In 1984 the band was approached by Jack Healy, head of Amnesty International USA, and was asked to join the "Conspiracy of Hope" tour to bring attention to human rights violations and encourage fans to fight them. Afterward Bono toured war-torn Nicaragua and El Salvador with groups seeking to help the victims of violence and poverty in those countries, and he grew increasingly interested in the plight of people in the less-developed world. His experiences informed the band's biggest-selling and most influential recording, *The Joshua Tree*, which ranked 26th when *Rolling Stone* magazine selected its top 500 albums of all time in 2003.

Described by the Edge as the "chairman and founding member of Over-Achievers Anonymous, with an irrepressible lust to be great and a lust for life," Bono decided, after participating in various benefits for humanitarian causes with other musicians, to deploy his fame and the access it brought to world leaders to commit himself to a second career as a global politician without portfolio. Dividing his time between fronting his remarkably durable band and meeting with presidents, prime ministers, economists, ministers, scientists, and philanthropists, Bono eventually helped found in 2002 Debt AIDS Trade Africa (DATA), a policy and advocacy organization that seeks to eradicate poverty, hunger, and the spread of AIDS in Africa through public awareness campaigns and in-country partnerships.

Despite his success at raising awareness, Bono has been criticized by many in the aid community for his willingness to work with leaders whom many progressives consider to be anathema (particularly Pres. George W. Bush) in order to try to secure additional money for AIDS programs and debt relief

*Bono.* PRNewsFoto/TED/AP Images

for impoverished African countries. Bono's most high-profile trip occurred in May 2002 when he traveled throughout Africa with U.S. Treasury Secretary Paul O'Neill, an excursion the *Washington Post* called a potential beginning of a "momentous...alliance between liberals and conservatives to launch a fresh assault on global poverty." Writing in the *New York Times*, James Traub characterized Bono as both "a kind of one-man state who fills his treasury with the global currency of fame" and "an emanation of the celebrity culture."

music and lyrics to the Broadway musical *Spider-Man: Turn Off the Dark*. Originally directed by Julie Tamor, the production was one of the most expensive in Broadway history, beset with costly overruns, script rewrites, and the departure of numerous members of the original cast and crew; however, it opened to a sold-out house in June 2011 (more than a year after its scheduled debut).

## LIVE AID

Organized by Boomtown Rats front man Bob Geldof and Ultravox vocalist Midge Ure, Live Aid drew an estimated 1.5 billion television viewers and raised millions of dollars for famine relief in Ethiopia. The benefit concert was held simultaneously at Wembley Stadium in London and JFK Stadium in Philadelphia on July 13, 1985.

Years of drought, civil war, and failed attempts at government control of the grain market in the early 1980s led to a catastrophic famine that threatened hundreds of thousands of lives in Ethiopia. After seeing a television news report on the subject in 1984, Geldof wrote the lyrics for "Do They Know It's Christmas?" Ure crafted the melody of the song, and Geldof recruited some of the biggest names in the British new wave scene to contribute vocals. The single, recorded in November 1984 and

marketed under the name Band Aid, sold over three million copies and inspired similar all-star benefit projects. Most notable among these was Quincy Jones's USA for Africa, which hinged on the recording of "We Are the World" in January 1985. The success of Band Aid and USA for Africa inspired Geldof and Ure to stage a fund-raising event that was described as a "global jukebox," collecting dozens of acts for a marathon 16-hour live music event.

Oz for Africa, a benefit held in Sydney, was to have been part of the Live Aid simulcast, but time zone differences proved impossible to reconcile. Footage from Oz for Africa, along with recorded performances from more than a half dozen cities around the world, was ultimately woven into the main satellite broadcast. This signal was carried by the British Broadcasting Corporation (BBC) in the United Kingdom and the American Broadcasting Company (ABC) in the United States, with a separate feed for the American cable television channel MTV. To ensure continuity in the broadcast, artists were given no more than 20 minutes of stage time, and equipment needs were kept to an absolute minimum.

With less than a month of preparation time, Geldof secured the services of an impressive array of artists. Groups reuniting for the event included the Who, Black Sabbath, and Crosby, Stills, Nash, and Young. Moreover, the surviving members of Led Zeppelin reconvened in Philadelphia, supported by Phil Collins on drums. Collins, who had performed at Wembley earlier in the day, had crossed the Atlantic on the Concorde to become the only artist to appear on both Live Aid stages.

Perhaps the most noteworthy performances of the day belonged to a pair of arena rock giants—U2 and Queen—with each excelling in its respective idiom. U2 devoted 12 minutes of its allotted time to its anthem "Bad," and lead singer Bono spent much of that time directly interacting with the Wembley crowd. An hour and a half later, lead singer Freddie Mercury powered through a condensed set of Queen's greatest hits, displaying a combination of superb vocal range, multi-instrumental mastery, and remarkable stage presence. The concert closed with renditions of "Do They Know It's Christmas?" (in London) and "We Are the World" (in Philadelphia).

## BOBBY MCFERRIN

American musician Bobby McFerrin (born March 11, 1950, New York, New York, U.S.) is noted for his tremendous vocal control and improvisational ability. He often sings a cappella, mixing folk songs, 1960s rock and soul tunes, and jazz themes with original lyrics. He prefers to sing without fixed lyrics, and he can imitate the sounds of various musical instruments with great skill.

McFerrin's parents both had distinguished vocal careers. His mother, a soprano, was a Metropolitan Opera judge who chaired the vocal department at Fullerton College, near Los Angeles, and his father, who sang at the Met, dubbed actor Sidney Poitier's singing on the 1959 *Porgy and Bess* soundtrack. In McFerrin's youth he was inclined to become a minister of music, but, after attending California State University at Sacramento and Cerritos College in Norwalk, California, he instead became a pianist and organist with the Ice Follies and with pop music bands. In 1977 he auditioned for and won a singing job. As a swinging jazz and ballad vocalist, by 1980 McFerrin was touring with popular jazz singer Jon Hendricks. Inspired by Keith Jarrett's improvised piano concerts, in 1982 he worked up the nerve to sing alone.

McFerrin issued his self-titled debut album in 1982, and it was followed by *The Voice* (1984), which was unusual because it featured no accompaniment; *Spontaneous Inventions* (1985), which featured music by Herbie Hancock and Manhattan Transfer; and *Simple Pleasures* (1988), which featured the hit song "Don't Worry, Be Happy." He also recorded television commercials and the theme song for *The Cosby Show* (1984–92); improvised music for actor Jack Nicholson's readings of Rudyard Kipling's children's stories; and released an album with cellist Yo-Yo Ma, titled *Hush*, in 1992.

McFerrin is perhaps best known for his spontaneity; in concert he might wander through the auditorium singing, make up songs on listeners' names, conduct his audience in choirs, or burst into a condensed version of *The Wizard of Oz*, complete with tornado sounds and munchkin, witch, and scarecrow voices. On record he could improvise all the parts in a vocal group himself, as he did in "Don't Worry, Be Happy." In 1995 McFerrin released *Paper Music*, an album he collaborated on with the St. Paul (Minn.) Chamber Orchestra that featured orchestral works by Mozart, Bach, Rossini, and other masters, with the melodies sung instead of played.

By the beginning of the 21st century, McFerrin's work had garnered 10 Grammy Awards. His later albums included *Circlesongs* (1997) and *Beyond Words* (2002).

## WHITNEY HOUSTON

American singer and actress Whitney Houston (born August 9, 1963, Newark, New Jersey, U.S.—died February 11, 2012, Beverly Hills, California) was one of the most successful pop vocalists of her generation. Her first four albums, released between 1985 and 1992, amassed global sales in excess of 86 million copies.

The daughter of Emily ("Cissy") Houston—whose vocal group, the Sweet Inspirations, sang backup for Aretha Franklin—and the cousin of singer Dionne Warwick, Whitney Houston began singing in church as a child. While still in high school, she sang backup for Chaka Khan and Lou Rawls and modeled for fashion magazines. At age 19 she signed with Arista Records, whose president, Clive Davis, groomed the gospel-based singer for crossover pop success. Her debut album, *Whitney Houston* (1985), yielded three number one singles: "Greatest Love of All," which became her signature; "Saving All My Love for You"; and "How Will I Know." *Whitney* (1987) delivered four more number ones and earned Houston a Grammy Award (for the single "I Wanna Dance with Somebody"). In 1992 she married singer Bobby Brown and made her motion-picture debut in *The Bodyguard*; the film featured her rendition of Dolly Parton's "I Will Always Love You," which stayed at number one for 14 weeks. The film's soundtrack dominated the Grammys the following year, with Houston winning the awards for album of the year, record of the year, and best female

*Whitney Houston, 1991.* PH2 Mark Kettenhofen—U.S. Department of Defense

pop vocal performance. In the mid-1990s she continued acting, in films such as *Waiting to Exhale* (1995) and *The Preacher's Wife* (1996), and the soundtrack of each film generated hit singles for her.

In 1998 Houston released *My Love Is Your Love*, which did not sell as well as previous efforts but was praised by the critics and earned her another Grammy Award. In 2001 she signed a new multialbum contract with Arista for $100 million, but personal difficulties soon overshadowed her recording career. Houston's tumultuous relationship with Brown (the couple divorced in 2007) provided fodder for the tabloids, as did her acknowledged drug use and financial issues. Her 2002 album, *Just Whitney*, was a personal response to her detractors, but its sales were disappointing compared with earlier efforts. Other than a lacklustre holiday album, *One Wish* (2003), Houston spent subsequent years in a state of virtual retirement.

In February 2009 she began a comeback effort with a four-song set at Clive Davis's annual pre-Grammy Awards gala. The performance was greeted warmly, and in June Houston announced that an album of new material would be available later that year. *I Look to You* was released in August to positive reviews, and standout songs included the up-tempo "Million Dollar Bill" (penned by Alicia Keys) and the title track, a slow-building ballad written by R. Kelly. In February 2012 Houston died in a Beverly Hills hotel shortly before Davis's pre-Grammy party. A coroner's report released the following month stated that the cause of death was accidental drowning, with heart disease and cocaine use listed as contributing factors.

## JOHN MELLENCAMP

Growing up in southern Indiana—with which he is strongly identified—singer-songwriter John Mellencamp (also called Johnny Cougar or John Cougar Mellencamp, born October 7, 1951, Seymour, Indiana, U.S.) began playing in rock bands as a teenager. His first two albums, released in the late 1970s, disappeared without a trace; however, repackaged as a heartland rocker, he had his first hit, "I Need a Lover," in late 1979. With two more big hits, "Hurts So Good" and "Jack and Diane," the album *American Fool* (1982) made Mellencamp a star. Although criticized by some at this stage of his career as a humourless, self-important Bruce Springsteen manqué—patronizing his working-class subjects rather than celebrating them—Mellencamp suddenly matured as a songwriter. His lyrics grew more empathic, and his music acquired an incisive, crackling power, largely owing to his supertight backing band. *Scarecrow* (1985) and *The Lonesome Jubilee* (1987) were his commercial and artistic high points, exploring the impact of Ronald Reagan's presidency on Middle America and producing the hits "Small Town," "R.O.C.K. in the USA," and "Cherry Bomb." He also was a chief sponsor of the first Farm Aid concert, in 1985, which benefited distressed American farmers, and remained active on behalf of similar causes.

Mellencamp followed *The Lonesome Jubilee* with a series of albums that were generally successful commercially and critically though not as well received as his work from the mid-1980s. The most notable of these included *Dance Naked* (1994), which went gold on the strength of its cover version of Van Morrison's "Wild Night"; *Mr. Happy Go Lucky* (1996), featuring the hit single "Key West Intermezzo (I Saw You First)"; the self-titled *John Mellencamp* (1998); *Trouble No More* (2003), an album of stripped-down covers that topped the blues charts; and the darkly introspective *Life Death Love and Freedom* (2008). In 2008 Mellencamp was inducted into the Rock and Roll Hall of Fame.

# MELISSA ETHERIDGE

American musician Melissa Etheridge (born May 29, 1961, Leavenworth, Kansas, U.S.) is known for her raspy-voiced rock-and-roll singing as well as her openness about her sexual orientation. Etheridge began playing the guitar at age 8 and writing songs by age 11. She honed her skills playing in local bands throughout her teens (emulating influences such as Bruce Springsteen and Pete Townshend of the Who) and briefly attended the Berklee College of Music in Boston before returning to Kansas. On her 21st birthday, Etheridge left home for Los Angeles, where she played in clubs and bars until 1986, when Chris Blackwell, founder of Island Records, signed her to a recording

contract. Her first album, *Melissa Etheridge* (1988), with its hit single "Bring Me Some Water," earned her a Grammy Award nomination. Success continued with the release of *Brave and Crazy* (1989) and *Never Enough* (1992), which garnered a Grammy for the single "Ain't It Heavy."

In early 1993, at a gay-and-lesbian celebration of the inauguration of Pres. Bill Clinton, Etheridge announced to the crowd what many of her most devoted fans had assumed: she was a lesbian. The album *Yes I Am* followed later that year, with the hit singles "Come to My Window" (another Grammy winner) and "I'm the Only One." Soon Etheridge's relationship with film director Julie Cypher became a matter of public record. The couple, who had been together since 1990, appeared on the cover of *Newsweek* magazine in 1996, and in 2000 they revealed in an article in *Rolling Stone* that musician David Crosby had supplied the sperm for the two children Cypher had borne. When she separated from Cypher later that same year, Etheridge chronicled the details of their relationship and breakup in her memoir, *The Truth Is…My Life in Love and Music*, and on her album *Skin*, which were both released in 2001. (Two years later Etheridge exchanged vows in a public ceremony with actress Tammy

Lynn Michaels, who gave birth to twins in 2006.)

In 2004 Etheridge was diagnosed with breast cancer, and after undergoing treatment she made a memorable appearance during the 2005 Grammy Awards ceremonies. Still bald from chemotherapy treatments, Etheridge sang a characteristically heartfelt rendition of Janis Joplin's "Piece of My Heart," bringing many in the audience to tears. Etheridge returned to touring the following year. She also wrote and performed the Academy Award-winning song "I Need to Wake Up" for the 2006 Oscar-winning documentary *An Inconvenient Truth*.

Following the release of her album *The Awakening* (2007), an audio autobiography of her career in music, Etheridge staged a concert tour in 2008 that was similarly designed to tell the story of her life through a progression of highly personal songs. That same year she released a Christmas-themed album, *A New Thought for Christmas*.

# CHAPTER 2

# College Rock and the Rise of Alternative

**T**he music industry was rescued from its economic crisis by the development in the 1980s of a new technology, digital recording. Vinyl records were replaced by the compact disc (CD), a technological revolution that immediately had a conservative effect. By this point the most affluent record buyers had grown up on rock; they were encouraged to replace their records and listen to the same music on a superior sound system. Rock became adult music; youthful fads continued to appear and disappear, but these were no longer seen as central to the rock process, and, if rock's 1970s superstars could no longer match the sales of their old records with their new releases, they continued to sell out stadium concerts that became nostalgic rituals (most unexpectedly for the Grateful Dead). For new white acts the industry had to turn to alternative rock. A new pattern emerged—most successfully in the 1980s for R.E.M. and in the '90s for Nirvana—in which independent labels, college radio stations, and local retailers developed a cult audience for acts that were then signed and mass-marketed by a major label. Local record companies became, in effect, research and development divisions of the multinationals.

## R.E.M.

R.E.M. was the quintessential college rock band of the 1980s. The members were lead singer Michael Stipe (born January 4, 1960, Decatur, Georgia, U.S.), guitarist Peter Buck (born December 6, 1956, Berkeley, California), bassist Mike Mills (born December 17, 1958, Orange, California), and drummer Bill Berry (born July 31, 1958, Duluth, Minnesota).

R.E.M., named for a dream-state condition (rapid eye movement),

*The CD cover of R.E.M.'s* And I Feel Fine…: The Best of the I.R.S. Years 1982–1987 *(2006).* PRNewsFoto/EMI Music Catalog Marketing/AP Images

formed in 1980 in Athens, Georgia, a university town about 65 miles (105 km) northeast of Atlanta that was already internationally noted for its local pop scene by the time R.E.M. released *Chronic Town*, its 1982 debut extended-play recording. Stipe, obsessed with his own passions and hatreds, was a rounded tenor who draped vague words in reassuring cadences, and Buck, with a wider-ranging view of rock, was a guitarist drawn to fun and ideas; they met at the record store where Buck worked and Stipe shopped. Their band was more melodic than earlier groups in Athens, such as Pylon, yet never as lighthearted as the B-52's. R.E.M. answered only to themselves.

This quality explains the unmatched regard that would accrue to this romantic band—the American equivalent of Irish rockers U2 and British alternative rock groups such as the Smiths, bands also interested in stretching the rock-band guitar tradition into something newly personal. Beginning with the shifting sonic tapestry of "Radio Free Europe" (first released in 1981), R.E.M. drew on influences as various as the Byrds, the Velvet Underground, Big Star, Patti Smith, the Rolling Stones, and the New York Dolls to regale fans with albums fashioned from unpredictable blends of nonmetal rock and impressionistic folk. Especially ambitious was the band's 1985 release, *Fables of the Reconstruction*, a tense blend of R.E.M.'s ideas about folk rock and those of Joe Boyd, an American expatriate who worked in the 1960s with British artists such as Nick Drake and Fairport Convention. R.E.M. also offered singles such as "Fall on Me" and "The One I Love," which broadened its audience. The tack was completed in 1991 when *Out of Time* reached number one on the British and American album charts and the single "Losing My Religion" became an enormous hit.

R.E.M. taught successive generations of American rockers how to be vague and specific at the same time; by juxtaposing evocative phrases to create poetic collages, they involved listeners in the creation of the meaning of their songs. The group spent the 1990s making balladic albums such as *Automatic for the People* (1992) and rowdier, noisier collections such as Monster (1994).

Soon after the release of *New Adventures in Hi-Fi* in 1996, drummer Berry, who had suffered health problems, left the band. With his departure R.E.M. again reinvented its sound with *Up* (1998), an adventurous album of sonic experimentation. The band continued to perform and record together into the 2000s—releasing *Reveal* (2001) and *Around the Sun* (2004)—but also branched

# ATHENS: THE BIRTHPLACE OF COLLEGE ROCK

It is said that in every musical generation something new crawls out of the American South. But few would have expected anything earthshaking from Athens, a small city in Georgia that calls itself the "Classic City." American college towns tend to be consumers rather than creators of musical trends. Athens, where one-third of the population are students at the University of Georgia, is the exception that proves the rule.

Fittingly, the first hit to emerge from the city, the knowingly kitschy "Rock Lobster" (1978) by the B-52's, became a favourite on college campuses across the country. A couple of years later, the Athens scene really took off—partly inspired by the B-52's nonironic emphasis on "fun" but far more by New York City and London punk's redefining of the possible. Athens's fertile party-and-club scene was based in houses around Baker Street and in clubs such as the Georgia Bar, the 40 Watt Club, and Tyrone's OC. Elsewhere in the country, students usually danced to records, but in Athens it was a matter of pride to dance to young local bands such as the Side Effects, the Tone Tones, the Method Actors, Pylon, Love Tractor, and the Brains. The music was strong on traditional instrumentation (guitars, bass, and drums), cover versions (notably Them's "Gloria"), and drunkenness. *People* magazine published a mass photograph of local bands in January 1983, but the only lasting success to emerge from this mélange of shifting allegiances was R.E.M., the college-radio stars whose first single came out in 1981 and whose album *Green* (1988) made them big-time mainstream stars.

Although R.E.M. never fetishized their home base, they stayed there and in a small way fostered the development of a distinct

Athens take on things—slightly eccentric thoughts allied to fairly straightforward rock. That approach was typified by R.E.M.'s discomfort with repeating themselves, by the B-52's "Love Shack" (a big hit in gay clubs in 1989), by B-52 Kate Pierson's work on Iggy Pop's single "Candy" (1990) and R.E.M.'s *Out of Time* (1991), and by all the darkly comic observations of singer-songwriter Vic Chesnutt, produced by R.E.M.'s Michael Stipe.

out individually to work with other performers. In 2007 R.E.M. was inducted into the Rock and Roll Hall of Fame and released the group's first live album, titled *R.E.M. Live*, later that year. *Accelerate* (2008), which followed and received great notices, emphasized electric guitars and Stipe's lustrous baritone while aiming allusive broadsides at the administration of Pres. George W. Bush. R.E.M. seemed displeased with the course U.S. politics had taken in the four years since the band had last recorded a studio album; however, the group must have taken solace in its old revved-up folk-rock sound because the new music emerged iconic.

*Accelerate* was R.E.M.'s highest-charting album since *New Adventures in Hi-Fi*, and the group supported it with an extensive world tour. The band returned to the studio for *Collapse*

*into Now* (2011), an album that combined power pop, straightforward rock, and acoustic ballads into a single audio palette, unified by Buck's masterful guitar work. In September 2011, after more than three decades at the forefront of rock music, the members of R.E.M. announced the dissolution of the band.

## THE REPLACEMENTS

The Replacements combined the intensity of punk with melodic hooks and heartfelt lyrics, providing an important bridge from the punk movement of the late 1970s to the alternative rock of the late 1980s. The principal members were Paul Westerberg (born December 31, 1960, Minneapolis, Minnesota, U.S.), Chris Mars (born April 26, 1961, Minneapolis), Bob Stinson (born December 17, 1959, Mound,

# CHILDREN BY THE MILLION SING FOR ALEX CHILTON

American singer and songwriter Alex Chilton (born December 28, 1950, Memphis, Tennessee, U.S.—died March 17, 2010, New Orleans, Louisiana) fronted the seminal power pop band Big Star, crafting a body of work whose influence far outstripped its volume.

Chilton was age 16 when he began his musical career as the lead singer of the Memphis blue-eyed soul group the DeVilles. The quintct achieved a measure of local fame, eventually coming to the attention of American Sound Studios executive Chips Moman and songwriter Dan Penn. Penn produced the group—now renamed the Box Tops—on the song "The Letter." "The Letter" was a surprise hit, spending four weeks at the top of the Billboard Hot 100 chart in 1967. It later resurfaced as a cover version by Joe Cocker. The Box Tops returned to the top 10 with "Cry like a Baby," but the group experienced diminishing success over the following years before disbanding in 1970.

In the wake of the Box Tops' demise, Chilton moved to New York City, but a career as a solo artist failed to materialize. He returned to Memphis in 1971, where he joined fellow songwriter Chris Bell to form the core of Big Star. The quartet released *#1 Record* in 1972, and the album's exquisitely crafted power pop met with critical acclaim. Melancholy lyrics, sweet harmonies, and jangly guitars combined on tracks such as "The Ballad of El Goodo" to create a sound that was widely described as ahead of its time. Distribution problems hampered the album's commercial success, however, and Bell exited the band prior to the release of the group's follow-up, *Radio City* (1974). Perhaps the standout track from *Radio City* was "September Gurls," now widely acclaimed as a Chilton masterpiece that anticipated the work of artists such as Tom Petty and Cheap

Trick. Big Star's final album, *Third* (also released as *Sister Lovers*; 1978), was a dark, meandering affair that lacked the focus of its predecessors. In spite of this, songs such as "Kangaroo" offered a glimpse of the noise-pop sound that would emerge in the 1980s with groups such as the Jesus and Mary Chain and My Bloody Valentine.

Chilton embarked on a solo career in the late 1970s, and he worked as a producer, recording the first single for the "psychobilly" (a fusion of punk and rockabilly) group the Cramps. Chilton's solo albums, which included *Like Flies on Sherbert* (1979) and *High Priest* (1987), met with mixed reviews, and the legacy of Big Star overshadowed much of his work throughout the 1980s and 1990s. Chilton seemed to embrace this fact, and he sometimes turned his back on music entirely. After a battle with alcoholism in the early 1980s, he moved to New Orleans, where he washed dishes and worked odd jobs to support himself. The advent of alternative rock during this era saw the emergence of R.E.M., Teenage Fanclub, and the Replacements—groups that were unabashedly creating music in the spirit of Big Star. The Replacements went so far as to name a song after Chilton, and the lyric "Children by the million sing for Alex Chilton" captured the newfound appreciation for Chilton's groundbreaking work. Chilton essentially retired from recording new material in the 21st century, but he remained a prolific live performer until his death.

Minnesota—died February 15, 1995, Minneapolis), and Tommy Stinson (born October 6, 1966, San Diego, California).

Formed in 1979 by guitarist-vocalist Westerberg, drummer Mars, and guitarist Bob Stinson—all in their teens—and Stinson's 12-year-old bassist brother, Tommy, the Replacements emerged from the thriving Minneapolis music scene of the early 1980s that also produced Prince and the influential hardcore band Hüsker Dü, with whom the Replacements were compared by virtue of the straight-ahead punk sound of their debut album, *Sorry Ma, Forgot to Take Out the Trash* (1981). With an attitude as petulant as that of their early songs, the Replacements were renowned for erratic live performances that ranged from inspired anarchy to drunken chaos. On their third recording, *Hootenanny* (1983), they began to include country and blues influences, which set the stage for three eclectic, critically acclaimed albums: *Let It Be* (1984), *Tim* (1985), and *Pleased to Meet Me* (1987). The albums document Westerberg's growing sophistication as a pop tunesmith, but they promised a commercial breakthrough that never came. An unstable blend of personalities, the Replacements dissolved after *All Shook Down* (1990), which was essentially a solo album by Westerberg, whose solo career was the most successful of those of the ex-Replacements.

## YO LA TENGO

The sound of Yo La Tengo (Spanish for "I've got it," alluding to the call of a baseball outfielder) consistently evolved over the course of more than a dozen albums, making the group a long-standing critical favourite despite its limited commercial success. The band was assembled in 1984 in Hoboken, New Jersey, by spouses Ira Kaplan (who handled vocals and guitar) and Georgia Hubley (who played drums). During their first years as a band they played with a number of bassists and lead guitarists whose tenures with the group were short, including guitarist Dave Schramm

and bassist Mike Lewis, with whom they recorded debut album *Ride the Tiger* (1986).

Schramm and Lewis departed before recording began on the band's sophomore release, *New Wave Hot Dogs* (1987), featuring Kaplan on lead guitar and Stephan Wichnewski on bass. By the time *President Yo La Tengo* (1989) was released, the band's sound had evolved from basic roots-rock to encompass dramatic juxtapositions of feedback-driven noise rock with melodic folk-influenced pop, drawing frequent comparisons to 1960s cult favourites the Velvet Underground. This comparison was alluded to in the 1996 film *I Shot Andy Warhol*, in which Yo La Tengo performed as a party band reminiscent of the legendary group.

*May I Sing with Me* (1992) marked James McNew's debut as the band's permanent bassist. In this best-known, three-member incarnation, Yo La Tengo expanded its stylistic palette to include elements of British Invasion pop and alternative rock subgenres such as droning shoegaze and keyboard-washed dream pop. The band's sixth album, *Painful* (1993), was released on Matador Records, which Yo La Tengo would continue to work with into the 21st century. *I Can Hear the Heart Beating as One* (1997), a critical favourite, combined clean melodic lines with feedback-laced, densely layered sound and gently ironic lyrics. Its inclusion of a lo-fi (unornamented) version of the Beach Boys' "Little Honda" was a characteristic move for a band that had become known for its diverse catalog of recorded cover songs. The low-key relationship-themed *And Then Nothing Turned Itself Inside Out* (2000), which takes its title from a quote by jazz musician Sun Ra, became the group's first entry in the Billboard 200.

In the early 21st century, Yo La Tengo composed instrumental scores for a number of films. The influence of these cinematic projects was felt on *I Am Not Afraid of You and I Will Beat Your Ass* (2006), which featured an orchestral sound bolstered by strings and horns. Following the release of that album, the group worked on several side projects, including a collaboration with Yoko Ono, while continuing to release studio albums such as *Popular Songs* (2009).

## THE PIXIES

The Pixies exhibited a unique blend of punk rock's aggression and pop music's infectious melodies, a sound that laid the foundation for alternative rock in the 1990s. The members were Black Francis (born Charles Michael Kitteridge Thompson IV, later known as Frank Black, born April 6, 1965, Boston, Massachusetts, U.S.), Joey Santiago (born June 10, 1965, Manila, Philippines), Kim Deal (born June 10, 1961, Dayton, Ohio), and David Lovering (born December 6, 1961, Burlington, Massachusetts).

The Pixies formed in Boston in 1986, when singer-guitarist Thompson (using the stage name Black Francis) and his former Boston University roommate, guitarist Santiago, decided to put together a band. In response to the duo's ad in a local newspaper for a "bassist into Hüsker Dü and Peter, Paul, and Mary," Deal joined the group, bringing along her friend Lovering as a drummer. The Pixies quickly earned a reputation as part of the local Boston club scene and released their full-length debut, *Surfer Rosa*, in 1988. The album was an instant critical favourite and received considerable airplay on college radio and in Europe. While rougher than the Pixies' later work, *Surfer Rosa* established the band's signature sound, an aggressive blast of searing guitars and Thompson's screeching vocals, which were oddly but effectively counterbalanced by enchanting pop melodics and Deal's gentler backup vocals. Equally distinctive were the strange, cryptic lyrics penned by Thompson, which over the years would encompass references ranging from his Pentecostal upbringing to UFOs to Salvador Dalí and Luis Buñuel's Surrealist film *Un Chien andalou* (1928; *An Andalusian Dog*).

In 1989 the group released *Doolittle*, its most revered album,

*The Pixies, 1988.* Steve Pyke/Premium Archive/Getty Images

which built upon the Pixies' existing formula and perfected the stop-and-start dynamics that would perhaps become its greatest legacy to later alternative bands, especially Nirvana. *Bossanova*, a surf music-inspired variation on the earlier albums, followed in 1990. By this time, tensions were rising in the band—Deal, once a co-songwriter, contributed little to the album, and the group had effectively disbanded by the time of the 1991 release of *Trompe le Monde* (*Fool the World*), which is generally considered the Pixies' weakest effort.

With another name change, Thompson went on to release several memorable albums as Frank Blank or Frank Black and the Catholics, including *Teenager of the Year* (1993), *Dog in the Sand* (2001), and *Honeycomb* (2005). Deal shifted her focus to her onetime side project, the Breeders, the band she had fronted with Tanya Donelly of Throwing Muses, whose place was taken by Deal's twin sister Kelley for the release of the candid, hook-laced *Last Splash* (1993), one of the landmark albums of the 1990s. In 2004 the Pixies reunited for a much-anticipated multicity tour, on which a limited amount of on-site CD recordings of each concert were instantly available to concertgoers. The tour was also captured in the documentary film *loudQUIETloud* (2006).

## PERE UBU

Formed in Cleveland in 1975, the American avant-garde art rock band Pere Ubu was a major force and influence in the development of post-punk music. The original members were David Thomas (born June 14, 1953, Miami, Florida, U.S.), Peter Laughner (born August 22, 1952, Cleveland, Ohio—died June 22, 1977), Tom Herman (born April 19, 1949, Buffalo, New York), Allen Ravenstine (born May 9, 1950), Scott Krauss (born November 19, 1950), and Tim Wright. Later members included Tony Maimone (born September 27, 1952, Cleveland, Ohio), Jim Jones (born March 12, 1950, Cleveland—died February 18, 2008, Cleveland), Chris Cutler (born January 4, 1947), Mayo Thompson (born February 26, 1944), Anton Fier (born June 20, 1956, Cleveland), and Eric Drew Feldman (born April 16, 1955).

Music critics Thomas and Laughner (both former members of Rocket from the Tombs), founded Pere Ubu, taking the band's name from the principal character in *Ubu roi* (1896; "King Ubu"), a farce by French writer Alfred Jarry. The band's combination of absurdist lyrics and often noisy and dissonant music endeared them to critics but did not lead to particularly impressive record sales. An almost endless stream of personnel and record-label changes further contributed to their relative obscurity, but it did not prevent Pere Ubu from producing consistently challenging work characterized by constant experimentation and innovation. The group broke up in 1982, but many members quickly reconvened, recording as David Thomas and, sequentially, the Pedestrians, His Legs, and the Wooden Birds. As with the first incarnation of Pere Ubu, the inimitable Thomas (a Jehovah's Witness who formerly called himself Crocus Behemoth) was the quirky and highly intellectual leader of the many different musical projects that once again congealed into Pere Ubu in 1987. Tales of alienation and fear and patterns of noise and sound eventually gave way to a more pop-oriented music on well-received recordings such as *The Tenement*

# KUSF AND COLLEGE RADIO

College radio stations—once considered little more than laboratories for students who had chosen broadcasting as an avocation—came to play an important gatekeeping role in the development of rock music beginning in the 1970s, in the aftermath of free-form FM rock radio and on the eve of the punk revolution. With a bent toward alternative rock, college stations gave artists such as the Police, U2, R.E.M., and Elvis Costello their initial radio airplay and provided outlets for all kinds of nonmainstream music. One such station, KUSF, broadcasting from the University of San Francisco (California), was also credited with giving early exposure to Nirvana, Sonic Youth, and Soundgarden. KUSF, which won four College Station of the Year awards from the radio trade publication *Gavin Report* and one from *The College Media Journal*, had numerous staff members who went on to success in the industry—most notably longtime deejay and adviser Howie Klein, who became the president of Reprise Records.

*Year* (1988), *Cloudland* (1989), and *Worlds in Collision* (1991).

Pere Ubu's music exploited new technology, and in the 1990s the band released hybrid CD-ROMs that blended music, video, and text. Signing with smaller record labels seemed to inspire the group, and *Ray Gun Suitcase* (1995) and *Pennsylvania* (1998) were viewed by many as worthy additions to the band's critically acclaimed oeuvre.

## THE JESUS AND MARY CHAIN

Influenced by the Sex Pistols and the Velvet Underground, as well as by the Beach Boys and Phil Spector-produced 1960s pop, the Jesus and Mary Chain created an arresting hybrid that was much celebrated by critics. While the group was only marginally successful commercially, it exerted an outsize influence on noise-pop and shoegaze bands such as My Bloody Valentine, Ride, and Lush. The original members were William Reid (born 1958, East Kilbride, East Kilbride, Scotland), Jim Reid (born 1961, East Kilbride), Douglas Hart, and Murray Dalglish. Later members included Ben Lurie, Bobby Gillespie, John Moore, and Steve Monti.

Brothers Jim and William Reid, guitarist-vocalists, formed the Jesus and Mary Chain in suburban Glasgow, Scotland. In 1984 they moved to London, where, under the tutelage of provocative promoter Alan McGee, they released a string of innovative postpunk singles beginning with "Upside Down" and elicited riotlike responses to truncated live performances that seldom exceeded 20 minutes. Multitracked guitar distortion and rudimentary snare and tom-tom drumming dominated *Psychocandy* (1985) which was heralded by some critics as one of pop music's most auspicious debuts. In 1986 the band's "Some Candy Talking" cracked the British Top 20; the next year "April Skies" made the British Top Ten.

Suffused in moody echoes, their follow-up album, *Darklands* (1987), marked a departure from the manic distortion of *Psychocandy*. *Automatic* (1989) was notable for its synthesized drum accompaniment and the singles "Blues from a Gun," which topped the Billboard alternative chart, and "Head On," which was a surprise hit on MTV. It was followed by *Honey's Dead* (1992), featuring their comeback hit "Reverence," and *Stone & Dethroned* (1994), which included "Sometimes Always," a song featuring Mazzy Star vocalist Hope Sandoval that was the group's only single to crack the Billboard Hot 100 chart. The 1998 album *Munki* was something of a career retrospective, visiting the various sounds that the group had embraced throughout its history. The band broke up shortly after *Munki*'s release, but reunited in 2007 for a series of well-received live appearances.

## SONIC YOUTH

Beginning as an avant-garde noise band, Sonic Youth became a highly influential forerunner of the alternative rock groups of the 1980s and '90s. The principal members were Kim Gordon (born April 28, 1953, Rochester, New York, U.S.), Lee Ranaldo (born February 3, 1956, Glen Cove, New York), Thurston Moore (born July 25, 1958, Coral Gables, Florida), Steve Shelley (born June 23, 1962, Midland, Michigan), Jim O'Rourke (born January 18, 1969), and Mark Ibold (born 1967, Cincinnati, Ohio).

Moore and Ranaldo met in New York City in the late 1970s, at the height of the postpunk "no wave" movement (dissonant, noisy, experimental music generally created by untrained musicians). Both performed in the guitar orchestras of avant-garde composer Glenn Branca. In 1981 Sonic Youth formed, with Moore and Ranaldo on guitar and Moore's girlfriend (later wife) Gordon on bass; the band went through a succession of drummers before Shelley became a fixture by 1986. The group's first recordings were heavy on noise and feedback, but, by the release of *Bad Moon Rising* in 1985, it was clear Sonic Youth was beginning to find its own voice. The band still specialized in creating mammoth walls of sound, but the rhythmic underpinnings gave the songs a greater sense of structure. This evolution led to the double album *Daydream Nation* (1988), which is generally regarded as the band's masterpiece.

The group eventually signed with a major label, DGC, but retained its underground edge and penchant for musical experimentation, which ranged from the straightforward pop approach of *Goo* (1990) and *Dirty* (1992) to the near-orchestral sweep of *Washing Machine* (1995) and *A Thousand Leaves* (1998). The group enlisted experimental musician Jim O'Rourke for *NYC Ghosts and Flowers* (2000), a paean to avant-garde composers such as John Cage. O'Rourke became a full-time member of Sonic Youth, appearing on tour and handling production duties for *Murray Street* (2002) and *Sonic Nurse* (2004). Although O'Rourke departed in 2005, the 2006 album *Rather Ripped* retained his orchestral influence.

With the conclusion of its contract with DGC, the group signed with independent label Matador for the 2009 release *The Eternal*. Enlisting Pavement bassist Mark Ibold for the album and subsequent tour, *The Eternal* recalled Sonic Youth's early 1990s rock sound. Each band member was also involved in a wide variety of side projects, and the group released a series of experimental albums on its own SYR label. In 2011 Moore and Gordon announced that they were separating, and the break-up of one of rock's most enduring couples cast doubt on the future of Sonic Youth.

## RED HOT CHILI PEPPERS

Heavily influenced by the Los Angeles punk music scene in the late 1970s, school friends Anthony Kiedis (born November 1, 1962, Grand Rapids, Michigan, U.S.), Flea (born Michael Balzary, October 16, 1962, Melbourne, Australia), Hillel Slovak (born April 13, 1962, Haifa, Israel—died June 25, 1988, Los Angeles, California), and Jack Irons (born July 18, 1962, Los Angeles) formed Tony Flow and the Miraculously Majestic

Masters of Mayhem. The group performed along the Sunset Strip in Los Angeles during the early 1980s, wearing only strategically placed tube socks, which, as a stage gimmick, became their trademark.

By 1983, under the name the Red Hot Chili Peppers, they had a loyal underground following and a recording contract with EMI. Their first album to reach the Billboard 200 charts was *The Uplift Mofo Party Plan* (1987). Just as the band was beginning to enjoy commercial success, Slovak died of a heroin overdose and Irons left the band, leaving Kiedis and Flea to reform with John Frusciante (born March 5, 1970, Queens, New York) and Chad Smith (born October 25, 1962, St. Paul, Minnesota). Their 1989 album, *Mother's Milk*, became a surprise hit. The album went gold by early 1990 and was followed by the more successful *Blood Sugar Sex Magik* (1991), which included the band's first Top Ten single, "Under the Bridge," as well as the Grammy Award-winning "Give It Away."

Through a number of lineup changes, the Red Hot Chili Peppers continued to release well-received albums, including *Californication* (1999), *By the Way* (2002), and Grammy-winning *Stadium Arcadium* (2006). The band went on hiatus in early 2008, and the following year Frusciante announced that he had left the group to pursue a solo career. He was replaced on lead guitar by Josh Klinghoffer, who had previously played with the group on the "Stadium Arcadium" tour. Putting aside various side projects, the band returned to the studio and released *I'm with You* in 2011. In 2012 the Red Hot Chili Peppers were inducted into the Rock and Roll Hall of Fame.

# CHAPTER 3

# Alternative Rock

**A**lternative rock burst into the mainstream when "Smells Like Teen Spirit"—the first major-label single from Nirvana—became a national hit. Suddenly, older, difficult, and even anarchic movements, as well as a previous decade of do-it-yourself college rock, acquired a flashy beachhead on pop radio. Ironically, most alternative rockers were born between the late 1950s and late '60s and grew up during the '70s amid the head-spinning studio refinement and growing social acceptance of the earliest rock music. Whether the richly accessible melodies of the Beatles or the free jams of Led Zeppelin, all music seemed conventional to alternative rockers. They yearned for something different, something apart from what was too accurately called, by the mid-1980s, classic rock. They therefore believed that their interest in such departures would be, by definition, unpopular.

On the face of it, their deduction seemed reasonable. Alternative rockers, after all, looked for inspiration to an earlier generation of cranky stylists in the United States and Britain. Of 1970s musicians, they revered the rough aggressiveness of the Sex Pistols and the Clash and the arty formal daring of, among many others, the Velvet Underground, the Stooges, and Patti Smith. Among 1980s musicians, alternative partisans sensed kinship with American upstarts such as the Replacements and Hüsker Dü, bands that had operated out of their own garages and, later, as part of an ever-expanding network of labels and clubs that shared their staunch independence. Both generations of alternative role models had enjoyed very little, if any, pop success. The exception was R.E.M., viewed to have bridged the admirable values of both decades and slowly built broad-based success on the band's own special terms.

By the late 1980s, however, music scenes in Seattle, Los Angeles, and Chicago gave rise to younger alternativists who wanted to balance maintaining stylistic independence with reaching larger audiences. Moreover, the record industry, always hot for something new, began to invest in such goals, thus boosting production values. In Hollywood, Jane's Addiction signed with Warner Brothers Records and made *Nothing's Shocking* (1988), an album on which they offered odd guitar tones and disrupted metres as clearly and forcefully as had been done on any classic rock recording. Just as the 1990s dawned, the Smashing Pumpkins began their ultimately very successful quest to make what their bassist, D'Arcy, called "beautiful music that varies" out of many-hued guitar tones that cracked and frazzled. In 1991 Nirvana and producer Butch Vig released "Smells Like Teen Spirit," from their epochal 1991 album, *Nevermind*. The sheer immediacy of its expert guitar distortions and layered orchestrations—influenced

by the organized noise of British pop groups such as the Cure and My Bloody Valentine—assured that "grunge," as the music based on those feedback sounds was called, would become an international pop phenomenon.

What alternative rockers hadn't counted on was that, by the time Nirvana released *Nevermind*, the young rock audience had tired of the same sounds the musicians had rejected; a few exhilaratingly growled notes from Nirvana, and suddenly the previous decade of slick, digitally metallicized "hair rock"—the sound of such million-selling bands as Warrant and Poison—seemed as hopelessly passé as the spandex pants worn by such bands. No matter how loudly some alternative rockers professed to despise the classic rock that preceded them, bands such as Soundgarden and Screaming Trees did in fact echo their childhood memories of the Beatles and Led Zeppelin. Alternative rockers had intended to make music for themselves; in the end, the movement created the sound of a resentful and distressed generation.

## PAVEMENT

Pavement epitomized 1990s college rock with foppish lyrics and punk-derived sonic textures that merged into free-floating poetry. The original members were lead singer, guitarist, and principal songwriter Stephen Malkmus (born May 30 1966, Santa Monica, California, U.S.) and guitarist Scott Kannberg (also known as Spiral Stairs, born August 30, 1966, Stockton, California). Manic original drummer Gary Young (born c. 1954, Marmaroneck, New York), a counterculture veteran who ran the studio where Pavement initially recorded, was replaced by Steve West (born 1967, Richmond, Virginia) in 1993. Percussionist Bob Nastanovich (born August 27, 1967, Rochester, New York) and bassist Mark Ibold (born 1967, Cincinnati, Ohio) joined in 1991 and 1990, respectively.

Formed in Stockton, California, in 1989, Pavement was among the first musical groups to come of age inside the "indie" rock subculture, forming their musical identities by listening to R.E.M. and collecting obscure records on small labels. Its first releases, later compiled into the 1993 album *Westing* (by Musket and Sextant), offered compressed snippets of industrial sound and shards of surprisingly melodic low-fi pop (from low fidelity; music made with rudimentary recording equipment such as four-track tapes). But *Slanted and Enchanted* (1992) revealed a new grandeur, with enigmatic anthems of subcultural devotion such as "Summer Babe" and "In the Mouth a Desert" treating the slacker life

as a birthright. Malkmus's forever puzzled, laid-back persona (priding himself on coasting) recast punk: instead of rebellion, Pavement emphasized the enchantments of rarefied self-expression.

Even so, the commercial breakthrough of alternative rock with Nirvana's *Nevermind* (1991) proved too obvious a target for Malkmus to resist, and 1994's *Crooked Rain, Crooked Rain* sniped at groups such as the Smashing Pumpkins and the Stone Temple Pilots, while also slicking up the pop enough to get Pavement some MTV exposure with the "Cut Your Hair" music video. But instead of further pursuing what Malkmus called "gold soundz," Pavement's next album, *Wowee Zowee!* (1995), spurned the Lollapalooza audience with sophisticated experimental jams. The subsequent *Brighten the Corners* (1997) and *Terror Twilight* (1999) were lyrical and contained elements that increasingly foreshadowed Malkmus's desire for a solo career. Malkmus announced the dissolution of Pavement in the fall of 2000, and he released his eponymous debut album in February 2001, followed by *Pig Lib* (2003), *Face the Truth* (2005), and *Real Emotional Trash* (2008), all with his new assemblage, the Jicks, who by 2008 included former Sleater-Kinney drummer Janet Weiss. Weiss, like Malkmus, lived in Portland, Oregon, where slacker collegiate types had bought homes and become parents. Even before the breakup of Pavement, Malkmus and Nastanovich had begun a side project with David Berman, recording as Silver Jews. Kannberg's post-Pavement band, Preston School of Industry, proved less interesting than either of Malkmus's groups.

Rumours of a possible Pavement reunion were a regular, if unfounded, occurrence in the world of rock journalism throughout the early 2000s. Years of speculation ended in September 2009, when the band announced that it would reunite the following year for a world tour. Warmly received by fans and critics alike, Pavement's 2010 tour served as a career retrospective, with band members falling into familiar onstage roles. The reunion, however, did not lead to any new recorded material.

## GRUNGE

The term *grunge* was first used to describe the murky-guitar bands that emerged from Seattle, Washington, in the late 1980s as a bridge between mainstream 1980s heavy metal–hard rock and postpunk alternative rock. In time, however, the grunge label came to be applied to a broad range of music, as well as the fashion trends associated with it.

Influenced by punk rock, by the hardcore-punk inheritors of its do-it-yourself ethic such as Hüsker Dü, and by the sound of 1970s heavy metal bands such as Black Sabbath, Led Zeppelin, and AC/DC, grunge came to fruition on Seattle's independent Sub Pop record label as Mudhoney, Nirvana, Screaming Trees, and Soundgarden followed in the footsteps of the pioneering Northwestern band the Melvins. Combining guitar distortion, anguished vocals, and heartfelt, angst-ridden lyrics, Nirvana and Pearl Jam won a rapidly increasing audience, moved to major labels, and released multimillion-selling albums. In the wake of their success, Seattle—already experiencing an economic boom as a result of the Microsoft Corporation's expansive growth—became a magnet for record executives looking for the next big thing. As the media spread the word, grunge became an international fad, and American department stores soon had sections of grunge clothing—knockoffs of the flannel shirts, thermal underwear, combat boots, and stocking hats favoured by Seattle bands and their fans.

Eventually, grunge faded—partly because of the death in 1994 of Nirvana's Kurt Cobain, who had become a generational spokesman, but also because of the disappointing record sales by many of the bands from Seattle who never did become the next big thing. Nevertheless, grunge played an enormous role in moving alternative rock into the pop mainstream.

## NIRVANA

Nirvana's breakthrough album, *Nevermind* (1991), announced the arrival of grunge and gave voice to the post-baby boom young adults known as Generation X. The members were Kurt Cobain (born February 20, 1967, Aberdeen, Washington, U.S.—died April 5, 1994, Seattle), Krist Novoselic (born May 16, 1965, Compton, California), and Dave Grohl (born January 14, 1969, Warren, Ohio).

From Aberdeen, near Seattle, Nirvana was part of the postpunk underground scene that centred on K Records of Olympia, Washington, before they recorded their first single, "Love Buzz," and album, *Bleach*, for Sub Pop, an independent record company in Seattle. They refined this mix of 1960s-style pop and 1970s heavy metal–hard rock on their first album for a major label, Geffen; *Nevermind*, featuring the anthemic hit "Smells Like Teen Spirit," was the first full expression of punk concerns to achieve mass market success in the United States.

Nirvana used extreme changes of tempo and volume to express anger and alienation: a quiet, tuneful verse switched into a ferocious, distorted chorus. In the fashion of many 1970s punk groups, guitarist-singer-songwriter Cobain set powerful rock against sarcastic, allusive lyrics that explored hopelessness, surrender, and male abjection ("As a defense I'm neutered and spayed," he sang in "On a Plain"). Imbued with the punk ethic that to succeed was to fail, Nirvana abhorred the media onslaught that accompanied their rapid ascent. Success brought celebrity, and Cobain, typecast as a self-destructive rock star, courted controversy both with his advocacy of feminism and gay rights and with his embroilment in a sequence of drug- and gun-related escapades—a number of which involved his wife, Courtney Love, leader of the band Hole.

Like *Nevermind*, the band's third album, *In Utero* (1993)—which contained clear articulations of Cobain's psyche in songs such as "All Apologies" and "Rape Me"—reached number one on the U.S. album charts. By this point, however, Cobain's heroin use was out of control. After a reputed suicide attempt in Rome in March 1994, he entered a Los Angeles treatment centre. In a mysterious sequence of events, he returned to Seattle, where he shot and killed himself in his lakeside home.

Unsurprisingly, Cobain's death signaled the end of Nirvana, but subsequent concert releases, notably *Unplugged in New York* (1994), which closed with a chilling cover of

Leadbelly's "In the Pines," and *From the Muddy Banks of the Wishkah* (1996), only added to the band's legend. After the demise of Nirvana, Novoselic formed the short-lived duo Sweet 75 before turning his attention to political causes. Grohl proved his mettle as a multi-instrumentalist, trading his drums for a guitar as the founder and lead vocalist of the Foo Fighters, one of the most successful alternative rock bands of the late 1990s and early 2000s. While hewing close to the hard rock idiom that had borne fruit for Nirvana, the Foo Fighters also exhibited a pop playfulness that was apparent both in their live performances as well as their music videos. Grohl also found the time to sit in as the drummer for the heavy metal super-group Queens of the Stone Age for their album *Songs for the Deaf* (2002). In 2002 the greatest-hits album *Nirvana* appeared and included the previously unreleased single "You Know You're Right." That year a collection of Cobain's journals was also published.

## KURT COBAIN

The angst-ridden poet of Generation X and lead guitarist and singer of Nirvana, Cobain's music bespoke a deeply personal despair that struck a chord of fellowship among young

*Kurt Cobain, c. 1991.* Michel Linssen/Redferns/Getty Images

51

# ROCK IN THE EMERALD CITY

If it was the worldwide reaction to the suicide of Kurt Cobain that confirmed Seattle's status as a major influence on early 1990s popular music, its arrival was announced by the band's hit "Smells Like Teen Spirit"—a forceful but melodic record that caught the anger-laden tone of a generation. The Seattle of the 1980s, in which Nirvana came to life, was a rainy city of lakes, rusty bridges, and more than a few disaffected (often drug-using) teenagers, a city whose image had yet to be shaped by the unlikely combination of Microsoft founder Bill Gates; *Frasier*, the popular television situation comedy set in Seattle; and gourmet coffee culture. Jimi Hendrix had grown up in the city in the 1950s but had to go to London to get noticed, and not much happened of note musically in Seattle until Nirvana formed in 1987 in nearby Aberdeen (save the contributions of the instrumental group the Ventures in the late '50s and early '60s and the outbreak of garage rock in the Northwest in the '60s that gave rise to the Kingsmen and Paul Revere and the Raiders in Portland, Oregon).

Nirvana's first records were for Sub Pop, Seattle's preeminent independent label, which created what came to be seen as the sound of Generation X with such groups as Tad, the Los Angeles-based latter-day girl group L7, Mudhoney, Soundgarden, and, eventually, Hole, the band formed by Cobain's future wife, Courtney Love. It was a vibrant if despair-ridden scene, well suited to Nirvana's debut, *Bleach*, a clear statement of the music that became known as grunge, a self-conscious antithesis to the cold professional lustre of much of 1980s pop. Pearl Jam, a more traditional rock band, also emerged in the city about the same time (Cobain, however, sneeringly dismissed them as "corporate"). There were those who felt that grunge's heyday had come and gone by the time Nirvana signed with major label Geffen Records and reached number one in 1991 with *Nevermind*, the album that would lead to mainstream acceptance of grunge and alternative rock in general.

adults struggling with their own frustrations. Cobain formed the alternative rock trio Nirvana in Aberdeen in 1986. The band, whose style derived from punk rock, combined the fury of that genre with anguished lyrics, defining a musical style that became known as grunge. The group's first album, *Bleach* (1989), was followed two years later by *Nevermind*, featuring the hit single "Smells Like Teen Spirit," which became something of an official anthem for Nirvana fans.

In 1992 Cobain married Courtney Love, leader of the group Hole. Cobain was hailed as the voice of his generation, but with the album *In Utero* he railed against his fame, "I do not want what I have got." In March 1994, while Nirvana was touring Europe, Cobain, who was known for his self-destructive behaviour and heroin use, was rushed to a hospital after slipping into a drug-and-alcohol-induced coma. After several days there, Cobain was released and returned to Seattle. On April 8, some three days after Cobain took his life, his body, with a gunshot wound to the head, was discovered.

## COURTNEY LOVE

Courtney Love (born Courtney Michelle Harrison, July 9, 1964, San Francisco, California, U.S.) is best known for her influential rock band Hole and for her marriage to Nirvana frontman Kurt Cobain.

Love began her career as an actress, appearing in two Alex Cox films, *Sid and Nancy* (1986) and *Straight to Hell* (1987). During this time, Love formed the band Sugar Baby Doll with Kat Bjelland and developed her signature style of babydoll dresses, ripped stockings, and smeared makeup. Following a stint playing bass in Bjelland's band Babes in Toyland, Love briefly served as the lead singer of Faith No More.

In 1989 Love formed Hole with guitarist Eric Erlandson (born January 9, 1963, Los Angeles), bassist Jill Emery (born 1962), and drummer Caroline Rue. Hole was known for its intense raw sound and unpredictable live shows, and the band quickly gained wide acclaim for its debut album, *Pretty on the Inside* (1991), produced by Sonic Youth's Kim Gordon.

Love married Cobain on February 24, 1992, and later that year she gave birth to a daughter, Frances Bean Cobain. The Hole roster evolved during this time as Love and Erlandson were joined by the drummer Patty Schemel (born April 24, 1967, Seattle, Washington) and the bassist Kristen Pfaff (born May 26, 1967, Amherst, New York—died June 16 1994, Seattle). Cobain committed suicide days before the release of Hole's second album, *Live Through This* (1994). Two months later, Pfaff died of a heroin overdose.

Love earned critical acclaim and a Golden Globe nomination for her role in the film *The People vs. Larry Flynt* (1996). In 1998 Hole released *Celebrity Skin*, an enormous commercial success, but the group disbanded in May 2002. Love began her solo career with the release of *America's Sweetheart* (2004). Persistent abuse of drugs and alcohol, however, resulted in a cycle of arrests followed by periods of court-ordered rehabilitation. She lost custody of her daughter in 2003 and again in 2005. By 2007 Love was touring with a new band and was preparing for the release of her second solo album, but her tabloid behaviour continued to overshadow her music. In 2009, at age 17, Frances Bean was legally emancipated from her mother, and a temporary restraining order was filed against Love to prevent her from contacting her daughter. *Nobody's Daughter* was released in 2010 as a Hole album, although it was essentially a Love solo effort. In spite of songwriting assistance from Billy Corgan of the Smashing Pumpkins, the album was met with a poor critical reception.

## PEARL JAM

With angry, stadium-style rock highlighted by lead singer Eddie Vedder's impassioned baritone vocals, Pearl Jam joined Nirvana as the musical voice of Generation X. The original members were Vedder (born Edward Louis Severson III, December 23, 1964, Chicago, Illinois, U.S.), rhythm guitarist Stone Gossard (born July 20, 1966, Seattle, Washington), bassist Jeff Ament (born March 10, 1963, Havre, Montana), lead guitarist Mike McCready (born April 5, 1966, Pensacola, Florida), and drummer Dave Krusen (born March 10, 1966, Tacoma, Washington). Later members included Jack Irons (born July 18, 1962, Los Angeles, California), Dave Abbruzzese (born May 17, 1968, Stamford, Connecticut), and Matt Cameron (born November 28, 1962, San Diego, California).

Pearl Jam came into being in Seattle in 1990 when Gossard and Ament of the glam-influenced rock combo Mother Love Bone decided to form a new band following the death of their group's lead singer, Andrew Wood. Named after the unusual homemade jam of Vedder's great-grandmother Pearl, the band released its first album, *Ten*, in 1991. Alternative rock had already begun to receive mainstream acceptance, thanks largely to the popularity of Nirvana—who, like Pearl Jam, were part of Seattle's vibrant music scene—and *Ten* (featuring the major hits "Jeremy," "Evenflow," and "Alive") became a multimillion-seller.

The group also earned a reputation for resisting the mainstream music industry. Notably, they refused to produce music videos for any of the songs on their second album, *Vs* (1993), and in 1994 they canceled a tour as the result of a heated battle over ticket prices. Instead, the band scheduled concerts at venues that were much smaller than the stadiums they usually played and experimented with unorthodox ticket distribution techniques.

*Vitalogy* (1994), the group's third multimillion-selling album, explored longing and loss, and it included the Grammy-winning single "Spin the Black Circle." Pearl Jam backed Neil Young on *Mirror Ball* (1995), then released *No Code* (1996), whose stylistic departure disappointed some fans. Despite good reviews, *Yield* (1998) and *Binaural* (2000) were not commercial successes. Pearl Jam, however, remained a popular concert draw, and its 2000 European tour was chronicled on 25 live and unedited CDs. The politically charged *Riot Act* (2002) was a solid rock album, but its intensity did not approach the eponymous *Pearl Jam* (2006). Critics and fans embraced the return to the arena-rock sound of *Vs*, and singles like "World Wide Suicide" recalled the anger and urgency of "Jeremy."

In 2007 Vedder made his solo debut with *Into the Wild*, the score for the Sean Penn film of the same name. The film recounted the true story of a young man who turned his back on society to live in the Alaska wilderness, and Vedder's award-winning soundtrack captured the mood with stripped-down instrumentation and lyrics that recalled traditional American roots ballads.

The band debuted its 2009 album, *Backspacer*, on the social networking site Myspace, and it was one of the first releases to take advantage of Apple's iTunes LP format—a software enhancement meant to more closely replicate the experience of a physical album by offering liner notes, lyric sheets, and photographs of the band. Director Cameron Crowe marked the 20th anniversary of the band with the documentary *Pearl Jam Twenty* (2011).

## SMASHING PUMPKINS

The Smashing Pumpkins were one of the most popular and influential alternative rock groups of the 1990s. Founded by guitarist and songwriter Billy Corgan (born March 17, 1967, Elk Grove, Illinois, U.S.) in Chicago in 1988, the band created a postpunk blend of progressive rock, grunge, and psychedelia that incorporated the brooding atmospherics of goth rock and the adventurous melodiousness of "dream pop" bands such as the Cocteau Twins.

In addition to Corgan, the band's founding members were guitarist James Iha (born March 26, 1968, Chicago), bassist D'Arcy (born D'Arcy

Elizabeth Wretzky, May 1, 1968, South Haven, Michigan), and drummer Jimmy Chamberlin (born June 10, 1964, Joliet, Illinois). Although the group found success with its debut single, "I Am One" (1990), it was the band's debut album, *Gish* (1991), with its arena-ready anthems, multitracked guitars, and high melodrama, that helped transform the rock landscape of the 1990s.

The Smashing Pumpkins got even bigger with the release of their second album, the multiplatinum *Siamese Dream* (1993), which featured the hits "Cherub Rock," "Today," and "Disarm." The follow-up, a double album, *Mellon Collie and the Infinite Sadness* (1995), debuted at number one on the Billboard charts on the way to selling over four million copies in the United States and earning seven Grammy nominations.

The Smashing Pumpkins were at the peak of their popularity when Jonathan Melvoin, the band's touring keyboardist, died of a heroin overdose. Thereafter, matters worsened as the band experienced a series of lineup changes. *Adore* (1998) not only met with mixed reviews but sold poorly, and *MACHINA/The Machine of God* (2000) sounded as if Corgan were going it alone, which he was by December 2000, when the group broke up—though it released a parting shot, *Machina II: The Friends and Enemies of Modern Music*, on the Internet in early 2001.

In 2005, Corgan and Chamberlin, who had played together briefly in another band, Zwan, announced that the Smashing Pumpkins were reuniting; however, they were the only original members who performed on the subsequent release, *Zeitgeist* (2007). Chamberlin left the group in March 2009, and Corgan, once again on his own, issued an open casting call for a new drummer. That June, after more than 1,000 applications had been reviewed, Corgan announced that Mike Byrne, age 19, would take over percussion duties for the latest incarnation of the Smashing Pumpkins. After releasing a series of singles and EPs, the Smashing Pumpkins—now featuring Corgan, Byrne, guitarist Jeff Schroeder, and former Veruca Salt bassist Nicole Fiorentino—unveiled *Oceania* (2012). The album, which consisted of 13 songs from the band's larger Teargarden by Kaleidyscope concept project, was hailed by critics as the group's best work since the early 1990s.

# RAGE AGAINST THE MACHINE

Rage Against the Machine was formed in Los Angeles in the early 1990s and comprised vocalist Zack

# RAP METAL

Heavy metal has tended to be one of rock's most porous genres, influencing (and in turn being influenced by) such disparate sounds as psychedelic, glam, punk, and alternative rock. Rap metal (and the related genre, nu metal) represented a fusion of heavy metal instrumentation and hip-hop conventions such as rapped lyrics and "turntabling."

Rap metal preceded nu metal, and its earliest examples featured rather straightforward collaborations between established rap and metal artists. In 1986 Aerosmith backed Run-D.M.C. on the single "Walk This Way," and the Beastie Boys released *Licensed to Ill*, a breakthrough album that combined hard rock samples with playful, intelligent rap that traversed the pop culture spectrum. Anthrax successfully brought rap metal into the 1990s when it joined Public Enemy for a remake of the latter's "Bring the Noise." The soundtrack for the film *Judgment Night* (1993) was arguably the high point of rap and rock's collaboration, as more than 20 rap, metal, and alternative artists combined efforts on an album that spotlighted both the strengths and limitations that such partnerships could exhibit. By the mid-1990s, groups such as Rage Against the Machine had established a niche as dedicated rap metal bands, combining sharp, politically aware lyrics with driving guitars. Other commercially successful artists included the funk-infused Incubus, deejay-turned-frontman Kid Rock, and the novelty act Insane Clown Posse.

de la Rocha (born January 12, 1970, Long Beach, California, U.S.), guitarist Tom Morello (born May 30, 1964, New York, New York), bassist Tim Commerford (also known as Tim Bob, born February 26, 1968, Irvine, California), and drummer Brad Wilk (born September 5, 1968, Portland,

Oregon). The band quickly became known for incendiary political lyrics, social activism, and a hard-driving sound that incorporated elements of hip-hop and heavy metal.

The group self-released a 12-song cassette in 1992, which led to a contract with Epic Records. That same year the band's eponymous debut album established a signature sound characterized by Morello's inventive guitar work (which sometimes mimicked a deejay's turntable scratching), Wilk's pounding rhythms, and de la Rocha's furious high-pitched rapping. Early hit "Killing in the Name" addressed police corruption, and other songs were similarly political. The group became involved in causes such as former Black Panther and death row inmate Mumia Abu-Jamal's quest for a new trial, jailed Native American activist Leonard Peltier's pursuit of parole, and the plight of sweatshop workers in less-developed countries.

*Evil Empire* (1996), which reprised the densely textured musical approach and militant lyrics of the band's debut album, entered the Billboard albums chart at number one. *The Battle of Los Angeles* (1999) was also successful commercially. In the summer of 2000 the group staged a concert outside the Democratic National Convention in Los Angeles, after which a small riot erupted between some audience members and police. In October of

that year, de la Rocha announced his departure from the band shortly before the release of *Renegades*, an eclectic collection of covers of rock and hip-hop artists, including Bob Dylan, the Rolling Stones, Afrika Bambaataa, and EPMD. The remaining three members went on to form Audioslave with former Soundgarden vocalist Chris Cornell. In 2007 Rage Against the Machine reunited for the first of several concert tours, and the following year the band returned to its politically active roots by performing a protest concert in close proximity to the 2008 Republican National Convention.

# GREEN DAY

Green Day infused the raw power of punk with a melodic pop sensibility and lyrics that captured the restlessness of American teenagers at the end of the 20th century and into the 21st. The principal members were Billie Joe Armstrong (born February 17, 1972, Oakland, California, U.S.), Mike Dirnt (born Michael Ryan Pritchard, May 4, 1972, Oakland), and Tré Cool (born Frank Edwin Wright III, December 9, 1972, Willits, California). Other members included Al Sobrante (born John Kiffmeyer).

Armstrong and Dirnt met while attending grade school in Crockett, California, and bonded over their love of classic punk groups such as the

*Billie Joe Armstrong of Green Day onstage in Caracas, Venezuela, Oct. 8, 2010.* AFP/Getty Images

Ramones and the Dead Kennedys. In 1987 they and drummer Sean Hughes formed their first band, a punk outfit called Sweet Children. Hughes was later replaced by Sobrante, a member of local group Isocracy. Sweet Children became a popular live act in the San Francisco Bay Area. In 1989 the group recorded an album, *39/Smooth*, that was released by local label Lookout Records under the new band name Green Day (it was later repackaged as part of the band's 1991 release, *1,039/Smoothed Out Slappy Hours*). Not long afterward, Sobrante was replaced by Tré Cool, a drummer from the mountains around Mendocino, California, who

59

had been playing in the punk band the Lookouts since age 12.

Green Day built a cult following and found a foothold in California's burgeoning punk revival scene, of which they were one of the main engines. The band's next album, *Kerplunk* (1992), was also released by Lookout Records, but it drew attention from bigger labels, including Reprise, which released Green Day's major-label debut, *Dookie*, in 1994. The album carried the band's catchy pop-punk sound and Armstrong's apathetic lyrics into the mainstream, earning a Grammy Award for best alternative music performance and selling more than 15 million copies.

Green Day's next two albums, *Insomniac* and *Nimrod* (1997), did well commercially but failed to match the smash success of *Dookie*, and *Warning* (2000) marked a waning in the band's popularity. After a four-year break from recording, Green Day released the stylistic gamble *American Idiot* (2004), a politically charged album with operatic scope. The hugely successful release combined the large-scale political commentary of Green Day's punk forebears with the charged intimate observations of their own previous albums and in doing so achieved unexpected relevancy and acclaim. *American Idiot* sold 12 million copies worldwide and received the 2005 Grammy Award

for best rock album. Moreover, a single from the album, "Boulevard of Broken Dreams," won the Grammy Award for record of the year in 2006. In 2009 a rock opera based on—and scored with the songs from—the album was produced at a theatre in Berkeley, California. Depicting the dead-end efforts of a trio of teenagers to escape the conventional life of their parents' suburb, the musical *American Idiot* made a triumphant move to Broadway the following year, gaining rave reviews and two Tony Awards, for scenic design and lighting design of a musical. Green Day received a second Grammy Award for best rock album for *21st Century Breakdown* (2009), another ambitious song cycle. The Broadway cast album for the *American Idiot* musical was awarded a Grammy in 2011.

## SLEATER-KINNEY

Sleater-Kinney arose from the feminist punk rock movement known as "riot grrrl" and was acclaimed for recordings that combined a lean and aggressive sound with passionate socially conscious lyrics. The group originated in Olympia, Washington, as a collaboration between friends Corin Tucker (born November 9, 1972, State College, Pennsylvania, U.S.) and Carrie Brownstein (born September 27, 1974, Seattle, Washington) of the early 1990s riot grrrl bands Heavens to Betsy and Excuse 17, respectively. (Sleater-Kinney was named after a street in Olympia.) The two singer-guitarists recruited drummer Lora MacFarlane (February 20, 1970, Glasgow, Scotland) to record their self-titled debut album, released in 1995. Though the songs on the recording were somewhat unrefined, the band's essential musical elements—Tucker's fierce, often caterwauling lead vocals and chugging rhythm guitar, as well as Brownstein's jagged lead guitar—were already in place.

Sleater-Kinney's sophomore release, *Call the Doctor* (1996), brought the band attention with its sharp attacks on consumer culture and gender inequality. On songs such as "I Wanna Be Your Joey Ramone," the group even skewers the very indie rock scene in which it had become widely celebrated. With *Dig Me Out* (1997), Sleater-Kinney moved to influential independent label Kill Rock Stars and also introduced new drummer Janet Weiss (born September 24, 1965, Hollywood, California). By this time Brownstein had also emerged as a strong secondary songwriter and vocalist. *The Hot Rock* (1999) further raised Sleater-Kinney's profile, and *All Hands on the Bad One* (2000), with its intimations of 1960s girl-group vocal harmonies, showed a marked turn toward pop songcraft while maintaining the band's distinct edge.

*One Beat* (2002) proved to be an even more expansive affair, incorporating classic rock song structures as well as instruments such as horns and synthesizers. Tucker's lyrics drew inspiration from her newfound role as a mother, as well as the aftermath of the September 11 attacks. Perhaps the group's most radical departure, however, was *The Woods* (2005). Working with noted producer Dave Fridmann, the band displayed a new sense of open-ended improvisation, along with its most dense and bombastic arrangements. Having earned a reputation that far outpaced its moderate commercial success, Sleater-Kinney disbanded at the conclusion of its 2006 concert tour.

Tucker subsequently released a solo album, *1,000 Years* (2010), under the name the Corin Tucker Band. Weiss, meanwhile, drummed for the indie rock groups the Jicks (the backing band of former Pavement frontman Stephen Malkmus) and Quasi. In addition, she and Brownstein—who had spent the intervening years as a writer and an actress—helped found the band Wild Flag, which debuted with a self-titled album in 2011. That same year Brownstein went on to star with co-developer Fred Armisen in *Portlandia*, a sketch comedy show on the Independent Film Channel.

## MODEST MOUSE

Modest Mouse was just one of a number of post-grunge alternative rock acts to emerge from the fertile creative ground of the American Pacific Northwest. Known for musical idiosyncrasy and darkly comical lyrics, the group was the brainchild of singer, songwriter, and guitarist Isaac Brock (born July 9, 1975, Issaquah, Washington, U.S.), whose austere upbringing brought a pronounced fatalism to the band's catalog. Other original members were Eric Judy (born 1974), and Jeremiah Green (born March 4, 1977).

With bassist Judy and drummer Green, Brock founded Modest Mouse in 1993, the trio rehearsing in a shed near Brock's mother's Washington home. The group released its debut album, *This Is a Long Drive for Someone with Nothing to Think About*, in 1996 on independent label Up Records. *The Lonesome Crowded West* (1997) earned the attention of major labels, and the band signed with Sony/Epic, releasing *The Moon & Antarctica* in 2000.

The band's early work was characterized by swings between slow, country-inflected tunes and jerky punk rock, with Brock's bleating, often abrasive vocals serving as a common thread. Later albums saw increasing musical experimentation and a broader instrumental palette. *Good News for People Who Love Bad News* (2004) adopted more concise song structures and radio-friendly production but was also the group's most eclectic record to date, featuring accents of psychedelia, jazz, and even dance music. It also proved a commercial breakthrough, selling more than one million copies on the strength of the backhandedly optimistic hit "Float On." Follow-up *We Were Dead Before the Ship Even Sank* (2007) debuted at the top of Billboard's Top 200 albums chart.

The core membership remained generally consistent, although Green briefly left the band in 2003 and 2004. Over time the group brought in additional musicians, including former Smiths guitarist Johnny Marr for several years. Brock, who had once worked as an artists-and-repertoire (A&R) agent for Seattle label Sub Pop Records, founded his own label in 2005, and he devoted much of his energy to signing and promoting emerging artists.

## WILCO

Wilco spun off from the group Uncle Tupelo in the mid-1990s and evolved from its alternative country roots into one of the most successful and multifaceted rock groups of its time. The original members were Jeff Tweedy (born August 25, 1967, Belleville, Illinois, U.S.), Ken Coomer (born November 5, 1960, Nashville, Tennessee), John Stirratt (born November 26, 1967, New Orleans, Louisiana), and Max Johnston.

Later members included Jay Bennett (born November 15, 1963, Rolling Meadows, Illinois—found dead May 24, 2009, Urbana, Illinois), Bob Egan (born July 12, 1956, Virginia, Minnesota), Glenn Kotche, Leroy Bach, Mikael Jorgensen, Nels Cline (born January 4, 1956, Los Angeles, California), and Pat Sansone (born June 21, 1969, Meridian, Mississippi).

Following the bitter breakup of alternative country band Uncle Tupelo, which had been based in Belleville, Illinois, near St. Louis, Missouri, cofounder Tweedy relocated to Chicago. Vocalist-guitarist Tweedy was joined there by former Uncle Tupelo members Coomer (drums), Stirratt (bass), and Johnston (multi-instrumentalist) in a new group, Wilco, a name derived from the trucker lingo "roger, wilco, okay." After recording their 1995 debut album, *A.M.*, they were joined by Bennett, a guitarist with a knack for playing many instruments and a background as a recording engineer. Bennett would prove crucial in the band's development as it moved beyond the country-flavoured rock songs of its debut. Tweedy, the primary songwriter and driving force in the band, retooled its approach on the 1996 album *Being There*. Adding keyboards and noisy textural elements to its roots rock foundation, the quintet morphed into one of the decade's most adventurous bands, a reputation cemented by boisterous live shows. In 1998 Tweedy and Wilco collaborated with British singer-songwriter Billy Bragg on the *Mermaid Avenue* album, in which they created music for lyrics left behind by Dust Bowl folksinger Woody Guthrie. The project produced one of Wilco's best-known songs, "California Stars." A second *Mermaid* volume followed in 2000.

The 1999 Wilco album *Summerteeth* found the band shifting its sound again into lush orchestral pop, a gambit employed in part to disguise some of Tweedy's most twisted and tortured lyrics, which were about a disintegrating relationship. The making of the 2002 album *Yankee Hotel Foxtrot* proved to be a turning point, with the band transforming a series of disappointments into a triumphant release. Coomer had been ousted during the recording sessions (he was replaced by drummer Kotche), and Bennett was fired soon after the album was finished, an acrimonious breakup glimpsed in Sam Jones's 2002 documentary *I Am Trying to Break Your Heart*. The album was greeted unenthusiastically by the band's label, Warner Brothers' Reprise, and the band was later dropped. Wilco began streaming the record on its Web site and went on tour in the fall of 2001, playing to energized audiences. *Foxtrot* was released the following spring by another Warner label, Nonesuch, and went on to become the most

# JAY BENNETT

Jay Bennett was best known for his role in shaping the sound of the alternative rock band Wilco. After recording with a number of bands, most notably the alternative rock quartet Titanic Love Affair, Bennett was recruited in 1994 by Jeff Tweedy to join Wilco. Wilco had already recorded one album that hewed closely to the alt-country model, but with the addition of Bennett, a multi-instrumentalist and gifted producer, the band's sound expanded in a dramatic way to include lush psychedelic influences and power pop sensibilities. The group also evolved as a live act, with Bennett providing a manic dreadlocked counterpoint to Tweedy's somewhat sedate stage presence. Bennett contributed to the albums *Being There* (1996) and *Summerteeth* (1999), and he assisted with the arrangement of the Wilco/Billy Bragg collaboration *Mermaid Avenue*, a collection of unfinished Woody Guthrie songs. The apex of Bennett's influence on the band's sound was the 2002 release *Yankee Hotel Foxtrot*, but the relationship between Bennett and Tweedy was strained, and Bennett was asked to leave the group just prior to the album's release. Bennett released a string of solo albums that showcased his skills as a producer, but he rarely toured.

commercially successful release in the band's career to date.

Soon after completing its fifth studio album, *A Ghost Is Born* (2004), the band was immersed in more turmoil. Tweedy checked himself into a rehab clinic for a longtime addiction to painkillers. The volatile lineup was shuffled again, with keyboardist Bach departing and guitarist Cline and multi-instrumentalist Sansone joining Tweedy, Stirratt, Kotche, and Jorgensen to create a sextet. This would prove to be the band's longest-lived incarnation. The unusual period of stability was characterized by widening success as a touring act and steady record sales for the gently introspective *Sky Blue Sky* (2007) and the career-spanning compendium *Wilco (The Album)*, released in 2009. On a track from the latter, "Wilco (The Song)," Tweedy even demonstrated a sense of humour, singing, "Wilco will love you, baby."

In January 2011 the band announced that it was leaving Nonesuch to form its own label, dBpm Records. Wilco's first album for the label, *The Whole Love* (2011), opened with an adventurous seven-minute sound collage, "Art of Almost," and closed with a 12-minute meditation, "One Sunday Morning (Song for Jane Smiley's Boyfriend)." In between were more concise examples of Tweedy's songwriting range, from Beatles-inspired chamber pop to autumnal folk, highlighting the band's increasingly accomplished interplay.

## WHITE STRIPES

The Detroit-based duo the White Stripes were known for combining punk, folk, country, and Mississippi Delta blues. Original band members were Jack White (born John Anthony Gillis, July 9, 1975, Detroit, Michigan, U.S.) and Meg White (born Megan Martha White, December 10, 1974, Grosse Pointe Farms, Michigan). There was much speculation about whether guitarist-vocalist Jack White and drummer Meg White were brother and sister, as they often claimed, or husband and wife. Despite the eventual discovery by the media of a marriage license (1996) and a divorce certificate (2000), the pair remained enigmatic about the precise nature of their relationship.

During the 1990s Meg held a variety of service jobs, and Jack worked as a furniture upholsterer. Exposed to a wide range of music by his employer, Brian Muldoon, Jack became interested in the sound of Detroit punk pioneers Iggy and the Stooges and the MC5. Jack (on guitar) and Muldoon recorded a blues-infused single under the name the Upholsterers. Trading one set of influences for another, in 1993 Jack signed on as drummer for the established "cow-punk" band Goober and the Peas. Jack gained experience onstage and in the recording studio, and the group's sound (a fusion of punk and rockabilly) and its stage persona (featuring cowboy hats and embroidered western suits) would reappear in his later work. In 1996 Goober and the Peas broke up, and Jack and Meg were married. That year the couple moved into Jack's childhood home, and they began to craft the sound of the White Stripes. The duo played at venues around Detroit, frequently appearing with Two-Star Tabernacle, a country-rock outfit that featured Jack and former Goober and the Peas front man Dan Miller. The White Stripes signed a contract with the independent Sympathy for the Record Industry label, and the duo's self-titled debut album was released in 1999. It was followed the next year by *De Stijl*.

In 2001 the White Stripes released their breakthrough album, *White Blood Cells*. Michel Gondry's eye-catching video for the single "Fell in Love with a Girl" received regular airplay on MTV, and the group became media darlings. The duo followed with *Elephant* (2003), a percussion-driven collection of songs that featured Meg's debut as a vocalist. *Elephant* earned a Grammy Award for best alternative music album, and it sold over a million copies on the strength of singles such as "Seven Nation Army." Jack appeared in the film *Cold Mountain* (2003), and he contributed five songs to its Grammy-nominated soundtrack. He also produced country legend Loretta Lynn's *Van Lear Rose* (2004), a collection of honky-tonk anthems that earned a pair of Grammy awards and introduced Lynn to a new generation of fans. The White Stripes earned another Grammy for their album *Get Behind Me Satan* (2005), and the song "Icky Thump," from their album of the same name (2007), became the band's first Top 40 hit on the Billboard singles chart.

The White Stripes went on hiatus in 2007 after Meg was afflicted with performance-related anxiety. They returned to the stage for a single performance in February 2009 for the final episode of *Late Night with Conan O'Brien*. Continuing to expand his body of work, Jack experimented with straightforward power pop as a member of the Raconteurs. The quartet produced a pair of well-received albums (2006 and 2008) and quickly became a fixture on the summer concert circuit. Meg married guitarist Jackson Smith (son of rock legend Patti Smith) in May 2009, and Jack undertook yet another side project. Enlisting members of the Kills and Queens of the Stone Age, Jack formed the Dead Weather, a bluesy psychedelic rock combo whose debut album, *Horehound*, was released in July 2009.

In March 2009 Jack founded Third Man Records, a Nashville record store, performance space, and label. As the rest of the music industry was trying to adjust its business model to accommodate digital downloads, White's label embraced the physical artifacts of the album era: the turntable, the gatefold cover, and, above all, high-quality vinyl releases. As Jack spent more time on Third Man and other projects—he produced *The Party Ain't Over*, the 2011 comeback album from rockabilly legend Wanda

Jackson—White Stripes fans began to suspect that the band's hiatus might be permanent. This was confirmed when in February 2011 Meg and Jack announced that they would no longer record or appear as the White Stripes. The following year Jack embarked on a solo career with the stylistically expansive Blunderbuss.

# EMO

Emo arose in Washington, D.C., in the mid-1980s. Guy Picciotto (who was later a founding member of the influential hardcore group Fugazi) and his band, Rites of Spring, launched the subgenre when they moved away from a punk scene that sometimes favoured attitude over substance, and they put the focus of the music and lyrics on personal pain and suffering. This confessional approach to singing punk music was dubbed emocore, or hard-core emotional, by fans in the 1980s. The lyrics in emo songs dealt primarily with tales of loss or failed romance, and they were often characterized by self-pity. The stories in emo music strongly resonated with teenage fans.

Over time, emo evolved to include radio-friendly pop punk bands, such as Weezer, Jimmy Eat World, Get Up Kids, Saves the Day, and Fall Out Boy, whose sound bore little resemblance to that of the Washington,

D.C., hardcore scene. Emo became less associated with a specific sound, and groups such as Death Cab for Cutie found themselves saddled with a label that took on an increasingly pejorative connotation. Like punk before it, the word *emo* was eventually applied to fashions and attitudes that had little to do with the music that initially defined the term.

## DEATH CAB FOR CUTIE

The American indie-rock group Death Cab for Cutie helped popularize the emo genre in the early 2000s. Original members were lead singer Ben Gibbard (born August 11, 1976, Bremerton, Washington, U.S.), guitarist Chris Walla (born November 2, 1975, Bothell, Washington), bassist Nicholas Harmer (born January 23, 1975, Bothell), and drummer Nathan Good. Later members included Michael Schorr and Jason McGerr.

Death Cab for Cutie founders Gibbard and Walla met in the mid-1990s at Western Washington University, in Bellingham, Washington, where they began to help each other write and record music in their dormitories. With Walla's help, Gibbard produced a cassette, *You Can Play These Songs with Chords*, which earned him a local following. Soon after, additional members were brought in and the band began performing as Death Cab for Cutie, a name taken from a song by 1960s psychedelic rock group the Bonzo Dog Doo-Dah Band.

In 1998 the band's debut album, *Something About Airplanes*, was released on Seattle's Barsuk Records, and it created buzz on the indie-rock scene. The group followed with *We Have the Facts and We're Voting Yes* (2000) and *The Photo Album* (2001); the latter was highly praised for its exploration of relationships. After touring, band members dispersed and devoted time to solo efforts. During this time Gibbard's new wave-influenced side project, the Postal Service, produced *Give Up* (2003). The title of Death Cab for Cutie's next album, *Transatlanticism* (2003), refers to the distances that had separated the band members during the album's preparation. The success of *Transatlanticism* led the band to sign with Atlantic Records in 2005. Plans, the group's major label debut, was released that year. In 2008 Death Cab for Cutie released *Narrow Stairs*, a darker album that hit number one on the Billboard charts in its first week of release. The group followed with *Codes and Keys* (2011), a comparatively upbeat album that found its muse in Gibbard's wife, actress and singer Zooey Deschanel (the couple split six months after the album's release).

## THE STROKES

Although their songs hinted at a rough-and-tumble life, the Strokes were composed mainly of privileged sons of the New York City elite. Singer Julian Casablancas (born August 23, 1978, New York, New York, U.S.), guitarist Nick Valensi (born January 16, 1981, New York), and drummer Fabrizio Moretti (born June 2, 1980, Rio de Janeiro, Braz.) began playing together in 1998 as schoolmates in Manhattan. Guitarist Albert Hammond, Jr. (born April 9, 1980, Los Angeles, California), and bassist Nikolai Fraiture (born November 13, 1978, New York), acquaintances of the original trio, joined shortly thereafter, solidifying the Strokes as a quintet in 1999.

Playing clubs on New York's Lower East Side, the group quickly became local favourites. Their debut EP, *The Modern Age* (2001), earned the adoration of the British music press, most notably of the magazine *NME*. The Strokes's lean hooks, laconic vocals, and spartan production—seen by many as a much-needed breath of fresh air in the rock world of the early 21st century—inspired a wave of followers before the group's first album had even been released. *Is This It* hit the shelves in the United Kingdom in the summer of 2001, with an American release following several months later (the controversial track "New York City

Cops" was removed from the American version of the album as a gesture of respect in the wake of the September 11 attacks). Already the toast of the music press, the Strokes also landed on tabloid pages as a result of their rock-star antics and celebrity liaisons.

By the 2003 release of their sophomore album, new wave-inspired *Room on Fire*, the Strokes phenomenon had already peaked, but the band retained a large following. Featuring another crop of infectious but coolly delivered rock songs, the album was considered by critics to be of a piece with its predecessor. Its first single, "12:51," topped out at number seven on the UK Singles Chart. *First Impressions of Earth* (2006) featured more robust, polished production and greater songwriting ambition but failed to produce a major hit song. After the ensuing concert tour, the band members spent the next several years pursuing other projects, including Moretti's well-received rock trio Little Joy and solo efforts by Hammond (the son of singer-songwriter Albert Hammond). The group returned to the studio for *Angles* (2011), an album of '80s-inspired power pop that received middling reviews.

## MY CHEMICAL ROMANCE

Singer Gerard Way (born April 9, 1977, Summit, New Jersey, U.S.) founded My Chemical Romance in 2001 in the immediate aftermath of the September 11 attacks, citing the tragedy as a motivation to "make a difference." The group's original lineup consisted of Way, brother Michael James (Mikey) Way (born September 10, 1980, Newark, New Jersey) on bass, drummer Matt Pelissier, and guitarists Ray Toro (born July 15, 1977, Kearney, New Jersey) and Frank Iero (born October 31, 1981, Belleville, New Jersey). The quintet began touring prior to releasing its first album, *I Brought You My Bullets, You Brought Me Your Love*, on independent label Eyeball Records in 2002, building a reputation for their gothic looks and dramatic performance style. The following year they signed with Reprise Records.

*Three Cheers for Sweet Revenge* (2004) featured modern-rock radio hits "I'm Not Okay (I Promise)," "Helena," and "The Ghost of You." These and other anthems of teenage angst earned the band a devoted following, and the album ultimately went platinum. That year Pelissier became the first of the original lineup to depart. Iero, Mikey Way, and Pelissier's replacement, Bob Bryar, also left the group at various points, though all three eventually returned.

*The Black Parade* (2006), a bombastic rock opera about the reflections of a dying cancer patient, was produced by Rob Cavallo, who had worked previously with pop-punk group Green Day on its similarly ambitious *American Idiot*. The ensuing multicontinent concert tour found My Chemical Romance at their most theatrical, with Gerard Way opening shows by being wheeled onstage on a hospital gurney and the rest of the band wearing matching black uniforms. *Black Parade Is Dead!*, released in 2008, was a live album recorded during this tour. The group tapped a similarly dramatic vein for *Danger Days: The True Lives of the Fabulous Killjoys* (2010), a concept album that traded angst for a broader rock appeal.

## TV ON THE RADIO

TV on the Radio craft multilayered musical collages that mix sonic experimentation with accessible pop hooks. The lineup included vocalist Tunde Adebimpe (born Babatunde Omoroga Adebimpe, February 25, 1975, St. Louis, Missouri, U.S.), multi-instrumentalist David Andrew Sitek (born September 6, 1972, Maryland), vocalist-guitarist Kyp Malone (born February 27, 1973, Pennsylvania), drummer Jaleel Bunton (born October 24, 1974, California), and bassist-keyboardist Gerard Smith (born September 20, 1974, New York, New York—died April 20, 2011, Brooklyn, New York).

The group was founded in 2001 when Adebimpe and Sitek met as neighbours in Brooklyn, New York. Finding much in common as visual artists and musicians, the pair self-released a demo recording, *OK Calculator* (2002), the title of which was a play on English rock group Radiohead's seminal album *OK Computer*. The two made their commercial debut on the independent Touch and Go label with the EP *Young Liars* (2003), and they brought Malone on board for the group's first full-fledged LP, *Desperate Youth, Blood Thirsty Babes* (2004). Though Bunton played drums on that album, he and Smith did not officially join the band until after its release. With a foundation of eccentrically timed drum loops and droning electronics adorned with jazzy horns and the striking interplay of Adebimpe and Malone's vocals, the album made TV on the Radio a critics' darling.

This success earned the group a contract with major label Interscope Records, which released *Return to Cookie Mountain* (2006), a densely layered recording whose stylistic reference points ranged from 1980s industrial music to the psychedelic soul of Parliament Funkadelic to 1950s doo-wop. Like the lyrics on the group's debut album, those on *Return* included meditations on war and societal unrest. Along with growing contributions from Bunton and

Smith, the album also featured a guest vocal performance by rock icon David Bowie, an avowed fan of the band.

*Dear Science* (2008) offered a brightening of the group's musical textures and lyrics, with an increased focus on hip-hop beats and major-key melodies. It debuted in the upper reaches of the Billboard albums chart and was named album of the year by *Rolling Stone* and *Spin*. It also topped the *Village Voice*'s influential annual "Pazz & Jop" critics' poll. As the accolades mounted, the band members turned their attention to other projects. In 2008 Adepimpe made his feature-film debut as an actor and singer in Jonathan Demme's *Rachel Getting Married*. Both he and Sitek had previously worked with art punk group the Yeah Yeah Yeahs, and they had a hand in that band's 2009 album *It's Blitz!*, which featured Adebimpe as a guest artist and Sitek as coproducer. Sitek also produced Scarlett Johansson's *Anywhere I Lay My Head* (2008), which featured the actress's interpretation of Tom Waits songs. Malone released a solo album titled *Rain Machine* in 2009, and the following year Sitek's pop group Maximum Balloon released its debut LP. The group returned to the studio for *Nine Types of Light* (2011), an ambitious departure that traded the driving bass of *Dear Science* for torch-song lyrics and rock-ballad instrumentation. Shortly after the release of the *Nine Types of Light*, Smith died of lung cancer.

## THE DECEMBERISTS

American indie-rock band the Decemberists are known for their highly stylized, literate songs. The band's principal members are lead singer and guitarist Colin Meloy (born October 5, 1974, Helena, Montana, U.S.), keyboardist and accordionist Jenny Conlee (born December 12, 1971, Seattle, Washington), guitarist Chris Funk (born November 28, 1971, Valparaiso, Indiana), drummer John Moen (born August 23, 1968, Brainerd, Minnesota), and bassist Nate Query (born September 5, 1973, Bellevue, Washington).

Formed in 2000 in Portland, Oregon, the Decemberists (with drummers Ezra Holbrook to 2002 and Rachel Blumberg from 2002 to 2005) initially hewed to a primarily folk-pop sound built around acoustic guitar melodies. Their first album, however, *Castaways and Cutouts* (2002), featured the baroque instrumentation and narrative song structures (as well as Meloy's idiosyncratically nasal voice) that would become the band's hallmarks.

In 2003 the group released *Her Majesty the Decemberists*, which built on the first album's sound to include prominent horn and string sections. Their EP (a format intermediate in

The Decemberists (left to right): *John Moen, Jenny Conlee, Colin Meloy, Nate Query, and Chris Funk.* Autumn De Wilde

length between a single and an album) *The Tain* (2004) consisted of a single song broken into multiple movements and foreshadowed the Decemberists' future direction. As the band grew more successful, its live shows developed a distinct theatrical bent, replete with elaborate stage designs and props, and the *Decemberists* became one of indie rock's most popular concert draws. Their third full-length record, Picaresque (2005), featured a wide-ranging set of songs that tell the stories of a diverse cast of characters, including a widowed peddler, spies who tragically fall in love, a pair of homeless runaways, and two men trapped inside the belly of a whale. The last of these tracks, "The Mariner's Revenge Song," was an eight-minute epic in the style of a sea shanty, which became one of the band's signature concert numbers, its performance augmented by the presence of a massive papier-mâché whale.

After the Decemberists signed in 2005 with major label Capitol Records, some observers speculated that the band might be required to make artistic compromises for the mainstream label. However, the group's first album with Capitol, *The Crane Wife* (2006), assuaged those fears. It featured elegant ballads about a man falling in love with and marrying a wounded crane that temporarily takes the form of a woman, alongside sprawling progressive-rock-infused jams, and was atop many critics' lists of the year's best albums.

In 2009 the band's uninterrupted hour-long rock opera *The Hazards of Love* debuted at number 14 on the Billboard album charts. The group's follow-up, *The King Is Dead* (2011), marked the Decemberists' return to both an independent label and the rustic folk-influenced sound of their earliest work, and it reached number one on the Billboard charts in the first week after its release.

# ARCADE FIRE

Arcade Fire was founded in 2003 in Montreal when transplanted Texan singer and guitarist Win Butler (born April 14, 1980) met multi-instrumentalist Régine Chassagne (born August 18, 1977) at an art opening. The two formed a songwriting partnership and eventually married. The group's original lineup was completed with Win's brother, William Butler (born October 6, 1982), playing synthesizer and percussion, along with keyboardist Richard Reed Parry (born October 4, 1977) and bassist Tim Kingsbury. The band's ranks continued to swell, including additional drummers, violinists, and others.

The seven-song EP *Arcade Fire* (2003) led to a recording contract with the independent North Carolina-based Merge Records, which released the full-length *Funeral* in 2004. Inspired by a spate of deaths in band members' families, the album's lyrics explored themes of mortality and mourning, yet the group's energetic performance, lush instrumentation, and romantic sense of melody yielded unlikely anthems such as "Wake Up" and "Rebellion (Lies)." Upon its release, *Funeral* was reviewed reverently by online music magazine Pitchfork, leading to a barrage of mainstream press coverage. Almost immediately

# POST-ROCK

The term *post-rock* was coined in 1994 by music critic Simon Reynolds in his discussion of the music of Talk Talk and Bark Psychosis. Post-rock generally applied to bands that used the typical instruments of a rock band—two guitars, a bass, and drums—with nontraditional rhythms, melodies, and chord progressions. Guitars created ambience by altering the colour and quality of the sound. Vocals, if they were included, were frequently treated not as a vehicle for lyrics but as an additional instrument. The focus was on the texture of the music and the sound produced rather than on melodic patterns and the basic structure of a rock song. Embracing "quiet as the new loud," post-rock shifted away from the hard, male-driven outbursts of rock music as that music became more commercialized; post-rock and other alternative genres were more independent and less commercially oriented.

The genre got its start in 1991 with landmark albums from two pioneer post-rock bands: Talk Talk's *Laughing Stock* and Slint's *Spiderland*. Some artists rejected the post-rock label, while others cheerfully embraced a genre that included such influential acts as Stereolab, Tortoise, and the Sea and Cake. Later examples of the genre included the orchestral rock of Godspeed You! Black Emperor, the soaring "Hopelandic" vocals of Sigur Rós, and the sample-rich ambient pop of M83.

it outsold every prior release in Merge's 15-year history. Additionally, Arcade Fire's success helped cement Pitchfork's reputation as an indie rock tastemaker.

On its ensuing concert tour in 2004 and 2005, the group appeared at major music festivals such as Chicago's Lollapalooza and southern California's Coachella. The band retreated to a church outside Montreal to record the bulk of *Neon Bible* (2007), which incorporated choral vocals, pipe organ, and even a live orchestra as part of a darker musical tapestry, with lyrics focusing on the conflict between spirituality and materialism in contemporary society.

Arcade Fire's third album, *The Suburbs* (2010), departed from the elegiac sound of its predecessor, incorporating synthesizers and new wave dance beats into a meditation on the cyclical nature of life. Despite the fact that the band continued to lack the marketing support of a major record label, the release debuted at number one on the Billboard album chart and in 2011 won album of the year at the Grammy Awards.

# CHAPTER 4

# The Rise of the Hip-Hop Nation

**A**lthough widely considered a synonym for rap music, the term *hip-hop* refers to a complex culture comprising four elements: deejaying, or "turntabling"; rapping, also known as "MCing" or "rhyming"; graffiti painting, also known as "graf" or "writing"; and "B-boying," which encompasses hip-hop dance, style, and attitude, along with the sort of virile body language that philosopher Cornel West described as "postural semantics." Hip-hop originated in the predominantly African American economically depressed South Bronx section of New York City in the late 1970s. As the hip-hop movement began at society's margins, its origins are shrouded in myth, enigma, and obfuscation.

Graffiti and break dancing, the aspects of the culture that first caught public attention, had the least lasting effect. Reputedly, the graffiti movement was started about 1972 by a Greek American teenager who signed, or "tagged," Taki 183 (his name and street, 183rd Street) on walls throughout the New York City subway system. By 1975 youths in the Bronx, Queens, and Brooklyn were stealing into train yards under cover of darkness to spray-paint colourful mural-size renderings of their names, imagery from underground comics and television, and even Andy Warhol-like Campbell's soup cans onto the sides of subway cars. Soon, influential art dealers in the United States, Europe, and Japan were displaying graffiti in major galleries. New York City's Metropolitan Transit Authority responded with dogs, barbed-wire fences, paint-removing acid baths, and undercover police squads.

The beginnings of the dancing, rapping, and deejaying components of hip-hop were bound together by the shared environment in which these art forms evolved. The first major hip-hop deejay was DJ Kool Herc (Clive Campbell), an 18-year-old immigrant who introduced the huge sound systems of his native Jamaica to inner-city parties. Using two turntables, he melded percussive fragments from older records with popular dance songs to create a continuous flow of music. Kool Herc and other pioneering hip-hop deejays such as Grand Wizard Theodore, Afrika Bambaataa, and Grandmaster Flash isolated and extended the break beat (the part of a dance record where all sounds but the drums drop out), stimulating improvisational dancing. Contests developed in which the best dancers created break dancing, a style with a repertoire of acrobatic and occasionally airborne moves, including gravity-defying headspins and backspins.

In the meantime, deejays developed new techniques for turntable manipulation. Needle dropping, created by Grandmaster Flash, prolonged short drum breaks by playing two copies of a record simultaneously and moving the needle on one turntable back to the start of the break while the other played. Sliding the record back and forth underneath the needle created the rhythmic effect called "scratching."

Kool Herc was widely credited as the father of modern rapping for his spoken interjections over records, but among the wide variety of oratorical precedents cited for MCing are the epic histories of West African griots, talking blues songs, jailhouse toasts (long rhyming poems recounting outlandish deeds and misdeeds), and the dozens (the ritualized word game based on exchanging insults, usually about members of the opponent's family). Other influences cited include the hipster-jive announcing styles of 1950s rhythm-and-blues deejays such as Jocko Henderson; the black power poetry of Amiri Baraka, Gil Scott-Heron, and the Last Poets; rapping sections in recordings by Isaac Hayes and George Clinton; and the Jamaican style of rhythmized speech known as toasting.

Rap first came to national prominence in the United States with the release of the Sugarhill Gang's song "Rapper's Delight" (1979) on the independent African American-owned label Sugar Hill. Within weeks of its release, it had become a chart-topping phenomenon and given its name to a new genre of pop music. The major pioneers of rapping were

# RAP

Rap is a musical style in which rhythmic and/or rhyming speech is chanted ("rapped") to musical accompaniment. This backing music, which can include digital sampling (music and sounds extracted from other recordings), is also called hip-hop, the name used to refer to a broader cultural movement that includes rap, deejaying (turntable manipulation), graffiti painting, and break dancing. Rap, which originated in African American communities in New York City, came to national prominence with the Sugar Hill Gang's "Rapper's Delight" (1979). Rap's early stars included Grandmaster Flash and the Furious Five, Run-D.M.C., LL Cool J, Public Enemy (who espoused a radical political message), and the Beastie Boys. The late 1980s saw the advent of "gangsta rap," with lyrics that were often misogynistic or that glamorized violence and drug dealing. Later stars include Diddy, Snoop Lion (formerly Snoop Dogg), Jay-Z, OutKast, Eminem, Kanye West, and Lil Wayne.

Grandmaster Flash and the Furious Five, Kurtis Blow, and the Cold Crush Brothers, whose Grandmaster Caz is controversially considered by some to be the true author of some of the strongest lyrics in "Rapper's Delight." These early MCs and deejays constituted rap's old school.

## GRANDMASTER FLASH AND THE FURIOUS FIVE

Formed in the Bronx, New York City, in 1976, Grandmaster Flash and the Furious Five were one of the first multimember rapping crews. The members were Grandmaster Flash (born Joseph Saddler, January 1, 1958), Cowboy (born Keith Wiggins, September 20, 1960—died September 8, 1989), Melle Mel (born Melvin Glover), Kid Creole (born Nathaniel Glover), Mr. Ness (also called Scorpio; born Eddie Morris), and Raheim (born Guy Williams).

The group was a staple of the earliest hip-hop shows in the Bronx and Harlem, and nonrapping member

*Grandmaster Flash accepting an award in 2006.* Rick Diamond—BET Networks/PRNewsFoto/AP Images

Grandmaster Flash was credited with being an inventor and innovator of many of the techniques and performing gimmicks associated with hip-hop deejaying. He also jury-rigged a drum machine into his turntable and created miniature audio dramas on his legendary 12-inch single "The Adventures of Grandmaster Flash on the Wheels of Steel" (1981) that presaged digital sampling. As recording artists on hip-hop's flagship label, Sugar Hill, the group was originally known for high-energy singles such as "Freedom" (1980) and "Birthday Party" (1981), which combined their rhyme skills with slick production. With their depiction of the harsh realities of ghetto life in "The Message" (1982), they became the pioneers of socially conscious protest rap, inspiring the likes of Public Enemy's Chuck D and Boogie Down Production's KRS-One to create provocative social commentary in the manner of Bob Dylan and Bob Marley. The group

# GIL SCOTT-HERON

Gil Scott-Heron (born April 1, 1949, Chicago, Ill.—died May 27, 2011, New York, New York) created music that lacerated the complacency of white middle-class America, most notably with his sardonic spoken-word anthem "The Revolution Will Not Be Televised." On his first album, *Small Talk at 125th and Lenox* (1970), Scott-Heron performed verse from his volume of poetry of the same title, accompanied by bongos and conga drums; highlights of that album included "The Revolution Will Not Be Televised" and "Whitey on the Moon." The following year he began recording a series of soul-jazz albums, among them *Pieces of a Man* (1971), which contained "Lady Day and John Coltrane" and "Home Is Where the Hatred Is," and *Winter in America* (1974), which featured "The Bottle." He also wrote two novels. Scott-Heron's career was marred by his addiction to drugs and alcohol, though he occasionally emerged to record music; his final solo album, *I'm New Here*, was released in 2010.

also tackled drug abuse in "White Lines" (1983). By the mid-1980s the group had disbanded, and later reunions were short-lived. In 2007 Grandmaster Flash and the Furious Five became the first hip-hop act inducted into the Rock and Roll Hall of Fame.

## SUGAR HILL RECORDS

Launched in 1979 by industry veterans Sylvia and Joe Robinson as a label for rap music (at that time a new genre), Sugar Hill Records, based in Englewood, New Jersey, was named after the upmarket section of Harlem and funded by Manhattan-based distributor Maurice Levy. Sylvia (born Sylvia Vanderpool) had a national hit in 1957 with "Love Is Strange" as half of the duo Mickey and Sylvia; Robinson was a former promotions man. Together they ran the All-Platinum label with some success during the 1970s.

At Sugar Hill a core session team of guitarist Skip McDonald, bass player Doug Wimbish, drummer Keith Leblanc, and percussionist Ed Fletcher provided the compulsive rhythm for most of the label's releases, including three milestone 12-inch (long-playing) singles in the genre that came to be called hip-hop. "Rapper's Delight" (1979) by the Sugarhill Gang was the first to make the Top 40; "The Adventures of Grandmaster Flash on the Wheels of Steel" (1981) was a 15-minute epic that sampled sections of Chic's "Good Times" (1979) and showcased the new sound of scratching; and "The Message" (1982) by Grandmaster Flash and the Furious Five, a heartfelt account of life in the ghetto, showed the potential of hip-hop for conveying social comment.

## THE NEW SCHOOL AND THE EVOLUTION OF GANGSTA

In the mid-1980s the next wave of rappers, the new school, came to prominence. At the forefront was Run-D.M.C., a trio of middle-class African Americans who fused rap with hard rock, defined a new style of hip dress, and became staples on MTV as they brought rap to a mainstream audience. Run-D.M.C. recorded for Profile, one of several new labels that took advantage of the growing market for rap music. Def Jam featured three important innovators: LL Cool J, rap's first romantic superstar; the Beastie Boys, a white trio who broadened rap's audience and popularized digital sampling (composing with music and sounds electronically lifted from other recordings); and Public Enemy, who invested rap with radical black political ideology, building on the social consciousness of Grandmaster Flash and the Furious Five's "The Message" (1982).

Rap's classical period (1979–93) also included significant contributions from De La Soul—whose debut album on Tommy Boy, *3 Feet High and Rising* (1989), pointed in a new and more playful direction—and female rappers such as Queen Latifah and Salt-n-Pepa, who offered an alternative to rap's predominantly male, often misogynistic viewpoint. Hip-hop artists from places other than New York City began to make their mark, including DJ Jazzy Jeff and the Fresh Prince (Will Smith), from Philadelphia; the provocative 2 Live Crew, from Miami; and M.C. Hammer, from Oakland, California, who experienced short-lived but massive crossover success with a pop audience.

The most significant response to New York hip-hop, though, came from Los Angeles, beginning in 1989 with N.W.A.'s dynamic album *Straight Outta Compton*. N.W.A. (Niggaz With Attitude) and former members of that group—Ice Cube, Eazy E, and Dr. Dre—led the way as West Coast rap grew in prominence in the early 1990s. Their graphic, frequently violent tales of real life in the inner city, as well as those of Los Angeles rappers such as Ice-T (remembered for his 1992 single "Cop Killer") and Snoop Lion and of East Coast counterparts such as Schoolly D, gave rise to the genre known as gangsta rap. As the Los Angeles-based label Death Row Records built an empire around Dr. Dre, Snoop, and the charismatic, complicated rapper-actor Tupac Shakur, it also entered into a rivalry with New York City's Bad Boy Records. This developed into a media-fueled hostility between East Coast and West Coast rappers, which culminated in the still-unsolved murders of Shakur and the wildly gifted MC known as the Notorious B.I.G.

By the late 1990s hip-hop was artistically dominated by the Wu-Tang Clan, from New York City's Staten Island, whose combination of street credibility, neo-Islamic mysticism, and kung fu lore made them one of the most complex groups in the history of rap; by Diddy (known by a variety of names, including Sean "Puffy" Combs and Puff Daddy), performer, producer, and president of Bad Boy Records, who was responsible for a series of innovative music videos; and by the Fugees, who mixed pop music hooks with politics and launched the solo careers of Wyclef Jean and Lauryn Hill.

Although long believed to be popular primarily with urban African American males, hip-hop became the best-selling genre of popular music in the United States in the late 1990s (at least partly by feeding the appetite of some white suburbanites for vicarious thrills). Its impact was global, with formidable audiences and artist pools in cities such as Paris, Tokyo,

Sydney, Cape Town, London, and Bristol, England (where the spin-off trip-hop originated). It also generated huge sales of products in the fashion, liquor, electronics, and automobile industries that were popularized by hip-hop artists on cable television stations such as MTV and The Box and

*Sean "Diddy" Combs.* PRNewsFoto/Sean John Fragrances EsteeLauder, Stuart Morton/Wireimage.com/AP Images

# NEW YORK: EAST COAST IN THE ASCENT

By the 1980s the record business in New York City was cocooned in the major labels' midtown Manhattan skyscraper offices, where receptionists were instructed to refuse tapes from artists who did not already have industry connections via a lawyer, a manager, or an accountant. Small labels such as Tommy Boy, Profile, and Def Jam set up offices in more accessible locations, and through their doors walked an army of rappers accompanied by "posses" of friends, bodyguards, and producers.

in hip-hop-oriented magazines such as *The Source* and *Vibe*. A canny blend of entrepreneurship and aesthetics, hip-hop was the wellspring of several staple techniques of modern pop music, including digital drumming and sampling (which introduced rap listeners to the music of a previous generation of performers, including Chic, Parliament-Funkadelic, and James Brown, while at the same time creating copyright controversies).

## RUN-D.M.C.

Run-D.M.C. brought hip-hop into the musical and cultural mainstream, introducing what became known as "new-school" rap. The members

were Run (born Joseph Simmons, November 14, 1964, New York, New York, U.S.), D.M.C. (born Darryl McDaniels, May 31, 1964, New York, New York), and Jam Master Jay (born Jason Mizell, January 21, 1965, New York, New York—died October 30, 2002, New York).

Formed in 1982 in Hollis—a middle-class, predominantly African American section of the New York City borough Queens—Run-D.M.C. was managed by Russell Simmons, who was the brother of group member Run and was cofounder of Def Jam, one of the most successful black-owned record companies. Run, whose nickname came from his quick turntable manipulation,

*Run-D.M.C.* Frank Micelotta/Getty Images

began his musical career as a deejay for old-school rapper Kurtis Blow. Later Run, D.M.C., and Jam Master Jay began performing in New York City clubs. In 1983 Profile Records released the group's groundbreaking single "It's Like That"/"Sucker MCs," which featured a spare, forceful rhythm track and overlapping vocals (group members interweaving lines and words). Not only was their sound different, so, too, was their dress. Whereas earlier rap stars fashioned their looks after the spangled superhero costumes of 1970s funk acts like Parliament-Funkadelic and Rick James, Run-D.M.C. appeared in their signature bowler hats, black leather jackets, unlaced Adidas athletic shoes, and black denim pants, establishing the more casual look of hip urban youth as de rigueur stage wear for rappers.

They were the first rappers to have a gold album—*Run-D.M.C.* (1984)—and the first rap act to appear on MTV, becoming popular with the cable channel's largely white

# PROFILE RECORDS

Hip-hop was scorned by the established music industry as a novelty idiom until 1986, when Run-D.M.C. enrolled Aerosmith's vocalist, Steven Tyler, and guitarist, Joe Perry, to take part in a revival of the hard rockers' hit "Walk This Way" from 10 years earlier. Released on the Profile label, the resultant record was accepted by many radio formats and became the first rap hit to make the Top Five on the pop chart. Its video was an MTV staple, and Run-D.M.C. became a major live attraction. Multimillion album sales enabled Profile's owner, Cory Robbins, to pay back the loan to his family that had funded the label's beginnings and to move into bigger offices (on Broadway in New York City's East Village neighbourhood). Although the label never found another act of stature comparable to Run-D.M.C.'s, its vital role had been to establish the commercial potential for rap, which other labels then exploited to better effect, notably Def Jam.

audience via their fusion of hardcore hip-hop and screaming guitar solos on hits such as "Rock Box" (1984) and a 1986 remake of Aerosmith's "Walk This Way" (featuring the song's hard-rocking originators). Other hits by Run-D.M.C. include "King of Rock" (1985), "My Adidas" (1986), which led to the first endorsement deal between hip-hop artists and a major corporation, and "It's Tricky" (1987). Although the group never

officially disbanded, their recording and performing activities decreased significantly in the 1990s. In 2002 Jam Master Jay was fatally shot at a recording studio in Jamaica, Queens. Run-D.M.C was inducted into the Rock and Roll Hall of Fame in 2009.

## RICK RUBIN

Rick Rubin (born March 10, 1963, Long Island, New York, U.S.) grew up listening to heavy metal and early punk, and he frequently took the train into Manhattan from his Long Island home to see New York punk pioneers the Ramones. While a student at New York University, he became interested in rap and immersed himself in the local scene. In 1983 he produced his first single, "It's Yours," by T La Rock and Jazzy Jay. Its success as a dance track in local nightclubs inspired him to create his own label, Def Jam Records.

After hearing "It's Yours," Russell Simmons, who was already a rising star in the hip-hop scene, joined Rubin at Def Jam. The two, based in Rubin's dormitory room, collected demo tapes from aspiring rappers and disc jockeys. In 1984 they had their first hit with LL Cool J's "I Need a Beat," a single that sold 100,000 copies. Rubin had created Def Jam to fill a niche that the mainstream recording industry had ignored, but the major labels took notice when its sales topped 300,000 albums in 1985. Columbia Records placed Rubin and Simmons under contract, and Def Jam's roster expanded to include the Beastie Boys, Public Enemy, and Run-D.M.C. (a group that included Simmons's brother Joseph).

Rubin left Def Jam in 1988 over a disagreement about the structure of the label's relationship with Columbia. He moved to Los Angeles and founded a new label, Def American, with the heavy metal acts Slayer and Danzig as his first artists. In 1991 he guided the Red Hot Chili Peppers to multiplatinum success with *Blood Sugar Sex Magik*, and with that success he established himself as a performer's producer. Whereas Phil Spector's work was characterized by the "wall of sound" and Sam Phillips made a career of the "Sun sound," there was no particular aural quirk that could be called "Rubinesque." His presence in the studio simply seemed to make good artists better.

Rubin's gift was perhaps most clearly demonstrated in 1993, when country legend Johnny Cash was at the nadir of his popularity, having been dropped by his label and facing an audience that was seemingly indifferent to his brand of music. The 1994 release *American Recordings* (Rubin had dropped the "Def" from the label's name the previous year) was a surprise smash hit. This success marked the beginning of a partnership that would earn five Grammy Awards and restart Cash's career. The 2002 release *American IV: The Man Comes Around* included Cash's interpretation of the Nine Inch Nails song "Hurt." The song, released only months before Cash's death, was transformed by Rubin from an industrial rock anthem into a poignant elegy, further demonstrating his ability to transcend genre.

Through the 2000s Rubin continued to lend his talents to established

*Rick Rubin at his home in Los Angeles, 2007.* © AP Images

# DEF JAM RECORDS

Rick Rubin and Russell Simmons managed several pioneer hip-hop acts, including Run-D.M.C., through their Rush Management agency, and in 1984 they set up their own Def Jam label; shortly thereafter, Columbia Records made a deal with the label and became its distributor. Def Jam's first success was LL Cool J, a soft-spoken "love" rapper whose style was compatible with black radio's still-conservative ideas of itself and its audience. Next up were the Beastie Boys, a trio of white New Yorkers who helped redefine rap as a cool alternative for white suburban kids, notably with the infectious, tongue-in-cheek anthem "(You Gotta) Fight for Your Right (to Party)" in 1986. Def Jam's next substantial act, Public Enemy, was altogether more confrontational, stoking the flames of antiwhite and antipolice rhetoric. Rubin went off to form Def American, leaving Simmons to sustain the most successful of the first generation of rap labels.

performers such as Neil Diamond, Jay-Z, and Tom Petty. In keeping with his unflappable, bearded guru image, he chose to avoid the 2007 Grammy Awards ceremony, and, although he won the Grammy for best producer, he characterized the previous year as "not unusually special." Nonetheless, Rubin exerted a quiet dominance on the industry's sales charts. He had production credit on two of the five nominees for album of the year (the Dixie Chicks' *Taking the Long Way* and the Red Hot Chili Peppers' *Stadium Arcadium*) and had contributed to a third (Justin Timberlake's *FutureSex/LoveSounds*).

In May 2007 Rubin was named cochairman of Columbia Records. The label was struggling with declining revenues as a result of the contraction of the compact disc market, and its parent company, the Sony Corporation, felt that Rubin

89

could provide a fresh alternative to its existing business model. Rubin's loose management style immediately clashed with executives, and his emphasis on creativity over commerce, exemplified by his relocation of the Columbia headquarters from Los Angeles to an I.M. Pei-designed office building in Santa Monica, California, evoked comparisons to Factory Records cofounder Tony Wilson. His studio talents were undiminished, however, and he collected a second Grammy as producer of the year in 2009 for his work on albums for Metallica, Neil Diamond, and Weezer, among others.

## LL COOL J

At age 16 James Todd Smith (born August 16, 1968, New York, New York, U.S.) took the stage name LL Cool J ("Ladies Love Cool James") and signed with fledgling rap label Def Jam. Distinguished by hard, fast, sinuous rhymes and artfully arrogant phrasing, his first single, "I Need a Beat," sold more than 100,000 copies. His first album, *Radio*, was released in 1985, the year he appeared in *Krush Groove*, the movie celebrating Def Jam's origins.

Thereafter he outlasted most of his competition by constantly creating daring, fresh modes of expression—gaining airplay with rap's first romantic ballad, "I Need Love" (1987),

and prefiguring West Coast rap with "Goin' Back to Cali" (1988), recorded in California. Criticized by some for his crossover success, LL responded by teaming with producer Marley Marl for the musically and thematically innovative album *Mama Said Knock You Out* (1990).

Following the huge commercial success of that album, the increasingly versatile LL began acting in films and on television. He starred in the situation comedy *In the House* (1995–99), and he continued to record, releasing the double-platinum *Mr. Smith* (1995); a string of solid albums followed. LL also branched into the world of fashion, debuting his James Todd Smith clothing line in 2004.

## THE BEASTIE BOYS

The Beastie Boys were the first white rap performers to gain a substantial following. As such, they were largely responsible for the growth of rap's mainstream audience. The principal members were MCA (born Adam Yauch, August 5, 1964, Brooklyn, New York, U.S.—died May 4, 2012, New York City), Mike D (born Mike Diamond, November 20, 1965, New York City), and King AdRock (born Adam Horovitz, October 31, 1966, South Orange, New Jersey).

Founded in New York City in 1981 by a group of arty middle-class Jewish kids responding to Manhattan's eclectic downtown music scene, the Beastie Boys evolved by 1983 from a hard-core punk quartet (including original guitarist John Berry and drummer Kate Schellenbach) into a trio—MCA, Mike D, and King AdRock. They signed with Def Jam, and early 12-inch singles and a brief tour with Madonna in 1985 finally brought them press attention. It was not until they toured with popular black rappers Run-D.M.C., however, that the Beastie Boys won credibility with the rap audience. Good timing and a clever blend of hard rock samples and parodic fraternity-boy posturing turned *Licensed to Ill* (1986) into a smash debut album, confirming the emotional and stylistic affinities some critics found between rap and hard rock. After moving from Def Jam to Capitol Records for their 1989 release, *Paul's Boutique*, the Beastie Boys strategically appropriated retro-funk influences, adding an acoustic dimension to digital sound-collage techniques learned from Rick Rubin and Grandmaster Flash.

The band launched the Grand Royal record label in 1992. In addition to the Beastie Boys, its roster included the alternative girl group Luscious Jackson, Australian singer-songwriter Ben Lee, and German techno act Atari Teenage Riot. *Check Your Head* (1992), the Beastie Boys' first release

Beastie Boys, c. 1980. L. Cohen/WireImage/Getty Images

on Grand Royal, featured a collection of radio-friendly rhymes that layered pop culture references over distorted funk instrumentation. The group's next album, *Ill Communication* (1994), had a similar sound, and the music video for the hit single "Sabotage"—a tongue-in-cheek homage to 1970s television police dramas—was in near-constant rotation on MTV. The band took an electronic turn on the Grammy-winning *Hello Nasty* (1998) and scored another hit with the single "Intergalactic." In 2001 Grand Royal folded as a result of slow sales and mounting debts, and the Beastie Boys returned to Capitol for the 2004 release *To the 5 Boroughs*.

The instrumental hip-hop album *The Mix-Up* (2007) represented a return to basics, and its fusion of funk, Latin, and lounge music won the band another Grammy. The

# GO-GO

Go-go, a style of funk heavy on bass and percussion, originated in Washington, D.C., in the late 1970s. Go-go bands were large ensembles with multiple percussionists who could maintain a steady beat for hours at a time. By 1982 go-go was the most popular music of the dance halls (called go-gos) in the black parts of the capital. The go-go pioneers were Chuck Brown and the Soul Searchers, who cultivated the steady, rigid use of the funk beat, and Trouble Funk, who packaged their powerful shows into some of the best studio recordings of the go-go era. Other steady go-go acts were Redds and the Boys, E.U. (Experience Unlimited), and Rare Essence.

Go-go bands were influenced by George Clinton and Parliament-Funkadelic, who frequently played four-hour concerts in the region. The tireless percussive rhythms of go-go also have connections to the Caribbean dance styles of soca and reggae. The rigid beats served some of the early rap sides for New York City hip-hop acts Afrika Bambaataa and Kurtis Blow; and rappers of the mid-1980s, such as Doug E. Fresh, Run-D.M.C., and the Beastie Boys, utilized the distinctive go-go beat in their music. The zenith of go-go's popularity was E.U.'s "Da Butt," from Spike Lee's film *School Daze* (1988).

Go-go recordings were almost exclusively released on independent labels, the most successful of which was D.E.T.T. Records, founded by Maxx Kidd. In 1985 Island Records made a brief attempt to record and market go-go groups, but the style never became nationally known, and its associations with hip-hop faded as urban rap styles changed in the 1990s.

trio's eighth studio album, *Hot Sauce Committee Part One*, was scheduled for release in 2009, but Yauch was diagnosed with cancer in July of that year, and the group suspended all recording and touring activity.

With Yauch's health improving, the Beastie Boys resumed recording and in May 2011 released *Hot Sauce Committee Part Two* (with the exception of one song, the track list was virtually identical to the unreleased Part One). Stylistically, it was similar to *Ill Communication*, and the star-studded video for the debut single "Make Some Noise" demonstrated that the group had not lost its sense of the absurd. In 2012 the Beastie Boys were inducted into the Rock and Roll Hall of Fame. Just weeks after that event, Yauch succumbed to cancer.

## PUBLIC ENEMY

Public Enemy was one of the most popular, controversial, and influential hip-hop groups of the late 1980s and early 1990s. The original members were Chuck D (born Carlton Ridenhour, August 1, 1960, New York, New York, U.S.), Flavor Flav (born William Drayton, March 16, 1959, New York), Terminator X (born Norman Lee Rogers, August 25, 1966, New York), and Professor Griff (born Richard Griffin, August 1, 1960, Long Island, New York).

Public Enemy was formed in 1982 at Adelphi University on Long Island, New York, by a group of African Americans who came primarily from the suburbs. Chuck D, Hank Shocklee, Bill Stephney, and Flavor Flav collaborated on a program on college radio. Reputedly, Def Jam producer Rick Rubin was so taken with Chuck D's booming voice that he implored him to record. Public Enemy resulted and brought radical black political ideology to pop music in an unprecedented fashion on albums with titles that read like party invitations for leftists and warning stickers for the right wing: *Yo! Bum Rush the Show* (1987), *It Takes a Nation of Millions to Hold Us Back* (1988), *Fear of a Black Planet* (1990), and *Apocalypse 91: The Enemy Strikes Black* (1991).

Acclaimed as Public Enemy's masterpiece, *Nation of Millions* revived the messages of the Black Panther Party and Malcolm X. On tracks such as "Night of the Living Baseheads," "Black Steel in the Hour of Chaos," and "Don't Believe the Hype," the strident, eloquent lyrics of Chuck D combined with bombastic, dissonant, and poignantly detailed backing tracks created by Public Enemy's production team, the Bomb Squad (Shocklee, his brother Keith, Chuck D, and Eric "Vietnam" Adler), to produce songs challenging the status quo in both hip-hop and racial politics. The Bomb Squad sampled (composed with other recordings) a wide variety of genres and sounds, including classic funk tracks by James Brown, jazz, the thrash-metal of Anthrax, sirens, and agitprop speeches. Flavor Flav provided a comic foil for Chuck D.

# HIP-HOP AND THE DIGITAL REVOLUTION

The radical development of digital technology that had begun in the 1980s was evident in the new devices for sampling and manipulating sound, which were used by dance music engineers who had already been exploring the rhythmic and sonic possibilities of electronic instruments and blurring the distinctions between live and recorded music. Over the next decade the uses of digital equipment pioneered on the dance scene fed into all forms of rock music making. For a hip-hop act such as Public Enemy, what mattered was not just a new palette of "pure" sound but also a means of putting reality—the actual voices of the powerful and powerless—into the music. Hip-hop, as was quickly understood by young disaffected groups around the world, made it possible to talk back to the media.

Comments by Professor Griff to the *Washington Times* in 1989 brought charges of anti-Semitism, which ultimately resulted in his leaving the group. Public Enemy's open admiration for the Nation of Islam leader Louis Farrakhan also brought it into conflict with Jewish organizations. While Public Enemy's activism inspired other artists to take up topical themes, the group's influence in the hip-hop community waned in the early 1990s as younger, more "ghettocentric" performers such as N.W.A. and Snoop Doggy Dogg (as he was then known) came to the fore. The group seemed to have folded after *Muse Sick N Hour Mess Age* (1994), but in 1998 they produced a new album of songs for Spike Lee's film *He Got Game* and went on tour.

## DE LA SOUL

De La Soul was formed in 1988 by three high-school friends—Posdnuos (born Kelvin Mercer, August 17, 1969, New York, New York, U.S.), Trugoy the Dove (born David Jolicoeur, September 21, 1968, New York), and Pasemaster Mase (born Vincent Mason, March 24, 1970, New York)—in Amityville, New

# TOMMY BOY RECORDS

*Dance Music Report* editor Tom Silverman started up Tommy Boy Records in 1981 in his Manhattan, New York City, apartment on West 85th Street. Producer Arthur Baker helped put the label on the map with hits by Afrika Bambaataa —"Looking for the Perfect Beat" (1982) and "Planet Rock" (1983)—whose robotic rhythms were inspired by European groups such as Kraftwerk. With radio slow to recognize this new idiom, exposure for hip-hop came mostly through 12-inch singles in dance clubs, but Tommy Boy's focused approach to artists-and-repertoire and promotion led to commercial breakthroughs with quirky character acts. Based in California, Digital Underground was led by the eccentric Shock-G, who brought a George Clinton-like sense of the absurd to the group's repertoire; their radio hit "The Humpty Dance" (1989) paved the way for the amusing and friendly vibe of De La Soul, hippielike rappers from Long Island, New York, whose album *3 Feet High and Rising* (1989) sampled the entire panoply of pop and had a particularly big impact in Britain and continental Europe.

York. Impressed by the trio's demo, "Plug Tunin'," "Prince Paul" Houston of the rap group Stetsasonic helped them secure a contract with Tommy Boy Records and produced their landmark debut.

Conceptual, densely layered, and replete with quirky interlude skits, *3 Feet High and Rising* (1989) influenced not only De La Soul's own self-constructed "family" of alternative rappers (ranging from A Tribe Called Quest to Queen Latifah) but also groups as disparate as Public Enemy (who were inspired by the collage-sampling technique of "Prince Paul") and gangsta rap pioneers N.W.A. (who incorporated interlude skits). Moreover, prior to the emergence of De La Soul, the primary source for hip-hop samples was the music of James Brown; in the wake of *3 Feet*

*High and Rising*, George Clinton's Parliament-Funkadelic catalog became the mother lode.

The group's second—and arguably best—album, *De La Soul Is Dead* (1991), dealt with weighty issues such as incest, mortality, and the buckling pressure of prior success. Despite the alternative that they offered to the proliferation of increasingly nihilistic and hypermaterialistic hip-hop in the mid-1990s, De La Soul's next releases, *Buhloone Mindstate* (1993) and *Stakes Is High* (1996), failed commercially. On the latter, De La Soul, having contributed so much to hip-hop's development lyrically and musically, forsook their usual coded poetry to take an unabashed stand against the pervasiveness of shallow lyrics and unimaginative sounds they believed to be too characteristic of the hip-hop era they had helped usher into existence. The group returned in 2000 with *Mosaic Thump*, the first volume in the proposed Art Official Intelligence trilogy. The album featured guest appearances by Busta Rhymes, the Beastie Boys, and Redman, among others.

Queen Latifah, 2003. PRNewsFoto/VH1/AP Images

## QUEEN LATIFAH

The success of Queen Latifah (born Dana Elaine Owens, March 18, 1970, Newark, New Jersey, U.S.) in the late 1980s launched a wave of female rappers and helped redefine the traditionally male genre. She later became a notable film actress.

Owens was given the nickname Latifah (Arabic for "delicate" or "sensitive") as a child and later adopted the moniker Queen Latifah. In high school she was a member of the all-female rap group Ladies Fresh, and, while studying communications at the Borough of Manhattan Community College, she recorded a demo tape that caught the attention of Tommy Boy Records, which signed the 18-year-old. In 1988 she released her first single, "Wrath of My Madness," and the following year her debut album, *All Hail the Queen*, appeared. Propelled by diverse styles—including soul, reggae, and dance—and feminist themes, it earned positive reviews and attracted a wide audience. Soon after, Queen Latifah founded her own management company. Her second album, *Nature of a Sista* (1991), however, failed to match the sales of her previous effort, and Tommy Boy did not re-sign her. After signing with Motown Records, she released *Black Reign* in 1993. The album was a critical and commercial success, and the single "U.N.I.T.Y.," which decried sexism and violence against women, earned a Grammy Award.

In 1991 Queen Latifah made her big-screen debut in *Jungle Fever*, and after several television appearances she was signed in 1993 to costar in the series *Living Single*. After the show ended in 1998, Queen Latifah returned to the big screen, playing a jazz singer in the 1998 film *Living Out Loud*. Her commanding screen presence brought roles in more films, including *The Bone Collector* (1999) and *Brown Sugar* (2002). In 1999 she began a two-year stint of hosting her own daytime talk show, and that year she published *Ladies First: Revelations of a Strong Woman* (co-written with Karen Hunter).

Queen Latifah's prominence in Hollywood was cemented in 2003, when she received an Academy Award nomination (best supporting actress) for her portrayal of Matron Mama Morton in the big-screen adaptation of the stage musical *Chicago* (2002). The film was followed by the comedies *Bringing Down the House* (2003), which Queen Latifah both starred in and produced, *Barbershop 2: Back in Business* (2004), *Beauty Shop* (2005), and *Last Holiday* (2006). She again brought her musical background to the screen for her role as Motormouth Maybelle in the film *Hairspray* (2007), a remake of the stage musical.

In 2008 Queen Latifah starred in *The Secret Life of Bees*, a drama about a white girl taken in by a family of beekeeping African American women in 1960s-era South Carolina. She later appeared in the romantic comedies *Valentine's Day* (2010), *Just Wright* (2010), and The Dilemma (2011). In *Joyful Noise* (2012) she starred opposite Dolly Parton as the director of a competitive church gospel choir. In addition, her voice was featured in several movies, including *Ice Age: The Meltdown* (2006) and its sequel, *Ice Age: Dawn of the Dinosaurs* (2009).

Throughout her acting career, Queen Latifah continued to record. Her other albums include *The Dana Owens Album* (2004) and *Trav'lin' Light* (2007), collections of jazz and pop standards that showcased her strong singing voice, and *Persona* (2009), an eclectic return to hip-hop.

## WILL SMITH

Will Smith (born September 25, 1968, Philadelphia, Pennsylvania, U.S.) was given the nickname "Prince Charming" in high school, which he adapted to "Fresh Prince" in order to reflect a more hip-hop sound when he began his musical career. He formed an alliance with schoolmate and deejay Jeffrey Townes, whom he met in 1981. They began recording as DJ Jazzy Jeff and the Fresh Prince and released their first single, "Girls Ain't Nothing but Trouble," in 1986, later followed by the album *Rock the House*. In 1988 the group released the groundbreaking single "Parents Just Don't Understand," which went on to win a Grammy Award (the first Grammy ever presented in the rap performance category).

*Will Smith, 2006.* Vince Bucci/Getty Images

Smith's act, notable for its wide crossover appeal, was sometimes characterized as "light rap" because of the lack of hard-core lyrics and themes in his compositions. Platinum-certified recordings and accompanying videos subsequently brought him to the attention of television producers. The television sitcom *The Fresh Prince of Bel-Air*, which began in 1990 and was loosely based on Smith's real-life persona, ran on NBC for six successful seasons, ending at the star's request.

During the series' run, Smith garnered two Golden Globe nominations and served as an executive producer for the final season.

Buoyed by his small-screen success, Smith expanded into cinema with *Where the Day Takes You* (1992). His first leading role was in the film version of John Guare's successful stage play *Six Degrees of Separation* (1993). The action comedy-thriller *Bad Boys* (1995), however, proved to be the turning point in his film career. While the movie was not a critical success, it made more than $100 million worldwide, proving Smith's star power. In 1996 he starred in that year's top-grossing movie, *Independence Day*. He was a hit at the box office again the next year with the science-fiction comedy *Men in Black*, for which he also recorded the Grammy-winning title song; sequels to the film appeared in 2002 and 2012. In 1998 Smith released his first solo album, *Big Willie Style*, which included the hit "Gettin' Jiggy wit It," and starred in the dramatic thriller *Enemy of the State*.

After releasing the album *Willennium* in 1999, Smith demonstrated his remarkable versatility as an actor, playing an enigmatic golf caddy in *The Legend of Bagger Vance* (2000); the boxer Muhammad Ali in the biopic *Ali* (2001), for which he received an Academy Award nomination; and a "date doctor" helping a romantically inept man find love in *Hitch* (2005). *Lost and Found*, Smith's fourth solo album, was released in 2005. The next year he starred in and coproduced *The Pursuit of Happyness*, and his performance as a single father who overcomes adversity earned him a second Oscar nomination for best actor. In *I Am Legend* (2007), Smith appeared as a scientist who is perhaps the last human on Earth following an epidemic. *Hancock* (2008) featured Smith as a superhero trying to revamp his unpopular image, and in *Seven Pounds* (2008) he played a man seeking redemption after accidentally killing seven people in a car accident. In addition, in the early 21st century Smith served as a producer for several films, and with his wife, actress Jada Pinkett Smith (married 1997), he helped create and produce the sitcom *All of Us* (2003–07).

## GANGSTA RAP

Gangsta rap came to dominate hip-hop in the 1990s, working as a reflection and product of the often violent lifestyle of American inner cities afflicted with poverty and the dangers of drug use and drug dealing. The romanticization of the outlaw at the centre of much of gangsta rap appealed to rebellious suburbanites as well as to those who had firsthand experience of the the harsh realities of the ghetto.

# LOS ANGELES: THE WEST COAST RESPONSE

After the buoyancy and optimism of the 1980s, black music in Los Angeles in the early '90s turned desolate. As economic recession and crack cocaine swept through Watts and East Los Angeles, a generation of artists chose to portray the world of the ghetto with unfettered realism. These were tough guys acting tough, and the sound they created was called gangsta rap. Over grinding electronic samples, they rapped about cops, crack, gangs, and lust (though seldom love).

Ice-T, who had experienced the world of gangs firsthand, introduced his steel-hammer-rhythm braggadocio on albums for Sire Records in the late 1980s, and N.W.A.'s *Straight Outta Compton* (initially released on group member Eazy-E's Ruthless label in 1988) was widely popular with both black and white teenage males reveling in their disaffection. When N.W.A. split, Ice Cube channeled the anger he had learned in south-central Los Angeles into a solo career—prompting outrage with several provocative tracks on *AmeriKKKa's Most Wanted* (1990). A third member of N.W.A., Dr. Dre, emerged as one of the most creative musical innovators of the decade, designing sublime soundscapes for his own records and those of other rappers, including Snoop Doggy Dogg for Death Row Records. The outrage of middle America over the violent content of so much rap discouraged most of the major labels, leaving a path clear for Interscope Records to sign some of the most controversial rappers, either directly or through label distribution deals.

Gangsta ("gangster") rap first came to prominence on the East Coast. Schoolly D, of Philadelphia, presented graphic tales of gangs and violence such as "PSK—What Does It Mean?" (1985); and Boogie Down Productions, formed in New York City by DJ Scott LaRock (Scott

Sterling) and KRS-One (Lawrence Krisna Parker), offered hard-hitting depictions of crack-cocaine-related crime on *Criminal Minded* (1987). In Houston, Texas, the Geto Boys' sex- and violence-dominated music was the subject of outrage in some corners. But gangsta rap became a national phenomenon in California, where a distinct school of West Coast hip-hop began with Eazy E's Los Angeles group N.W.A. (Niggaz With Attitude).

In Oakland, Too $hort had become a major regional force, and his profane and sexually explicit style influenced N.W.A. member Ice Cube's early writing. It was N.W.A.'s controversial album *Straight Outta Compton*, however, that shifted hip-hop's geographic centre. The most distinguishing characteristic of N.W.A.'s approach was the very plain way that violence was essayed: as plainly as it occurred in the streets of south-central Los Angeles and neighbouring Compton, argued the group. Hyperrealism was often conflated with myth and declarations of immortality; exaggeration became a kind of self-protective delusional device for listeners who were actually involved in the dangerous lifestyle N.W.A. was chronicling.

In the mainstream press and among African Americans nationwide, N.W.A., by virtue of their name, single-handedly reignited a debate about the word "nigger." Its appropriation by black youth transformed it into a positive appellation, argued Ice Cube. For many, the persistent misogyny in N.W.A.'s work, which was alternately cartoonish and savage in its offensiveness, was less defensible.

As N.W.A. splintered, the group's importance multiplied with each solo album. Ice Cube's *AmeriKKKa's Most Wanted* (1990) employed Public Enemy's production team, the Bomb Squad, and introduced New York City listeners to the West Coast sound, known by this point as gangsta rap. In 1992 N.W.A. producer and sometime rapper Dr. Dre released the California rap scene's most influential and definitive record, *The Chronic*; its marriage of languid beats and murderous gangsta mentality resulted in phenomenal sales. Most significantly, it launched Death Row Records and the career of Snoop Doggy Dogg.

As early as 1988, other important artists from California began making an impression. Like Too $hort, Ice-T relied on his self-styled image as a pimp to propel sales; though his lyrics were well-respected, his single "Cop Killer" (1992), like gangsta rap in general, raised controversy. N.W.A.'s influence could be heard in groups like Compton's Most Wanted, DJ Quik, Above the Law, and countless other gangsta groups, but by the early 1990s groups

*Dr. Dre, 2003.* PRNewsFoto/Coors Light/AP Images

## DR. DRE

Born to teenage parents who aspired to singing careers, André Young (born February 18, 1965, Los Angeles, California, U.S.) took the stage name of Dr. Dre in the early 1980s. He performed as a hip-hop deejay and as part of the group World Class Wreckin' Cru at clubs and parties in Los Angeles's south-central district. In 1986 he founded N.W.A. with fellow rappers Eazy-E and Ice Cube. The group's second album, *Straight Outta Compton* (1988), was a breakthrough for the nascent gangsta rap movement, featuring explicit descriptions (and often glorifications) of street violence and drug dealing. While Dre appeared prominently as a rapper in N.W.A., his most lauded role was as a producer, crafting ambitiously noisy, multilayered sonic collages to back the group's inflammatory lyrics.

Dre left N.W.A. in 1992 and cofounded Death Row Records with Marion ("Suge") Knight. That year his solo debut, *The Chronic*, introduced the "G-funk" production style, characterized by plodding tempos, synthesizer washes, and copious musical "sampling" of 1970s funk records, especially those by Parliament-Funkadelic. *The Chronic*'s multiplatinum success helped make this sound dominant in mainstream hip-hop in the mid-1990s. In 1996 Dre left Death Row to form Aftermath Records and solidified his

had surfaced whose approach was the antithesis of N.W.A.'s violence and misogyny. The jazzily virtuosic improvisers Freestyle Fellowship and the Pharcyde, of Los Angeles, and Souls of Mischief, of Oakland, owed more to East Coast abstractionists De La Soul and A Tribe Called Quest than to gangs. Nevertheless, by the mid-1990s Death Row Records and Bad Boy Records were engaged in a "coastal battle." Life imitated art imitating life; the violence that had been confined to songs began to spill over into the world, culminating in the tragic murders of New York City rapper Notorious B.I.G. (Christopher Wallace), and California rapper Tupac Shakur (2Pac).

# DEATH ROW RECORDS

Among the individuals responsible for the flourishing of hip-hop in Los Angeles in the 1990s was a white man, Jimmy Iovine, a former engineer on recordings by Bruce Springsteen and the new head of Interscope Records. Although Interscope had a stable of success-ful alternative rock acts—including Nine Inch Nails and Bush—its greatest impact came from its alliance with Death Row Records. Founded by Marion ("Suge") Knight, Death Row rapidly became the home of gangsta rap. Essentially it was an outlet for the talents of N.W.A's Dr. Dre. The attention drawn to gansta rap's violent lyrics tended to mask the unschooled but innovative nature of the music, shaped by producer Dre's distinctive slurred, lazy studio sound.

Among the Death Row releases to top the pop charts were *Doggystyle* (1993) by Snoop Doggy Dogg, who emerged from a cameo role on Dre's own work, and the gritty *All Eyez on Me* (1996) by Tupac Shakur. As the decade progressed, Death Row became increasingly enmeshed in legal proceedings—both financial and criminal—that were reflective of its gangsta rhetoric. Snoop was found innocent of a murder charge, then left the label. Shakur died in Las Vegas, Nevada, as a result of gunshot wounds—a victim of the rivalry between East Coast and West Coast rappers that exploded into murder. Knight was sentenced to nine years for assault, and Interscope severed all connections with Death Row.

shift from recording his own albums to producing other artists' work. Some of his most notable protégés include rap-pers Snoop Doggy Dogg and Eminem. Among the artists he collaborated with in the early years of the 21st century were Mary J. Blige, Jay-Z, and 50 Cent.

## SNOOP LION

For many, Snoop Lion (born Cordozar Calvin Broadus, Jr., also known as Snoop Doggy Dogg and Snoop Dogg, October 20, 1971, Long Beach, California, U.S.) was

**103**

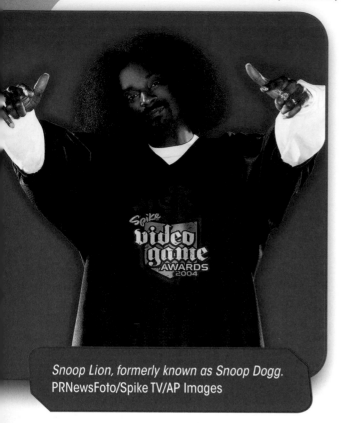

*Snoop Lion, formerly known as Snoop Dogg.*
PRNewsFoto/Spike TV/AP Images

became the first debut record to enter the Billboard 200 at number one.

While recording *Doggystyle*, Snoop was arrested in connection with a drive-by shooting. Although he was ultimately cleared of all charges, the incident entangled him in court for years, contributing to a long delay before the release of his next album, *Tha Doggfather* (1996). By that time the gangsta rap movement had begun to ebb. For a few years Snoop's records failed to generate excitement comparable to that of his debut, but his carefully cultivated—and at times cartoonish—public persona made him a popular icon. His West Coast slang and exaggerated verbal tics entered the popular American vocabulary. Snoop was a frequent guest on radio and television talk shows and amassed a substantial number of film credits. In 2008 he starred in *Snoop Dogg's Father Hood*, a reality television series chronicling his home life.

In July of 2012, in a self-professed desire to leave the world of gangsta and hip-hop behind and embrace reggae, which he calls the "music of love,' Snoop announced at a news conference that, after a spiritually moving experience on his trip to Jamaica earlier that year, he was changing his name from Snoop Dogg to Snoop Lion. He told reporters that the idea for the name change came from a Rastafarian priest, who

the epitome of West Coast hip-hop culture. His signature drawled lyrics took inspiration from his early encounters with the law. After high school he was in and out of prison for several years before seriously pursuing a career in hip-hop. Eventually he came to the attention of famed producer-rapper Dr. Dre, who featured him on his single "Deep Cover" and on his landmark album *The Chronic* (both 1992). Snoop's prominent vocals on the hit singles "Dre Day" and "Nuthin' but a 'G' Thang" fueled a rapid ascent to stardom. His own album *Doggystyle* (1993)

# NOTORIOUS B.I.G.

The Notorious B.I.G. (born Christopher Wallace, May 21, 1973, Brooklyn, New York, U.S.—died March 9, 1997, Los Angeles, California) transformed from drug dealer and street hustler to one of hip-hop's premier artists as chronicled in his platinum-selling debut album, *Ready to Die* (1994). Weeks before the release of his second album, *Life After Death*, he was killed during a drive-by shooting. The event was widely perceived to be the bloody fallout of a feud between East Coast and West Coast rap communities. The rapper's death catapulted his associates into the limelight. Diddy, who had discovered and signed the Notorious B.I.G. (who was also known as Biggie Smalls) to his label, recorded "I'll Be Missing You" as a tribute to the late rapper, featuring his widow, Faith Evans, on vocals. The song was a massive hit, and both Diddy and former B.I.G collaborator Mase followed with full-length albums that topped the Billboard album charts.

in essence said that a lion was a far more fitting animal for the singer.

## NATE DOGG

Nate Dogg (born Nathaniel Dwayne Hale, August 19, 1969, Long Beach, California—died March 15, 2011, Long Beach) was an integral part of the West Coast rap sound, contributing soulful vocal hooks as a guest artist on numerous G-funk and gangsta rap songs beginning in the 1990s. Early in the '90s he formed the rap group 213 with Snoop Dogg and Warren G; the demonstration tape that 213 recorded impressed producer Dr. Dre and resulted in contributions by Nate Dogg and Snoop to cuts on Dr. Dre's classic 1992 album *The Chronic*. In 1994 Nate Dogg and Warren G released the platinum single "Regulate," and thereafter Nate Dogg was in great demand as a collaborator, notably on "Area Code" with Ludacris (2001) and "Shake That" with Eminem (2005). He recorded the solo albums *G-Funk Classics, Vol. 1 & 2* (1998) and *Music & Me* (2001). Nate Dogg never fully recovered from strokes that he suffered in 2007 and 2008.

## TUPAC SHAKUR

Lesane Parish Crooks (born June 16, 1971, Brooklyn, New York, U.S.— died September 13, 1996, Las Vegas, Nevada) was the son of Alice Faye Williams, a member of the Black Panther Party, and she renamed him Tupac Amaru Shakur—after Peruvian revolutionary Tupac Amaru II—when he was a year old. He spent much of his childhood on the move with his family, which in 1986 settled in Baltimore, Maryland, where Shakur attended the elite Baltimore School of the Arts. He distinguished himself as a student, both creatively and academically, but his family relocated to Marin City, California, before he could graduate. There Shakur took to the streets, selling drugs and becoming involved in the gang culture that would one day provide material for his rap lyrics. In 1990 he joined Digital Underground, an Oakland-based rap group that had scored a Billboard Top 40 hit with the novelty single "The Humpty Dance." Shakur performed on two Digital Underground albums in 1991, *This Is an EP Release* and *Sons of the P*, before his solo debut, *2Pacalypse Now*, later that year.

*2Pacalypse Now* was a radical break from the dance party sound of Digital Underground, and its tone and content were much closer to the works of Public Enemy and West Coast gangsta rappers N.W.A. The lack of a clear single on the album limited its radio appeal, but it sold well, especially after Vice Pres. Dan Quayle criticized the song "Soulja's Story" during the 1992 presidential campaign. That same year Shakur joined the ranks of other rappers-turned-actors, such as Ice Cube and Ice-T, when he was cast in the motion picture *Juice*, an urban crime drama. The following year he appeared in *Poetic Justice*, opposite Janet Jackson, and he released his second album, *Strictly 4 My N.I.G.G.A.Z*. The album did not stray far from the activist lyricism of his debut, but singles such as "Holler If Ya Hear Me" and "Keep Ya Head Up" made it much more radio-friendly.

With increased fame and success came greater scrutiny of Shakur's gangsta lifestyle. A string of arrests culminated with a conviction for sexual assault in 1994; he was incarcerated when his third album, *Me Against the World*, was released in 1995. Shakur was paroled after serving eight months in prison, and he signed with Suge Knight's Death Row Records for his next release. That album, *All Eyez on Me* (1996), was a two-disc paean to the "thug life" that Shakur embodied. It debuted at number one on the Billboard charts and sold more than five million copies within its first year of release. Quick to capitalize on his most recent success, Shakur returned to Hollywood, where he starred in *Bullet* (1996) and *Gridlock'd* (1997).

On the evening of September 7, 1996, Shakur was leaving a Las Vegas casino, where he had just attended a prizefight featuring heavyweight champion Mike Tyson, when he was shot by an unknown assailant. The incident, believed by many to be the result of an ongoing rivalry between the East Coast and West Coast rap communities, shocked the entertainment world. Shakur died six days later. In spite of his relatively short recording career, Shakur left an enduring legacy within the hip-hop community. His popularity was undiminished after his death, and a long succession of posthumous releases (many of them were simply repackaged or remixed existing material, and most were of middling quality), ensured that "new" 2Pac albums continued to appear well into the 21st century.

One particularly notable posthumous release occurred in April 2012 at the Coachella Music Festival in Indio, California. There, a video projection of Shakur that gave the eerie 3-D appearance of a hologram was shown on stage. Performing with Shakur were Dr. Dre and Snoop Lion (then Snoop Dogg). The optical technology gave rise to speculation as to how onstage performing—of both the living and the dead—might change.

## NAS

Nas (born Nasir bin Olu Dara Jones, September 14, 1973, Queens, New York, U.S.), the son of a jazz musician, grew up in public housing in Queens. He dropped out of school in the eighth grade and searched for a creative outlet, finally settling on hip-hop. His breakthrough came in 1992, when his song "Half Time" (credited to Nasty Nas) appeared on the soundtrack to the film *Zebrahead*. Columbia Records soon signed him to a contract. His debut recording as Nas, *Illmatic* (1994), drew widespread acclaim for its poetic narration of hard-edged inner-city life.

The more pop-oriented approach of *It Was Written* (1996) helped that album reach an even wider audience than its predecessor but ignited a recurring tension in Nas's career between the appetite of the pop audience and the demands of hip-hop purists. By 2000, sales and airplay of his records had declined somewhat; at the same time, he became embroiled in a public feud with fellow rapper

Jay-Z over which of the two was the preeminent voice in East Coast hip-hop. The schism inspired *Stillmatic* (2001), a comeback album that was well received by both critics and consumers. The two rappers publicly settled their differences in 2005, and shortly thereafter Nas signed with Def Jam, of which Jay-Z was president at the time. Nas's first album for the label was *Hip Hop Is Dead* (2006). A Greatest Hits compilation with Columbia Records followed in 2007, though Nas continued to record new music for Def Jam. His self-titled *Nas* (2008) was a fiercely challenging work, and *Distant Relatives* (2010)

paired Nas with Damian Marley, the youngest son of reggae legend Bob Marley, in an effort to raise funds for education in Africa.

## DIDDY

Hip-hop mogul Diddy seemed to amass names and titles with equal ease. Born Sean John Combs (November 4, 1970, New York, New York, U.S.) but variously known as Sean "Puffy" Combs, Puff Daddy, P. Diddy, and Diddy, the rapper, record producer, clothing designer, and entrepreneur controlled an entertainment empire that was worth

*Nas (left) and C-Sick (Charles Dumazer).* PRNewsFoto/Red Bull Big Tune/ AP Images

over $500 million in the early 21st century.

Combs was born and raised in Harlem in New York City, where his father was murdered when Combs was three. Nine years later the family moved to suburban Mount Vernon, New York, where Combs attended prep school and supposedly received the nickname "Puffy" for his habit of puffing up his chest during football practice. He attended Howard University in Washington, D.C., but he left college after two years to become an intern at Uptown Records in New York City; within a year he had moved up to vice president. In December 1991, 9 people were crushed to death and 29 were injured as crowds pushed their way into a charity basketball game Combs had promoted at the City College of New York.

In 1993 Combs was fired from Uptown, and he turned his energies to his own label, Bad Boy Entertainment. He soon discovered and befriended a street hustler named Christopher Wallace, who rapped as Biggie Smalls and recorded as the Notorious B.I.G. By 1994 Wallace was a rising rap star, and Combs had negotiated a $15 million deal to move Bad Boy to Arista Records, which gained him a growing industry-wide reputation as a rap impresario and entrepreneur. In spring 1997 the Notorious B.I.G. was murdered, and Combs's first album, *No Way Out*—released that summer under the moniker Puff Daddy—included the single "I'll Be Missing You," a musical eulogy featuring the voice of Wallace's widow and the melody from the Police's "Every Breath You Take." Several more singles from *No Way Out* dominated the pop charts in 1997.

In 1998 Combs toured in support of *No Way Out* and maintained his presence on the airwaves; for the movie *Godzilla* he enlisted guitarist Jimmy Page to concoct the single "Come with Me," a thunderous reworking of Page's Led Zeppelin song "Kashmir." That year Combs took home two Grammy Awards, for rap album (*No Way Out*) and rap performance ("I'll Be Missing You"), and he also launched the Sean John clothing line.

Legal troubles, however, soon overshadowed Combs's music and fashion achievements. In 1999 he was found partially liable for the City College stampede and was made to pay settlements on several resulting claims. Later that year, he pleaded guilty to second-degree harassment after an altercation with a record company executive, and in December 1999 he was present during a shooting at a Manhattan nightclub. Charged with several crimes, including illegal gun possession, he was acquitted in 2001 on all counts. He subsequently made a symbolic break with his past by changing his name to P. Diddy

# TIMBALAND

Influential hip-hop and R&B producer Timbaland (born Timothy Mosley, March 10, 1971, Norfolk, Virginia, U.S.) grew up in Virginia with rappers Missy ("Misdemeanor") Elliot and Magoo. At age 19, he began to learn how to use studio equipment under the direction of producer and musician DeVante Swing, whose pronunciation of the shoe manufacturer Timberland resulted in a new name for his protégé. Timbaland's inventive production skills were first evidenced on Aaliyah's 1996 hit "One in a Million." Soon afterward Timbaland signed with Blackground Records as both a solo act and part of the rap duo Timbaland and Magoo. In 1997 the two put out their first album, *Welcome to Our World*; featuring the contributions of Elliot and Aaliyah, along with the hit song "Up Jumps da Boogie," it achieved platinum sales status.

By the late 1990s Timbaland had developed a signature sound that made him a much sought-after and often-imitated hip-hop and rhythm-and-blues producer. He used original beats—rather than samples—to create complex syncopated rhythms and complemented them with quiet background rapping or obscure sounds, such as a whinnying horse. With an uncanny knack for crafting commercially successful singles and albums, Timbaland produced hits for Jay-Z, Ginuwine, Elliot, Ludacris, and Snoop Dogg. In the early 2000s Timbaland moved beyond the genres of hip-hop and rhythm and blues to produce albums for rock and pop stars, including Nelly Furtado, Justin Timberlake, Beck, Bjork, and Madonna. In addition to his notable work as a producer, Timbaland continued to release albums, both as a solo artist and in conjunction with Magoo. He created new record labels under the umbrella of Interscope—Beat Club and Mosley Music Group—and received a Grammy Award (2006) for his work on "Sexy Back" with Timberlake.

and releasing his second album, *The Saga Continues* (2001). He claimed another Grammy in 2004 for his collaboration with the rapper Nelly on "Shake Ya Tailfeather," and later that year he was honoured by the Council of Fashion Designers of America as their menswear designer of the year. He publicly dropped the "P." from his name in 2005 and released his third album, *Press Play*, the following year as Diddy.

In addition to his music career, Combs occasionally acted. In 2001 he appeared as a death row inmate in the critically acclaimed *Monster's Ball*. He later portrayed a record executive in the comedy *Get Him to the Greek* (2010). His television credits include the 2008 adaptation of Lorraine Hansberry's play *A Raisin in the Sun*.

## MISSY ELLIOTT

From an early age, Missy Elliott (born July 1, 1971, Portsmouth, Virginia, U.S.) demonstrated a knack for performance. Her big break came in 1991 when Jodeci band member DeVante Swing signed Elliott's group, Sista, to his Swing Mob Records label. Lack of funds prevented the release of Sista's debut album, however, and the group subsequently broke up. Elliott, known as Missy Misdemeanor at this time, teamed up with childhood friend Timbaland to

cowrite and coproduce songs for the American rhythm-and-blues artists Jodeci and Aaliyah. Elliott was only 25 years old when the head of the Elektra Entertainment Group offered her a deal that would enable her to write, produce, and record music under the umbrella of her own Gold Mind record label.

Elliott's first album, *Supa Dupa Fly* (1997), went platinum and was nominated for a Grammy Award, and her follow-up, *Da Real World* (1999), spent almost a year on the Billboard rhythm-and-blues chart. *Miss E…So Addictive* (2001), featured the crossover dance track "Get Ur Freak On," and the album won Elliott her first two Grammy Awards. She won a third Grammy for "Work It," a single from her 2002 album *Under Construction*. Her 2005 album, *The Cookbook*, contained the Grammy-winning single "Lose Control." In addition to her Grammy wins, Elliott collected the Black Entertainment Television (BET) Award for best female hip-hop artist numerous times, and her music videos earned her accolades as well as a regular presence on MTV.

## LAURYN HILL

Lauryn Hill (born May 26, 1975, South Orange, New Jersey, U.S.) embarked on an entertainment career at an early age. She and high school classmate Prakazrel ("Pras")

*Lauryn Hill, 2001.* Scott Gries/Getty Images

Michel performed together under the name Tranzlator Crew and were joined shortly thereafter by Michel's cousin Wyclef Jean. As a teenager, Hill also acted on the television soap opera *As the World Turns* and alongside Whoopi Goldberg in the film *Sister Act 2: Back in the Habit*. With the money she earned from her acting jobs, she helped finance her group, renamed the Fugees in 1993.

The Fugees were eventually signed to a division of Columbia Records, but their debut album, *Blunted on Reality* (1994), attracted less-than-spectacular reviews. Critics commented that Hill overshadowed her partners and that she should strike out on her own. The group's second album, *The Score* (1996), which featured an impressive remake of Roberta Flack's 1973 hit "Killing Me Softly with His Song," was much better received, selling more than 17 million copies and earning two Grammy Awards. Hill, who had been pursuing a degree in history at Columbia University, abandoned her studies, and the group's members decided to pursue their individual interests.

In 1996 Hill established the Refugee Project, an organization designed to aid underprivileged youths, and the following year she and Rohan Marley (Bob Marley's son) had their first child. In early 1998 she began putting together a solo album, flying to Jamaica to record the work at the Bob Marley Museum Studio. *The Miseducation of Lauryn Hill* was released that August, and in November she gave birth to her and Marley's second child. Fueled by the release of the single "Doo Wop (That Thing)," the album went multiplatinum, and in 1999 Hill was nominated for 10 Grammy Awards. She won five, including those for best new artist and album of the year.

Hill's sound, often categorized as "neo-soul," bridged hip-hop and mainstream popular music. *The Miseducation of Lauryn Hill* was also notable for its deeply personal lyrics, which addressed such themes as the meaning of self, family, and community. She followed her debut solo recording with a two-disc live album taken from her appearance on MTV's *Unplugged 2.0* series in 2002. The album, which featured an unpolished performance by Hill on acoustic guitar, was punctuated throughout with extended, tear-filled meditations on the burdens of celebrity. Although *Unplugged 2.0* sold poorly, Hill proved that she could still be a significant draw when she co-headlined the

*Wyclef Jean, 2007.* PRNewsFoto/Nickelodeon—Don Bowers/AP Images

Smokin' Grooves tour with OutKast later in 2002. After that tour, she left the public eye but contributed single songs to film soundtracks.

## WYCLEF JEAN

Born in a suburb of Port-au-Prince, Wyclef Jean (born Nel Ust Wyclef Jean, October 17, 1969, Croix des Bouquets, Haiti) was raised by relatives after his parents immigrated to the United States. At age nine he and his younger brother joined their parents in Brooklyn, New York. The family moved to Newark, New Jersey, when he was a teenager. Jean's father, a Nazarene minister, prohibited rap music and encouraged Jean to channel his musical talents into the church choir. Nonetheless, Jean joined Tranzlator Crew (later known as the Fugees), a rap group founded by Prakazrel ("Pras") Michel and Michel's friend Lauryn Hill, in the late 1980s.

Jean studied music at Five Towns College in Dix Hill, New York, before dropping out to concentrate on his rapping. He continued to perform with Michel and Hill, and in 1994 they released their debut album, *Blunted on Reality*. Though the album was only moderately successful, the trio continued to record and in 1996 released their sophomore effort *The Score* as the Fugees. The recording, which innovatively blended elements of jazz, soul, reggae, and hip-hop, sold more than 18 million copies and won two Grammy Awards.

The members of the group then embarked upon solo efforts, a trajectory some observers attributed to an ill-fated affair between Jean and Hill. In 1997 Jean released *Wyclef Jean Presents the Carnival Featuring Refugee All Stars*, which mirrored the syncretic style of his efforts with the Fugees. Between albums, he collaborated with performers including Carlos Santana, for whom he produced the song "Maria, Maria," and Whitney Houston, for whom he cowrote the hit "My Love Is Your Love." In 2000 Jean followed up with *The Ecleftic: 2 Sides II a Book* and in 2002 released *Masquerade*. Further efforts included *Sak Pasé Presents Welcome to Haiti: Creole 101* (2004) and *Carnival Vol. II: Memoirs of an Immigrant* (2007).

In 1998 Jean founded the Wyclef Jean Foundation (later known as Yéle Haiti). The organization raised money and engineered programs to assist victims of poverty in Haiti. Following the Haiti earthquake of 2010, Yéle Haiti raised several million dollars for those affected. Jean announced in August of 2010 that he would run for president of Haiti, but he was deemed ineligible because he was not a resident of the country.

## ERYKAH BADU

Neo-soul vocalist Erykah Badu (born Erica Wright, February 26, 1971, Dallas, Texas, U.S.) was the eldest of three children. Although she was never formally trained in music, she majored in dance and theatre at Grambling State University in Louisiana after graduating from the High School for the Performing and Visual Arts in Dallas. She dropped out of Grambling in 1993 to pursue a singing career and formed the group Erykah Free with her cousin while also working as a waitress and a drama teacher. In 1995, while the group was opening for singer D'Angelo, Badu came to the attention of Kedar Massenburg, who was just starting his own record company. Badu disbanded Erykah Free when Massenburg offered her a contract; she thought that she would receive more individual attention as a solo artist at a smaller label. In January 1997 "On & On," Badu's first single, was released and quickly became a hit. The next month, her debut album, *Baduizm*, for which she wrote all but one of the songs, was released. It rose to number two on the Billboard album chart, thanks to the crossover appeal of Badu's bluesy vocals—which were frequently compared to those of jazz legend Billie Holiday—backed by down-tempo hip-hop beats.

Her sound drew from the roots of African American popular music, and she cited among her early influences Miles Davis, Al Jarreau, Chaka Khan, Stevie Wonder, and Marvin Gaye.

Badu's follow-up album, *Erykah Badu Live*, reached the top five on the Billboard pop charts. The combined sales of the two albums exceeded three million copies, and both efforts were certified as platinum. That year, she captured two NAACP Image Awards, four Soul Train Awards, an American Music Award, and two Grammy Awards. Her second album of original material, *Mama's Gun* (2000), sold well on the strength of singles such as "Bag Lady," and she followed with *Worldwide Underground* (2003), a collection that was marketed as an EP (extended play) in spite of its 50-minute length. In 2008 she released *New Amerykah, Part One: 4th World War*, a bass-heavy album that blended elements of funk with Badu's socially aware lyrics. A flurry of publicity greeted *New Amerykah, Part Two: Return of the Ankh* upon its release in 2010. The controversial video for that album's first single, "Window Seat," featured Badu completely disrobing while she walked through Dealey Plaza in downtown Dallas, the site of the assassination of U.S. Pres. John F. Kennedy.

# CHAPTER 5

# Hip-Hop in the 21st Century

**A**s the century turned, the music industry entered into a crisis, brought on by the advent of digital downloading. Hip-hop suffered at least as severely as or worse than other genres, with sales tumbling throughout the decade. Simultaneously, though, it solidified its standing as the dominant influence on global youth culture. Even the massively popular "boy bands," such as the Backstreet Boys and *NSYNC, drew heavily on hip-hop sounds and styles, and rhythm and blues and even gospel had adapted so fully to the newer approach that stars such as Mary J. Blige, R. Kelly, and Kirk Franklin straddled both worlds.

In the early 2000s, hip-hop's creative centre moved to the American South. Following the success of the increasingly experimental OutKast and the stable of New Orleans-based artists that emerged from two record companies—Cash Money and No Limit Records (which was both founded and anchored by Master P)—the chant-based party anthems of such rappers as Juvenile, 8Ball & MJG, and Three 6 Mafia brought the sounds of the "Dirty South" (an often profane form of hip-hop that emerged in the U.S. South) to the mainstream.

Dr. Dre remained a crucial figure; his New York City-born protégé, 50 Cent, achieved multiplatinum status with 2003's *Get Rich or Die Tryin'*, and Eminem became perhaps the world's biggest pop star when *8 Mile* (2002), the loosely autobiographical film in which he starred, enjoyed huge popular and critical success (his "Lose Yourself" won the Academy Award for best song). However, Dr. Dre remained mostly silent for the remainder of the decade, working on technology for a new brand of headphones but never releasing an album after 1999. Eminem, whose outlaw status was challenged by his Hollywood success, seemed adrift, and the Los Angeles style exemplified by Dr. Dre in the 1990s lost much of its power.

Dr. Dre's legacy, though, was visible in the extent to which hip-hop had become a producers' medium. In the 21st century the music— born from the sonic creations of the deejay—saw its greatest innovations in the work of such studio wizards as Timbaland, Swizz Beatz, and the Neptunes. The focus on producers as both a creative and a commercial force was concurrent with a widespread sense that the verbal dexterity and poetry of hip-hop was waning. The genre had truly become pop music, with all of the resultant pressures of accessibility, and the intricacy and subversive nature of earlier MCs had largely been pushed to the "alternative"/"underground" scene spearheaded by rappers such as Mos Def and Doom (MF Doom). The dissatisfaction with the state of mainstream hip-hop was sufficiently common that in 2006 Nas released an album titled *Hip Hop Is Dead*.

Still, major stars continued to emerge. Many of the biggest figures continued to rise from the South, including Atlanta's T.I. and Lil Wayne from New Orleans. Hip-hop celebrity now often came hand-in-hand with multimedia success, such as a burgeoning film career for Ludacris. The genre continued to be assimilated deeper into nonmusical culture, with some of the genre's early stars—LL Cool J, Ice Cube, Queen Latifah, Ice-T—established as familiar faces in movies and television. Snoop Dogg (aka Snoop Lion) headlined rock festivals alongside Bruce Springsteen. Perhaps no one represented the cultural triumph of hip-hop better than Jay-Z. As his career progressed, he went from performing artist to label president, head of a clothing line, club owner, and market consultant—along the way breaking Elvis Presley's record for most number one albums on the *Billboard* magazine charts by a solo artist. Candidate Barack Obama made references to Jay-Z during the 2008 presidential campaign, and on the rapper's 2009 album *The Blueprint 3*, he claimed to be a "small part of the reason" for Obama's victory.

Kanye West, one of Jay-Z's producers, emerged as one of the most fascinating and polarizing characters in hip-hop following the success of his 2004 debut album *The College Dropout*. Musically experimental and fashion-forward, West represented many of hip-hop's greatest possibilities with his penetrating, deeply personal lyrics. However, his endless self-promotion and often arrogant aura also demonstrated some of the elements that now tried the patience of many listeners.

Regardless of hip-hop's own internal struggles, the music's global impact constantly continued to expand. No single artist may have better personified hip-hop in the 21st century than M.I.A. Born in London, raised in her family's native Sri Lanka, and trained as a graphic designer, M.I.A. wrote politically radical lyrics set to musical tracks that drew from wildly diverse sources around the world. Not only was her album *Kala* named the best album of 2007 by *Rolling Stone*, but M.I.A. was also listed as one of *Time* magazine's "100 Most Influential People"—illustrating the reach and power of a music born decades earlier on litter-strewn playgrounds.

# OUTKAST

Formed in 1992, the American rap duo OutKast put Atlanta, Georgia, on the hip-hop map and redefined the G-Funk (a variation of gangsta rap) and Dirty South music styles with their strong melodies, intricate lyrics, and positive messages.

André Lauren Benjamin (born May 27, 1975, Atlanta, Georgia, U.S.)

and Antwan André Patton (born February 1, 1975, Savannah, Georgia) joined forces at a performing arts high school in Atlanta. Discovering their mutual admiration for hip-hop and the funk musicians that became their stylistic touchstones (Parliament-Funkadelic, Sly and the Family Stone, and Prince), they formed a rap group, 2 Shades Deep. Recording in a basement studio under the guidance of the Organized Noize production team (hitmakers for Xscape and TLC), Benjamin and Patton, now known respectively as Dré and Big Boi and collectively as OutKast, had a breakthrough single with "Player's Ball" in 1993.

In 1994 OutKast released their first album, *Southernplayalisticadillacmuzik*. A critical and commercial success, it highlighted the duo's originality and penchant for catchy hooks. *ATLiens* (1996), their follow-up, featured the hit "Elevators (Me and You)" and sold 1.5 million copies. OutKast's third effort, the double-platinum *Aquemini* (1998), employed more live instruments and earned a Grammy nomination for the single "Rosa Parks." As OutKast deepened the sophistication of its frequently life-affirming lyrics and broadened its musical eclecticism, it never lost its unique sense of humour. The group's image also became a signature, especially the increasingly flamboyant wardrobe of Dré (renamed André 3000), and their theatricality and stylish music videos became OutKast hallmarks.

Backed by the hit single "B.O.B" ("Bombs over Baghdad"), OutKast's fourth studio album, *Stankonia* (2000), was a huge crossover success. It earned Grammys for best rap album and best performance by a rap duo/group for the heartfelt "Ms. Jackson," and it placed at or near the top of most critics' yearly "best of" lists. In 2003 the duo released the double album *Speakerboxxx/The Love Below*, which highlighted the solo abilities of both artists as they each took the lead on one disc. In the process OutKast both renewed its mastery of "old school" rap, largely on the Big Boi-dominated *Speakerboxxx*, and continued its assault on the boundaries of hip-hop, primarily on *The Love Below*, on which André 3000 sang as much as he rapped and included funk stylings. The album topped the charts and won three Grammy Awards in 2004: album of the year, best rap album, and best urban/alternative performance for the boisterous "Hey Ya!" In 2006 André 3000 and Big Boi starred in the musical *Idlewild* and recorded the soundtrack. The duo subsequently turned to individual pursuits, with Big Boi recording the critically acclaimed solo album *Sir Lucious Left Foot: The Son of Chico Dusty* (2010) and André 3000

devoting his time to production and guest vocal work for an assortment of high-profile artists.

# MARY J. BLIGE

Called the Queen of Hip-Hop Soul, Mary J. Blige (born January 11, 1971, Bronx, New York, U.S.) spent her childhood in Savannah, Georgia, and in a housing project in Yonkers, New York. Her early musical influences included singing in a Pentecostal church and listening to her mother's collection of soul records. When a recording of the 17-year-old Blige singing Anita Baker's "Caught Up in the Rapture" (made in a karaoke booth in a local shopping mall) came to the attention of Uptown Records in 1988, the rhythm-and-blues label put Blige, who had dropped out of high school, under contract. She sang backup for various artists until the 1992 release of her first solo album, *What's the 411?*, produced primarily by rapper Diddy.

That album revealed the pain of Blige's childhood while presenting a unique sound that mixed classic soul with hip-hop and urban contemporary rhythm and blues, redefining soul music and influencing a generation of artists. Blige's glamorous but street-tough image softened over time; however, her music remained personal, emotional, and spiritual. Among Blige's host of hit singles are "Be Without You" (1994), "Not Gon' Cry" (1996), and "Take Me as I Am" (2005). Her hit albums include *Share My World* (1997) and *Growing Pains* (2008), both of which reached number one on the Billboard charts, and *No More Drama* (2001), Blige's fifth album, which presents an artist who is happy with the woman she has become. Her 2006 release, *Reflections* (2006), provides a retrospective of her work. Blige's 2008 tour with Jay-Z made her one of hip-hop's top-grossing live acts, and the following year she won a Grammy Award for best contemporary rhythm and blues album for *Growing Pains*. *Stronger with Each Tear* (2009) was

criticized for its overreliance on guest vocalists and Auto-Tune technology, but Blige rebounded in convincing fashion with *My Life II…The Journey Continues (Act I)*, released in 2011, which played to Blige's strengths, balancing soulful ballads with infectious dance tunes that recalled her earliest hits.

## JAY-Z

Jay-Z (born Shawn Carter, December 4, 1970, Brooklyn, New York, U.S.) grew up in Brooklyn's often dangerous Marcy Projects, where he was raised mainly by his mother. His firsthand experience with illicit

*Mary J. Blige and Jay-Z performing on stage in Atlanta, Georgia, Apr. 8, 2008.* Annette Brown/Getty Images

drug dealing would inform his lyrics when he began rapping under the stage name Jazzy, soon shortened to Jay-Z (a name that may also have been derived from the proximity of the J and Z subway lines to the Marcy Projects). Jay-Z and two friends founded their own company, Roc-a-Fella Records, to release his debut album, *Reasonable Doubt* (1996), which climbed the Billboard charts, reaching number 23 on the pop chart and number 3 on the rhythm-and-blues chart.

A string of successful albums followed at a rate of at least one per year through 2003. *Vol. 2: Hard Knock Life* (1998) not only was the first of Jay-Z's releases to top the Billboard 200 album sales chart but also won a Grammy Award for best rap album. In 2001 he pleaded guilty to assault relating to a 1999 nightclub stabbing and received three years' probation. In 2003, with the release of The *Black Album*, Jay-Z announced his retirement as a performer. In 2004 he assumed the presidency of Def Jam Recordings, making him one of the most highly placed African American executives in the recording industry at the time.

Postretirement, Jay-Z stayed remarkably active, collaborating with the rock group Linkin Park in 2004 and appearing as a guest vocalist on the recordings of numerous other artists, including Kanye West and Beyoncé; Jay-Z and Beyoncé were married in 2008. He developed a large portfolio of business ventures and investments, including Roc-a-Fella Films, a clothing line, and a stake in the New Jersey Nets of the National Basketball Association, which he later helped relocate to his hometown of Brooklyn. He formally returned to recording in 2006 with *Kingdom Come*. In December 2007 he stepped down as Def Jam president shortly after releasing the album *American Gangster*.

Jay-Z proved that he remained one of rap's most bankable acts when he embarked on a highly successful tour with Mary J. Blige in 2008. The following year he won a Grammy Award for best rap performance for "Swagga Like Us," a collaboration with T.I., Kanye West, and Lil Wayne, and that September he released *The Blueprint 3*, which featured guest vocals from Alicia Keys and production by West and Timbaland. The album continued to generate Grammy-winning singles for more than a year, with "Run This Town," a collaboration with Rihanna and West, and "D.O.A. (Death of Auto-Tune)" being honoured in 2010 and "Empire State of Mind," a collaboration with Keys, and "On to the Next One" scoring wins in 2011. He continued his streak of Grammy success in 2012, winning best rap performance for "Otis," a single from *Watch the Throne* (2011), an ambitious and highly regarded collaboration with West. In 2010 Jay-Z published a memoir, *Decoded*.

## BLACK EYED PEAS

The Black Eyed Peas originated in the underground hip-hop movement of the 1990s. After the dissolution of their group Atban Klann, rappers will.i.am (born William James Adams, Jr., March 15, 1975, Los Angeles, California, U.S.) and apl.de.ap (born Allan Pineda Lindo, November 28, 1974, Angeles City, Pampanga, Philippines) recruited MC and dancer Taboo (born Jaime Luis Gomez, July 14, 1975, East Los Angeles, California) to form the Black Eyed Peas. The group's debut recording, *Behind the Front* (1998), gained attention for its positive socially conscious lyrics and musical dexterity.

*Bridging the Gap* (2000), boasting guest appearances by hip-hop performers Mos Def, De La Soul, and

*The Black Eyed Peas (from left to right): will.i.am, Fergie, apl.de.ap, and Taboo.* PRNewsFoto/Volkswagen of America, Inc., Meeno/AP Images

Wyclef Jean, continued in a similar vein. With the addition of vocalist Fergie (born Stacy Ann Ferguson, March 27, 1975, Hacienda Heights, California) in 2001, however, the group abandoned the hip-hop underground for the pop mainstream. *Elephunk* (2003) yielded the upbeat club-friendly hit singles "Where Is the Love?" (a collaboration with Justin Timberlake), "Hey Mama," and "Let's Get It Started" (titled "Let's Get Retarded" on the album) and went on to sell more than two million copies. Its follow-up, *Monkey Business* (2005), featuring the exuberant top-five hits "Don't Phunk with My Heart" and "My Humps," was even more commercially successful.

After an extensive concert tour in support of *Monkey Business*, the group was dormant for several years. In 2006 Fergie released a multi-platinum solo record, *The Dutchess*. Will.i.am, who produced much of that album, released his own *Songs About Girls* the following year. The Black Eyed Peas returned in 2009 with *The E.N.D.*, which cemented their prominence in the pop music world. Between the singles "Boom Boom Pow" and "I Gotta Feeling," the group occupied the number one position on the Billboard Hot 100 for an unprecedented 26 straight weeks in the middle of that year. In 2010 they won three Grammy Awards, including best pop vocal album.

# EMINEM

Marshall Bruce Mathers III (born October 17, 1972, St. Joseph, Missouri, U.S.) had a turbulent childhood, marked by poverty and allegations of abuse. At age 14 he began rapping in clubs in Detroit, Michigan, and, when unexcused absences kept him in the ninth grade for the third year, he quit school, determined to make it in hip-hop music. As Eminem, he made a name for himself in the hip-hop underground, but his first album, *Infinite* (1996), sold poorly, and he continued to work menial jobs.

When Eminem placed second in the freestyle category at the 1997 Rap Olympics in Los Angeles, he came to the attention of Dr. Dre. By this time Eminem had developed the persona of the inhibitionless Slim Shady, who gave voice to Eminem's id in often vulgar and violent lyrics. With Dr. Dre as his producer and mentor, Eminem released *The Slim Shady LP* early in 1999. Benefiting from the inventive channel-surfing music video for the hit song "My Name Is" and the instant credibility of Dr. Dre's involvement, the album went multiplatinum, and Eminem won two Grammy Awards and four MTV Video Music Awards.

Grounded in his life experience but seemingly reflecting a troubled psyche, Eminem's songs outraged many, including the Gay & Lesbian

*Eminem in* 8 Mile *(2002).* © Universal Pictures/PRNewsFoto/AP Images

Alliance Against Defamation, which denounced him as a homophobic misogynist. His tumultuous relationship with his wife, Kim, was chronicled in songs in which he rapped about killing her. In 2000 Eminem was charged with assault when he allegedly pistol-whipped a man he saw kissing her; the couple divorced in 2001, and their relationship remained rocky (in 2006 the couple remarried and divorced again). His mother also sued him for defaming her in song and in interviews.

In 2000 Eminem released *The Marshall Mathers LP*—the fastest-selling album in the history of rap. The incredible success of the album brought more controversy. To silence critics, in 2001 Eminem performed a duet with openly gay musician Elton John at the Grammy Awards, where *The Marshall Mathers LP* was nominated for best album of the year. Later that year he recorded the album *Devil's Night* with D12 (also known as the Dirty Dozen), a Detroit-based rapping sextet, and toured with the group. He also created his own record label, Shady Records. The D12 collective, 50 Cent, and other rappers signed to and released albums with the label.

When he finished touring in 2002, Eminem made his acting debut in the semiautobiographical *8 Mile*. The gritty film was a critical and commercial success. The following year he won an Academy Award for "Lose Yourself," a song featured in the movie. Eminem's later works include *The Eminem Show* (2002) and *Encore* (2004). While both albums proved successful, neither brought Eminem the attention garnered by his previous two. In 2005 he issued a greatest-hits set—*Curtain Call: The Hits*—that topped the charts. Eminem then stepped out of the public eye, resurfacing briefly in 2006 to eulogize friend and D12 member Proof, who was killed outside a Detroit nightclub.

In 2008 Eminem published the memoir *The Way I Am*, which included photos, drawings, and lyrics. The following year he released *Relapse*, his first collection of new material in five years. While it featured solid production from Dr. Dre, the album met with middling reviews because of its over-the-top attempts to shock and its somewhat dated catalog of pop culture references. Nevertheless, *Relapse* won the 2010 Grammy Award for best rap album, and Eminem shared the Grammy for best rap duo or group with Dr. Dre and 50 Cent for the single "Crack a Bottle." Eminem's 2010 release *Recovery* was a response to the criticisms leveled at *Relapse*, and it was his sixth album to top the Nielsen SoundScan chart for weekly sales. At the 2011 Grammy Awards Eminem repeated in the best rap album category, winning for *Recovery*, and the album's lead single, "Not Afraid," was honoured for best rap solo performance.

## LIL WAYNE

Lil Wayne (born Dwayne Michael Carter, Jr., September 27, 1982, New Orleans, Louisiana, U.S.) grew up in New Orleans's impoverished 17th Ward. There he came to the attention of Cash Money Records head Brian ("Birdman") Williams, and he soon became a member—with Juvenile, B.G., and Young Turk—of the label's all-star group Hot Boys and won notice for the albums *Get It How U Live!* (1997) and *Guerrilla Warfare* (1999). Lil Wayne's first solo LP, *Tha Block Is Hot*, arrived later in 1999 and went double platinum, with its title track reaching the Billboard Top Ten, but two subsequent releases were less successful.

Lil Wayne, who was also known by the nickname Weezy, found a new avenue to success in 2003 with his first underground mixtape, *Da*

*Lil Wayne, 2008.* Kevin Winter/Getty Images

*Drought*. His 2004 album *Tha Carter* reached number five on the Billboard Hot 100 chart and number two on the Hot R&B/Hip-Hop chart and spawned a hit single, "Go DJ." During this time Lil Wayne came into his own as an artist, with lyrics that were both profound and clever and that spoke to a wide range of people. His contribution in 2004 to the single "Soldier" (by Destiny's Child) was the first in a long line of guest performances with other artists. Two popular mixtapes preceded the critically praised album *Tha Carter, Vol. 2* (2005), which sold more than 1.8 million records. His reputation continued to grow throughout 2006 and 2007, with numerous mixtapes, CDs, and collaborations.

In 2008 more than a million copies of *Tha Carter III*, which contained the ubiquitous singles "A Milli" and "Lollipop," were sold in its initial week, and it went on to sell more than 2.8 million units, becoming the best-selling album of the year. In the wake of its success, Lil Wayne could be seen on most of that year's music awards shows, and in February 2009 he took home Grammy Awards for best rap album, best rap song, best rap solo performance, and best rap performance by a duo or group.

Later that year he pleaded guilty to attempted criminal possession of a weapon; the charge stemmed from a 2007 incident in which a loaded gun was found on his tour bus. In March 2010 Lil Wayne received a one-year sentence, and while in jail he released his eighth album, *I Am Not a Human Being*. With time off for good behaviour, Lil Wayne was freed from jail in November after serving eight months.

Shortly after his release, Lil Wayne debuted the single "6 Foot 7 Foot," and in March 2011 he embarked on a North American tour with Nicki Minaj and Rick Ross. The full-length follow-up to *I Am Not a Human Being* was slow to materialize, however, and its release date was pushed back multiple times. Lil Wayne acknowledged those delays with his *Sorry 4 the Wait* mixtape, and he remained a presence on the hip-hop scene as a frequent guest vocalist. In August 2011, after a boisterous performance at the MTV Video Music Awards, he released *Tha Carter IV*, which featured guest performances by John Legend, Busta Rhymes, and OutKast's André 3000.

## LUDACRIS

Ludacris (born Christopher Bridges, September 11, 1977, Champaign, Illinois, U.S.) exemplified the Dirty South school of hip-hop, and his magnetic, larger-than-life rapping persona propelled him to stardom. Though born in Illinois, Chris Bridges spent his formative years in Atlanta, where he later attended Georgia State University. During a stint as a radio disc jockey, he met noted hip-hop producer Timbaland, on whose single "Fat Rabbit" he made his rapping debut in 1998. Adopting the moniker Ludacris (a play on his given name and the word ludicrous; he is also known as DJ Chris Lova Lova), he recorded an independently released debut album, *Incognegro* (2000). Through word of mouth the album managed to enter the Billboard 200 chart, and Ludacris was soon signed to the record label Def Jam South, which repackaged *Incognegro* as *Back for the First Time* (2000). That major label debut ultimately reached number four in the Billboard 200.

Follow-up efforts such as *Word of Mouf* (2001) and *Chicken-N-Beer* (2003) solidified Ludacris's status as a top-selling artist, reaching number three and number one, respectively, on the Billboard chart. *Release Therapy* (2006) also topped the chart and earned Ludacris a Grammy Award for best rap album. Later albums include *Theater of the Mind* (2008) and *Battle of the Sexes* (2010). Signature elements of Ludacris's records include comical, sometimes chauvinistic wordplay, larger-than-life imagery, a fascination with marijuana, and an elastic vocal delivery that alternates between laconic drawl and booming swagger.

As his musical reputation grew, Ludacris developed a secondary career as an actor, taking supporting roles in such films as the dramas *Crash* and *Hustle & Flow* (both 2005), two installments (2003, 2011) of the *Fast and the Furious* action series, and the holiday comedies *Fred Claus* (2007) and *New Year's Eve* (2011). In addition, he made frequent guest appearances on other artists' records, including collaborations with Missy Elliott, OutKast, LL Cool J, and Mariah Carey.

## M.I.A.

Although Maya Arulpragasam was born in London (July 18, 1975), she spent much of her childhood in northern Sri Lanka. When the civil war between the Tamil minority in the north and the Sinhalese government in the south intensified in the 1980s, her father joined the militant Tamil Tigers, and the rest of her family fled Sri Lanka, eventually returning to London. There Arulpragasam studied visual arts, often creating works that were influenced by the conflict she had witnessed as a child. She received her first exposure to the music industry as the graphic designer for the British pop punk group Elastica, and she familiarized herself with the recording equipment used by dance music producers.

Dubbing herself M.I.A., she recorded the single "Galang" in 2003. Although only 500 copies of the song were pressed, it became an instant hit

*M.I.A., 2009.* Kevin Winter/Getty Images

in the European club scene, and word spread quickly on the Internet about its unique fusion of politically aware world music, bass-infused hip-hop, and South London dancehall patois. Anticipation of a full-length album intensified among her fans with the release of *Piracy Funds Terrorism*, a 2004 mix tape produced with American producer Diplo. Although segments of M.I.A.'s 2005 debut album had been circulating on the Internet for almost a year, its release was still greeted with much critical interest. The album title, *Arular*, was the name her father adopted while a Tamil Tiger, and the album cover featured M.I.A.'s face surrounded by a collage of cartoon tanks and AK-47s. The compilation was a huge success on the club circuit, based on the strength of singles such as "Galang" and "Bucky Done Gun," and M.I.A.'s politics lent a new gravity to the dance music genre. M.I.A.'s second album, *Kala*, was released in 2007, and it featured guest production appearances by Diplo and American hip-hop icon Timbaland. More aggressive and sample-heavy than its predecessor, Kala spawned the hit "Paper Planes," which catapulted to success when it was used in the theatrical trailer for the 2008 Judd Apatow film *Pineapple Express*.

In 2009 M.I.A. earned an Academy Award nomination for the song "O, Saya," a collaboration with Indian composer A.R. Rahman for the *Slumdog Millionaire* (2008) soundtrack, and her single "Paper Planes" garnered a surprise Grammy Award nomination for record of the year. M.I.A., who was nine months pregnant and due to deliver on the day of the Grammy Awards ceremony in February 2009, performed with rappers T.I., Jay-Z, and Kanye West and provided one of the more memorable images of the ceremony (three days later she gave birth to a boy). Such mainstream exposure gave her a platform to voice her support for humanitarian aid for civilians in the Tamil region of Sri Lanka, although critics claimed that her lyrics and music videos betrayed a veiled sympathy for the militant Tamil separatist movement. She released her third album, Maya, to mixed reviews in July 2010.

## KANYE WEST

Kanye West (born June 8, 1977, Atlanta, Georgia, U.S.), the child of a photographer and former Black Panther father and a college professor mother, grew up in Chicago and attended Chicago State University for one year before dropping out to pursue a career in music. Early on he demonstrated his considerable abilities as a producer, contributing to Jermaine Dupri's album *Life in 1472* (1998) before relocating to the New York City area, where he made his name with his production work for Roc-a-Fella Records, especially on rapper Jay-Z's album *Blueprint* (2001).

West's skillful use of accelerated sample-based beats soon made him much in demand as a producer, but he struggled to be allowed to make his own recordings (partly because of the perception that his middle-class background denied him credibility as a rapper). When he finally released his debut solo album, *The College Dropout* (2004), it was massively successful: sales soared, and critics gushed over its sophisticated sound and clever wordplay, which blended humour, faith, insight, and political awareness on songs such as "Through the Wire" and the gospel-choir-backed "Jesus Walks," which won a Grammy Award for best rap song—to go along with the awards for best rap album and best rhythm-and-blues song for "You Don't Know My Name."

Abetted by his flamboyant personality, West quickly rose to stardom. His second album, *Late Registration* (2005), repeated the commercial success of his first—with a number of hit singles, including "Diamonds in Sierra Leone" and "Gold Digger"—and earned West three more Grammy Awards. He also gained notoriety for his widely quoted assertion that the federal government's slow response to the Hurricane Katrina disaster in

Kanye West (left) *interrupting an acceptance speech by Taylor Swift at the MTV Video Music Awards, Sept. 13, 2009.* Christopher Polk/Getty Images

New Orleans in 2005 demonstrated that U.S. Pres. George W. Bush "doesn't care about black people"—a comment that Bush later characterized as one of the worst moments of his presidency.

Throughout his career West continued to produce for high-profile artists such as Ludacris, Alicia Keys, and Janet Jackson. He also founded

GOOD Music, a record label under the auspices of Sony BMG. His third release, *Graduation* (2007), produced the hit singles "Good Life" and "Stronger" and garnered him four more Grammy Awards. In 2008 West released *808s and Heartbreak*, an album that dwelled on feelings of personal loss and regret. Its sound differed radically from his previous releases, as West chose to sing (with the assistance of a vocal production tool called an Auto-Tuner) rather than rap his lyrics.

West spent much of late 2009 rehabilitating his image after he rushed the stage at the MTV Video Music Awards, preempting Taylor Swift's acceptance speech for best female video, to declare that "Beyoncé had one of the best videos of all time." Video footage of the incident quickly went viral on the Internet, and West found himself vilified in the media. A series of apologies, some of them appearing as a stream-of-consciousness narrative on West's Twitter feed, soon followed.

The brashness that caused him such trouble in 2009 fueled a triumphant return to music the following year, with *My Beautiful Dark Twisted Fantasy*, a monumentally complex exploration of the nature of success and celebrity. With potent rhymes that were in equal parts boastful and self-effacing, instrumentation that ranged from tribal drums to soaring orchestral accompaniment, and a list of guest performers that included Jay-Z, Rihanna, Kid Cudi, and Chris Rock, that album represented some of West's most ambitious work. He followed it with *Watch the Throne* (2011), a Billboard chart-topping collaboration with Jay-Z that featured the Grammy-winning single "Otis." West also collected a trio of Grammys, including best rap album, for *My Beautiful Dark Twisted Fantasy*.

# K'NAAN

K'Naan (born Keinan Abdi Warsame, 1978, Mogadishu, Somalia) grew up in Mogadishu in an artistic family—his grandfather was a celebrated poet and his aunt a popular singer—and as a child he, too, displayed a gift for reciting verse. He became drawn to American hip-hop after his father, who was living in New York City, sent him records, and he later taught himself English in part by phonetically imitating the rap songs he admired. When civil war broke out in Somalia in 1991, he fled with his mother and two siblings, settling first in New York City, where he reconnected with his father, and then in a community of Somali immigrants in Toronto.

As a teenager K'Naan began to write songs to help him process the turmoil he experienced in Mogadishu. After dropping out of school in 10th grade, he honed his performance skills at open-mic nights in Toronto and contributed poems to Somali Web sites. Eventually, he attracted a manager, who secured him an opportunity to participate in an event in Geneva in 2000 marking the 50th anniversary of the creation of the Office of the UN High Commissioner for Refugees. K'Naan's impassioned spoken-word performance, which openly criticized the UN's involvement in the Somali civil war, received a standing ovation. It also captured the attention of Senegalese singer Youssou N'Dour, who invited him to appear on the album *Building Bridges* (2001), a compilation of songs by musicians living in exile.

In 2005 K'Naan released *The Dusty Foot Philosopher*, a rap album that fused traditional African instrumentation to the familiar structures of American hip-hop. Among its standout tracks, "Soobax" (Somali: "Come Out") was a direct challenge to the warlords of his native land, rapped and sung in a mix of English and Somali, and "What's Hardcore?" was a withering commentary on the macho pretenses of some gangsta rappers. Critics lauded K'Naan's lyrical playfulness and political engagement, and the album won a Juno Award in Canada for best rap recording.

After putting out a live recording, *The Dusty Foot on the Road* (2007), K'Naan expanded his audience with

*Somali-Canadian rapper and singer K'Naan.* Direct Current Media

*Troubadour* (2009). The album, recorded in Jamaica at studios that once belonged to Bob Marley, was another globally inspired concoction, featuring elements of reggae and Ethiopian jazz beneath K'Naan's ebullient rhymes. Though some critics felt that the record was unfocused because of a surfeit of prominent guest stars, many saw it as K'Naan's most accessible work.

In 2010 the determinedly optimistic track "Wavin' Flag," already a hit in Canada, was remade as a celebrity-studded charity single to benefit victims of the January earthquake in Haiti. Another version of the song, a remix by K'Naan, became the official anthem of Coca-Cola's 2010 World Cup campaign. Amid such popularity, it was little surprise when in April he won two more Juno Awards, for artist of the year and songwriter of the year.

# CEE LO GREEN

Thomas DeCarlo Burton (born May 30, 1974, Atlanta, Georgia, U.S.) grew up in Atlanta as the son of two ordained Baptist ministers, both of whom died when he was young; sometime after his father's death, he assumed his mother's maiden name, Callaway. As an adolescent, he engaged in gang activity and committed petty theft, and, after dropping out of school in the ninth grade, he was sent to a military academy, where he eventually earned a GED. Having early displayed an affinity for music—he sang in his church and played the piano at home—by his late teenage years he sought to pursue it as a career.

In 1991 Callaway, along with three friends, formed the hip-hop act Goodie Mob. Three years later the group appeared on the first album by fellow Atlanta rappers OutKast, and their own debut, *Soul Food* (1995), soon followed. With its optimistic attitude and its incorporation of live instrumentation infused with the sounds of classic soul and funk music, *Soul Food* became a touchstone for an emerging sub-genre of hip-hop based in the South. Callaway, who rapped and sang under the pseudonym Cee-Lo, earned particular praise for his spirited high-pitched delivery. Goodie Mob later recorded *Still Standing* (1998), which won further acclaim, as well as other collaborations with OutKast. *World Party* (1999) was considered an artistic and commercial disappointment, however, and Cee-Lo subsequently left the group.

Appending a surname to his moniker, Cee-Lo embarked on a solo career with the stylistically varied rhythm-and-blues (R&B) record *Cee-Lo Green and His Perfect Imperfections* (2002). The album further showed off Green's rich tenor, garnering him comparisons to soul singer Al Green. *Cee-Lo Green…Is the Soul Machine* (2004) boasted a similarly wide-ranging sound.

For his next project, Green teamed up with the hip-hop producer Danger Mouse (born Brian Burton). As Gnarls Barkley (a pun on the name of basketball star Charles Barkley), the pair released *St. Elsewhere* (2006), an offbeat R&B album on

*Cee Lo Green.* PRNewsFoto/Procter & Gamble, Susan Goldman/AP Images

which Green mused upon such dark themes as paranoia and suicide over slick sample-based arrangements. Mostly because of the single "Crazy," a buoyant pop-soul confection that became a surprise worldwide hit, Gnarls Barkley brought Green mainstream popularity for the first time.

After winning two Grammy Awards, the collaborators, who played up their eccentric image by frequently performing in extravagant costumes, returned with *The Odd Couple* (2008).

Green scored his first solo hit with "F--k You!" (2010), an infectious up-tempo track rooted in 1960s soul on which he assumed the role of a heartbroken lover gleefully casting spite upon his ex-girlfriend's well-to-do new mate. The single (which was sanitized for radio and other contexts as "Forget You") served as the centrepiece of his lushly orchestrated album *The Lady Killer* (2010) and earned four Grammy nominations; it won for best urban/alternative performance. In 2011 Green ventured into television, becoming a coach on the singing competition *The Voice* and the host of the show *Talking to Strangers*, on which he interviewed other musicians. The following year his sultry single "Fool for You" won Grammy Awards for best R&B song and best traditional R&B performance.

# CHAPTER 6

# Club Sounds: Trip-Hop, House, Industrial, and Techno

**B**y the 21st century, electronic music had evolved far beyond its origins with krautrock pioneers Kraftwerk. Club anthems typically featured driving rhythms and pounding bass, but those seeking a break from the beat could find satisfaction in the ambient sounds of trip-hop and trance. As techno artists and club DJs achieved mainstream success, traditional rock acts branched out by incorporating elements of electronic music.

## HOUSE

Born in the early 1980s in Chicago clubs that catered to gay, predominantly black and Latino patrons, house fused the symphonic sweep and soul diva vocals of 1970s disco with the cold futurism of synthesizer-driven Eurodisco. Invented by deejay-producers such as Frankie Knuckles and Marshall Jefferson, house reached Europe by 1986, with tracks on Chicago labels Trax and DJ International penetrating the British pop

# THE WAREHOUSE

While go-go was the rage in Washington, D.C., and hip-hop was ascendant in New York City, gay Chicago was laying the foundation for the most lastingly influential of early 1980s African American dance musics, house. The name came from a club, the Warehouse, where deejay Frankie Knuckles eschewed the contemporary gay dance music style, the ultrafast Hi-NRG. Instead, he made new music by mixing together snatches of other material—gloomily anxious Joy Division tracks, synthesizer-driven Eurodisco, snatches of psychedelia, and old soul hits.

House mixes rapidly made their way to vinyl, notably on Trax and Rocky Jones's DJ International label, which, respectively, produced the first big local hit, Farley Funk's "Love Can't Turn Around" (1986), and the first international house hit, Steve ("Silk") Hurley's "Jack Your Body." The house sound was, in the words of DJ Chip E, "a lot of bottom, real heavy kick drum, snappy snare, bright hi-hat, and a real driving bassline to keep the groove."

charts. In 1988 the subgenre called acid house catalyzed a British youth culture explosion, when dancers discovered that the music's psychedelic bass lines acted synergistically with the illegal drug ecstasy (MDMA, or 3,4-methylenedioxymethamphetamine, a hallucinogen and stimulant).

By 1990 the British scene had divided. Following the bacchanalian spirit of acid house, some preferred manic music designed for large one-time-only raves (all-night parties in warehouses or fields). Others favoured the more "mature," club-oriented style of soulful house called garage (named after New York City's Paradise Garage club). Following early homegrown efforts by the likes of the British musician known as A Guy Called Gerald, Britain also started producing its own mutations of the Chicago sound. Pioneered by the British electronica band Leftfield, another subgenre called progressive house excised the style's gay-disco roots and explored production techniques that gave the music a hypnotic quality. Bombastic introductions and soaring female vocals characterized handbag (or diva) house, and anthemlike choruses and pulsating beats distinguished epic house. NU-NRG (a gay, hard-core style) and tech-house (which took an abstract minimalist approach) were other significant subgenres that emerged.

Despite these European versions, house cognoscenti still looked to America's lead—the lush arrangements of auteur-producers such as Masters at Work, Armand Van Helden, and Deep Dish, the stripped-down severity and disco cut-ups of newer Chicago labels such as Relief and Cajual. On both sides of the Atlantic, the continuing proliferation of subgenres testified to house music's adaptability, appeal, and seemingly inexhaustible creativity.

## THE PET SHOP BOYS

The Pet Shop Boys recorded a string of international hits, several of which topped the charts in the United Kingdom in the late 1980s. The band comprised Neil Tennant (born July 10, 1954, Gosforth, Tyne and Wear, England) and Chris Lowe (born October 4, 1959, Blackpool, Lancashire).

Formed in London in 1981 by vocalist Tennant (then a writer for the music magazine *Smash Hits*) and keyboardist Lowe, the Pet Shop Boys arrived at a clever pairing of ironic, coolly delivered lyrics and catchy synthesizer-based dance music, underlain by emotional tension. Influenced by the music of gay nightclubs, the duo (who broke their carefully maintained sexual ambiguity when they came out in 1994) incorporated the sounds of disco, Hi-NRG, house, and techno. Their first single, "West End Girls," recorded with American producer Bobby ("O") Orlando, became a hit in France and Belgium in 1984, but it was not until two years later that a rerecorded version of the song shot to number one in Britain, the United States, and several other countries. Subsequent hits included "Opportunities (Let's Make Lots of Money)" from the duo's first album, *Please* (1986), and "It's a Sin," "Rent," "Heart," and "What Have I Done to Deserve This?" from *Actually* (1987).

In 1988 the Pet Shop Boys starred in their own film, *It Couldn't Happen Here*, a surreal cross-country journey scored with the duo's hits, including their remake of Elvis Presley's "Always on My Mind." In 1989 the pair, who rarely performed live, undertook a tour that was elaborately staged by the painter and film director Derek Jarman. Their songs continued to place high on the

British singles charts in the 1990s, and their 1993 album, *Very*, made the American Top 20 and reached number one in Britain. The duo remained a potent force on the dance scene into the 21st century, and *Yes* (2009) was the group's highest charting album in more than a decade.

## TECHNO

With its glacial synthesizer melodies and brisk machine rhythms, techno was a product of the fascination of middle-class African American youths in Detroit, Michigan, for European electronic dance music. Influenced by Kraftwerk's Teutonic electro-pop and Alvin Toffler's concept of "techno rebels," a clique of deejay-producers—Derrick May, Juan Atkins, and Kevin Saunderson—began drawing attention to their innovative music in 1985. Crossing the Atlantic as an adjunct to Chicago house music, their early tracks—Rythim Is Rythim's "Strings of Life," Model 500's "No UFOs," and Inner City's "Good Life"—incited pandemonium on Europe's dance floors. Unlike house, Detroit techno was primarily all-instrumental, and its beats were more complex than the disco-derived, four-to-the-floor kick-drum that underpinned house.

As the Detroit sound became a mainstay of the European rave scene (the neo-psychedelic subculture based around ecstasy-fueled all-night dance parties), white producers took the music in a harder-edged direction, replacing its dreamy elegance with aggressive riffs and druggy sample textures. Pioneered by Joey Beltram from New York City, Belgian artists such as 80 Aum and Human Resource, and second-wave Detroit labels Underground Resistance and +8, this new brand of techno was called hardcore, signifying both its militant attitude and ecstasy-driven hedonism. Meanwhile, British styles such as the minimalist bleep-and-bass and breakbeat hardcore were bringing hip-hop influences into the mix. By the mid-1990s, techno had fragmented into myriad subgenres, the most important being trance (characterized by metronomic beats and cosmic melodies), electronica (atmospheric experimentalism designed for album-length home listening), jungle (based around sped-up hip-hop breakbeats and floor-quaking reggae bass), and gabba (an ultrafast furor closer to heavy metal than dance music). Although purist connoisseurs pined for the lighter touch of the Detroit originators and their inheritors Carl Craig and Jeff Mills, a rowdy, rock-and-roll mutant of techno invaded the American mainstream in 1997, with the success of albums by the Prodigy and the Chemical Brothers.

Encompassing a huge range of substyles, from multimillion-selling

# RAVE 'TIL DAWN

Britain's rave culture and the sound that powered it were the product of a cornucopia of influences that came together in the late 1980s: the pulse of Chicago house music and the garage music of New York City, the semiconductor technology of northern California and the drug technology of southern California, the early electronic music of Munich and Frankfurt am Main, Germany, and the surge in car ownership and foreign holiday taking among the residents of the greater London area.

Designed for clubs where the volume was high and bass tones were dominant, the music that resulted was the sound of creative electronic repetition. It was produced with both samples and rhythm machines (typically the Roland 808 synthesizer for drums and the Roland 303 for bass). Because it first emerged in clubs such as the Ku and Amnesia on Ibiza, in the Spanish Balearic Islands—a favourite vacation spot for fun-loving young Britons—the sound was initially called Balearic Beat. There had been warehouse parties in London since about 1983, but the new We Generation—the name coined by its members, perhaps under the influence of the hallucinogen and stimulant ecstasy—came to full life on the M25, London's giant orbital ring road, on which "ravers" gathered in their cars before driving to vast, open-air, all-night dance parties.

Recorded music achieved total supremacy: the only notion of performance was in the skill of the deejay. The music's heart was "in the mix." Having previously sought attention by association with stars, the deejays finally became stars themselves (including some former vocalists who reemerged in this new guise, notably Boy George). Like rock and roll in the mid-1950s, this sound swept the world, decentralizing what had become a very centralized music business, producing a new family of music, such as techno, hardcore, trance, trip-hop, jungle, and bass and drum, and a new generation of artists, such as Orbital (named after the M25), the Prodigy, and the Chemical Brothers—all unthinkable without the constantly tumbling price of microprocessors.

pop to the darkest depths of the underground and even influencing mainstream rock bands such as U2, techno established itself as the cutting edge of Western popular music at the end of the 20th century.

## THE CHEMICAL BROTHERS

The Chemical Brothers pioneered the big beat dance music genre in the 1990s. Members Ed Simons (born June 9, 1970, London, England) and Tom Rowlands (born January 11, 1971, Oxfordshire) met at Manchester University in 1989. Already fans of hip-hop, the pair quickly became avid participants in the "Madchester" rave scene, then buzzing thanks to the synergy of house music and the drug ecstasy. Rowlands and Simons attended nightclubs such as the much ballyhooed Hacienda and illegal warehouse raves in nearby Blackburn. They started their deejay career at the small Manchester club Naked Under Leather.

Relocating to London, the duo recorded early tracks such as "Song to the Siren" under the name the Dust Brothers, borrowed from the American production team who would later demand they stop using the name. In 1994 the Chemical Brothers began their deejay residency at the Heavenly Social club, whose anything-goes music policy attracted those alienated by the increasingly stratified nature of British dance culture. Rowlands's and Simons's anti-purist deejay mix of rap, techno, and rock crystallized into their own sound on "Chemical Beats," which combined fast hip-hop break beats and acid techno sounds. Crucially, what gave the track its rock attack was the way the Roland 303 synthesizer-bass riff supplied the mid-frequency blare of a distorted electric guitar.

Not only did "Chemical Beats" provide the blueprint for the duo's 1995 debut album, *Exit Plane Dust*, but it also sired an entire genre, big

# THE LOVE PARADE

Germany's annual Love Parade was the temporary centre of the world of electronic dance music during its two-decade run. First organized in 1989 in West Berlin by planetcom, a company affiliated with the defunct E-Werk club, the parade was registered with the city as a political demonstration for "peace, joy, and pancakes" and until 1997 was held on the Kurfürstendamm, Berlin's main shopping street. The first Love Parade consisted of a couple of vans playing techno music for a crowd of about 300 fans, but the event soon grew into a festival that attracted corporate sponsorship, heavy coverage by MTV Europe, and many more spectators; in 1997 estimates of crowd size ranged from 750,000 to 1,500,000 people. Each year, Berlin authorities threatened to ban the Love Parade for environmental or safety reasons, and permits for the event had by 2006 become too difficult to secure, forcing its relocation to the Ruhr region. Although the parade itself got most of the media attention, the real point for the fans was the hundreds of parties in nearby clubs during the weekend, when nearly every major star of the electronic dance music world appeared. Organizers ended the event after a tragic stampede at the 2010 Love Parade in Duisburg killed 21 and injured more than 500.

beat. The Chemicals' 1997 follow-up, *Dig Your Own Hole*, kept them ahead of a growing legion of imitators by expanding their sonic spectrum, which ranged from the crude adrenal inrush of "Block Rockin' Beats" (the reductio ad absurdum of the "Chemical Beats" formula, already perfected on 1996's exhilarating "Loops of Fury") to the fragile psychedelic ballad "Where Do I Begin?" (with vocals by neo folksinger Beth Orton). "Setting Son," which topped the U.K. singles charts and featured

Oasis's Noel Gallagher, sounded like a hip-hop update of the Beatles' psychedelic rock masterpiece "Tomorrow Never Knows."

A hit on MTV and modern rock radio in the United States, "Setting Son" pushed *Dig Your Own Hole* to U.S. sales of more than 700,000. Along with Prodigy, the Chemical Brothers were trailblazers for "electronica," a media and music industry buzzword for a disparate bunch of British posttechno acts belatedly impacting the American mainstream. The triumph was sweet but brief. By 1999 the electronica–big beat sound had been codified by copyists (the best of whom, Fatboy Slim, was even more successful than the Chemicals). And it had been literally "commercial-ized" by the advertising industry, which used its high-energy rhythms to pep up innumerable television commercials.

Seeking a fresh path, the Chemical Brothers' *Surrender* (1999) alternated between a gentler, house-influenced sound and further forays into rhapsodic psychedelia. "Before, our music was about a disorienting, punishing kind of joy," Rowlands declared. "*Surrender* is a nicer way of achieving that—lifting you up instead of blasting you out of a cannon." In the United Kingdom, the album enhanced the Chemical Brothers' stature as "proper" album artists and revered elder statesmen of "rave 'n' roll." But in the United States, caught between a mainstream that had already tired of electronica and a rave underground scene that always regarded it as a crass sellout, *Surrender*'s absence of ballistic thrills confused consumers and resulted in disappointing sales, as did the Chemical Brothers' releases in the 2000s, though these efforts fared better with the British critics and audience.

## TRIP-HOP

Coined by the British dance magazine *Mixmag* but rejected by many of its purported practitioners, trip-hop originated in Bristol, England, a West Country port known for its leisurely pace of life. Spawned from the town's postpunk bohemia, Massive Attack—a multiracial collective of deejays, singers, and rappers including Daddy G. (born Grant Marshall, December 18, 1959, Bristol, England), 3-D (born Robert Del Naja, January 21, 1965, Brighton, England), and Mushroom (born Andrew Vowles, c. 1968)—created *Blue Lines* (1990), widely regarded as the first trip-hop album. Citing influences from Isaac Hayes's orchestral soul and the Mahavishnu Orchestra's jazz-rock to the dub reggae of Studio One, Massive Attack talked of making music for "chilling out" at home rather than for dancing—hence the torrid tempos of trip-hop.

Trip-hop as a term really achieved currency in 1994–95 thanks to other Bristolians, former Massive Attack rapper Tricky (born Adrian Thaws, January 27, 1968, Bristol) and Portishead, a group formed by Massive protégé Geoff Barrow (born December 9, 1971, Southmead, England). Featuring the forlorn vocals of Martina Topley-Bird alongside Tricky's croaky, mumbled rhymes, Tricky's debut album, *Maxinquaye* (1995), is a masterpiece of paranoid ambience. Songs such as "Aftermath" and "Ponderosa" drew inspiration from the slough of despondency into which Tricky slid with help from alcohol and marijuana, but they also serve as stark visions of mid-1990s Britain: politically deadlocked, culturally stagnant, and with many young people using drugs to numb the pain of their blocked idealism. Portishead's *Dummy* (1994) was similarly desolate-sounding thanks to the torch-singer persona of vocalist Beth Gibbons (born January 4, 1965, Keynsham, England), but Barrow's attractive film-score-influenced arrangements made the album a cult success and nearly ubiquitous as background music at trendy cafés and dinner parties. Portishead's eponymous second album, released in 1997, covered much the same ground but lacked some of the cachet of its predecessor. Massive Attack remained active into the 2000s, though by the release of the group's fourth album, *100th Window* (2003), only 3-D remained from the original lineup.

Although globally popular, trip-hop has remained a largely British genre. Its leading labels (Ninja Tune, Jazz Fudge, and Mo' Wax—whose founder, James Lavelle, cited *Blue Lines* as the inspiration for his pursuit of a career in music) are based in the United Kingdom, as are the genre's top artists, some of whom first made their mark in trip-hop but moved on to other musical pursuits, including Funky Porcini, DJ Vadim, Wagon Christ (Luke Francis Vibert), DJ Food, and U.N.K.L.E. The notable exception is DJ Shadow (born Josh Davis, January 1, 1973, Hayward, California, U.S.), an American, who honed his version of trip-hop in northern California. A hip-hop fan disillusioned by rap's commercialization, Shadow created emotionally evocative song suites such as "In/Flux" (1993), "Lost and Found" (1994), and "Midnight in the Perfect World" (1997), which, although artfully woven out of samples from movie soundtracks and vintage funk records, were essentially brand-new compositions. Shunning rappers and singers, Shadow preferred to use sound bites from spoken-word albums whenever his abstract music required emotional focus. The sleeve art of his 1996 debut, *Endtroducing*, depicts the teeming rack of a used

# BRISTOL: THE CAPITAL OF TRIP-HOP

Until 1990 if a musician came from Bristol—the English port city whose wealth was built on the slave trade—there was little to be gained from admitting it. But the success of the trio Massive Attack, especially in Britain, so changed perceptions that by the end of the decade, in the eyes of many, Bristol was the place to be from. Nellee Hooper, PJ Harvey, Portishead, Tricky, and Roni Size reinforced the city's growing reputation for harbouring single-minded eccentrics who achieved critical acclaim and substantial sales despite ignoring conventional concepts of commerciality. No single venue, studio, or record label provided cohesion, as each project tended to work in its own club or workshop space; but several key players had worked together during the mid-1980s as part of a group of deejays known as the Wild Bunch.

Hooper was the first to surface, in 1989, as arranger and coproducer of the internationally successful album *Club Classics Vol. One* (titled *Keep on Movin'* in the United States) by the London-based Soul II Soul, but it was Massive Attack that put Bristol on the musical map with their album Blue Lines in 1991. Low-key hip-hop-style raps by the group's members provided coherence and context for the contributions of guest vocalists such as soul diva Shara Nelson, reggae veteran Horace Andy, and rapper Tricky in a suite of musical soundscapes whose atmospheric, dub-drenched style defied classification as rock or soul, dance or alternative. Somebody called it "trip-hop," and the name stuck. Other producers across the country were inspired to write soundtracks for the movies in their heads, but the three most notable responses came from Bristol: Portishead's *Dummy* (1994) and Tricky's *Maxinquaye* (1995), both full of gloomy paranoia and suppressed passion, and Massive Attack's own follow-up, *Protection* (1995), featuring guest vocalist Tracey Thorn from Everything but the Girl.

vinyl (record) store. It is a celebration of hip-hop's culture of "digging in the crates," the hunter-gatherer approach to salvaging obscure samples from unlikely sources. Like Tricky and Massive Attack, Shadow proved that this is a valid modern aesthetic, which at its best can alchemize stale cheese into soulful gold. In 2006 he surprised trip-hop fans with his album *The Outsider*, on which he embraced "hyphy" (from hyper and fly), the mixture of old-school hip-hop beats and more-contemporary rapping styles that had emerged in the Oakland–San Franciso Bay Area.

## PORTISHEAD

Portishead popularized trip-hop in North America by fusing dance music conventions such as drum loops and samples with atmospheric, cabaret-style vocals. Principal members included lead singer Beth Gibbons (born January 4, 1965, Keynsham, Bath and North East Somerset, England), producer Geoff Barrow (born December 9, 1971, Walton-in-Gordano, North Somerset), and guitarist Adrian Utley (born April 27, 1957, Northampton, Northamptonshire).

Barrow, who was active in the Bristol music scene in the early 1990s, got his start in the recording industry writing songs for Neneh Cherry and doing production work for trip-hop pioneers Massive Attack.

Gibbons had been earning a living as a nightclub singer when she and Barrow met in 1991 while participating in a job-training program at the Bristol unemployment office. They collaborated on a number of songs and dubbed themselves Portishead, after the town where Barrow grew up. Meanwhile, Barrow continued working as a producer and remixed songs for a diverse collection of groups that included Primal Scream, Ride, and Depeche Mode. During this time, Portishead's core lineup was completed with the additon of Utley, a veteran jazz guitarist who had previously recorded with guitar virtuoso Jeff Beck.

The group's debut album, *Dummy* (1994), was widely hailed as a dark masterpiece. Gibbons's vocals, which alternately evoked Billie Holiday's growl and Judy Collins's plaintive soprano, served as an anchor for the instrumental experimentation of Barrow and Utley, who integrated sound loops, samples from 1960s film soundtracks, and theremin solos into a sonic mélange that achieved massive crossover success. The album's retro sound and melancholy lyrics appealed to an adult alternative rock market that had traditionally eschewed dance music, and the heavy rotation of videos for the singles "Sour Times" and "Numb" on MTV sparked additional sales. *Dummy* went on to capture the 1995

*Portishead (left to right): Geoff Barrow, Adrian Utley, and Beth Gibbons, 2007.* ©John Minton/Portishead

Mercury Prize for album of the year, and it was certified gold in the United States.

The band's second album, the self-titled *Portishead* (1997), was a solid follow-up to *Dummy*, and the haunting video for the single "Only You" became a staple on MTV. After the release of the live album *PNYC* (1998), the band went on an extended hiatus, with individual members pursuing solo projects. Gibbons teamed with former Talk Talk bassist Paul Webb (who billed himself as Rustin Man) to produce *Out of Season* (2002). The album represented a radical departure from the electronic wizardry of Portishead, with acoustic guitars and simple piano melodies taking the place of samplers.

Portishead reunited in 2005, playing a handful of live dates and collecting material for a new album. The appropriately titled *Third* reached the Billboard Top Ten in its first week of release in 2008, and critics praised the band's reinvention of itself. Although the group had not totally forsaken its trip-hop roots, the driving beats of songs such as "We Carry On" and "Machine Gun" offered a harder, more industrial sound than any of Portishead's previous works.

## INDUSTRIAL MUSIC

Coined by British postpunk experimentalists Throbbing Gristle in the 1970s, the term *industrial music* simultaneously evoked the genre's bleak, dystopian worldview and its harsh, assaultive sound ("muzak for the death factories," as Throbbing Gristle put it). Believing that punk's revolution could be realized only by severing its roots in traditional rock, industrial bands deployed noise, electronics, hypnotic machine rhythms, and tape loops. Instead of rallying youth behind political slogans, industrial artists preferred to "decondition" the individual listener by confronting taboos. Key literary

influences were J.G. Ballard's anatomies of aberrant sexuality and the paranoid visions and "cut-up" collage techniques of William S. Burroughs.

By the early 1980s Throbbing Gristle and its allies—Nurse with Wound, Current 93, Coil, 23 Skidoo—had shifted from fetishizing horror to a neo-pagan fascination with occult magic and mystical arcana. Throbbing Gristle's leader, Genesis P-Orridge, formed the less abrasive Psychic TV and a cultlike "fan club" called Temple Ov Psychick Youth. However, many of Orridge's acolytes were alienated when their guru abandoned the "dark side" for the ecstatic trance dancing and "positivity" of the acid house scene in 1988. The industrial legacy was reaching the dance floor by another route, too— the regimented rhythms of electronic body music (Front 242, Nitzer Ebb), Canada's Front Line Assembly and Skinny Puppy, and Chicago's Wax Trax! label. In the 1990s industrial invaded the U.S. mainstream, with Ministry and Nine Inch Nails offering a kind of cyber-grunge counterpart to the raging guitars of post-Nirvana alternative rock.

## NINE INCH NAILS

The "band" Nine Inch Nails was essentially a stage name for singer and multi-instrumentalist Trent Reznor (born Michael Trent Reznor, May 17,

# CYBERPUNK: INDUSTRIAL LITERATURE

The word "cyberpunk" was coined by writer Bruce Bethke, who wrote a story with that title in 1982. He derived the term from the words cybernetics, the science of replacing human functions with computerized ones, and punk, the cacophonous music and nihilistic sensibility that developed in the youth culture during the 1970s and '80s. Science-fiction editor Gardner Dozois is generally credited with having popularized the term.

The roots of cyberpunk extend past Bethke's tale to the technological fiction of the 1940s and '50s, to the writings of Samuel R. Delany and others who took up themes of alienation in a high-tech future, and to the criticism of Bruce Sterling, who in the 1970s called for science fiction that addressed the social and scientific concerns of the day. Not until the publication of William Gibson's 1984 novel *Neuromancer*, however, did cyberpunk take off as a movement within the genre. Other members of the cyberpunk school include Sterling, John Shirley, and Rudy Rucker.

1965, Mercer, Pennsylvania, U.S.). Nine Inch Nails began in Cleveland in 1988 while Reznor was working at a recording studio. He wrote, arranged, performed, and produced the majority of the material, bringing in other musicians for live performances. The band quickly gained popularity with its debut release, *Pretty Hate Machine* (1989), which went triple platinum in the United States and signaled a breakthrough into the American mainstream for industrial music. After a drawn-out legal battle with his recording company, TVT, Reznor set up his own label called Nothing Records and released the EP album *Broken* (1992), which earned a Grammy Award. Reznor signed glam shock rocker Marilyn Manson to the Nothing label, and the two fed on each other's successes throughout the 1990s.

*Trent Reznor, 2005.* L. Cohen/WireImage/Getty Images

Reznor's second full-length album, *The Downward Spiral* (1994), debuted at number two on the Billboard album chart. It was eventually certified quadruple platinum on the strength of such singles as "Closer" and "Hurt." (An emotional acoustic version of the latter song later became a surprise hit for country legend Johnny Cash.) Nine Inch Nails appeared as a headliner at the 1994 Woodstock festival, and "Happiness in Slavery," a single recorded at that performance, earned Reznor a second Grammy. In 1995 Nine Inch Nails opened for David Bowie on his North American tour, but a new album was slow to follow, and much of Reznor's time was spent in the production studio with label mate Marilyn Manson.

The double album *The Fragile* appeared in 1999—hitting the top of the charts in its first week of release— but it faded quickly when no clear singles emerged. *With Teeth* (2005) also bowed at number one, and its industrial dance floor anthems signaled a return to the sound of *The Downward Spiral*. Given the half-decade wait between previous Nine Inch Nails releases, a veritable flurry of activity followed. The concept album *Year Zero* (2007) was accompanied by an ambitious viral marketing campaign, and instrumental samples used in its creation were collected in *Ghosts I– IV* (2008). Reznor signaled his break with the traditional music distribution model when he released the sixth full-length Nine Inch Nails album, *The Slip* (2008), as a free digital download from his Web site.

At the conclusion of the 2009 "Wave Goodbye" tour, Reznor disbanded Nine Inch Nails as a live act. In 2010 he formed the electronic group How to Destroy Angels with his wife, percussionist Mariqueen Maandig, and British musician Atticus Ross. In collaboration with Ross, Reznor also began to compose for motion pictures, and their music for *The Social Network* (2010) won the Academy Award for best original score.

# CHAPTER 7

# Dance Pop

It seems that there will always be a place in rock for unabashedly pop performers. Whether aiming squarely at the teen and pre-teen set with bubble gum ballads or crossing into the mainstream by way of the dance charts, high-energy tunes featuring charismatic vocalists continued to occupy a crucial niche in the rock spectrum.

## KYLIE MINOGUE

Singer and actress Kylie Minogue (born May 28, 1968, Melbourne, Victoria, Australia) became a pop superstar in Australia and Europe in the late 1980s and continued to enjoy success into the early 2000s.

Minogue, who had been acting since she was a child, first garnered fame in Australia and Great Britain for her work on the popular soap opera *Neighbours* (1985–88). She subsequently left television for a singing career, making her recording debut in 1988 with the album *Kylie*—as part of the London hit factory Stock, Aitken & Waterman—and registering her first number one single, "I Should Be So Lucky." Her cover of Little Eva's "Locomotion" broke into the American Top Ten, where she would not reappear for another 14 years. With media savvy and a strong work ethic, the diminutive (5 feet [1.5 metres] tall) Minogue saw her career skyrocket in Europe. She became a favourite of the tabloids, and Minogue cultivated her sexy image to further publicity.

Minogue left Stock, Aitken & Waterman in the early 1990s, and her musical career later slumped as she assumed a punky look and recorded with "indie" rockers. She returned to her pop roots in 2000 with her comeback single, "Spinning Around," from the album *Light Years*. Minogue had further success the following year with *Fever*, which contained the blockbuster single "Can't Get You Out of My Head." In the United States the album reached number three in 2002, outselling all of her previous albums there combined. Her renewed popularity continued with the release of *Body Language* (2003), and in 2004 she won her first Grammy Award, for best dance recording, with the single "Come into My World."

In 2005 Minogue announced that she had been diagnosed with breast cancer. She subsequently underwent surgery, and, after a recovery period of more than a year, she began touring again in late 2006. The following year her 10th studio album, *X*, was released. She was made a Member of the Order of the British Empire in 2008.

## GWEN STEFANI

As teenagers in Orange County, California, Gwen Stefani (born October 3, 1969, Fullerton, California,

U.S.) and her brother Eric helped found No Doubt, which fused ska with new wave-style pop. The group's breakthrough came with its third album, the chart-topping *Tragic Kingdom* (1995), which included the hit singles "Just a Girl," "Spiderwebs," and "Don't Speak." As the band's popularity grew, the spotlight was very much on the stylish Stefani, who became almost instantly identifiable by her fire-engine red lips and platinum blonde hair and who branched out to collaborate on recordings with rapper Eve and techno artist Moby. No Doubt followed *Tragic Kingdom* with *Return of Saturn* (2000) and *Rock Steady* (2001), winning a Grammy Award (Best Pop Performance by a Duo or Group) for the latter's "Hey Baby." In 2002 Stefani married Gavin Rossdale, the front man for the British alternative rock group Bush.

When No Doubt went on hiatus, Stefani released her first solo album, *Love.Angel.Music.Baby* (2004). Reminiscent of some of Stefani's earliest influences, including Prince and Madonna, the album was considered innovative in part because of an eclectic mix of collaborators that included Linda Perry (formerly of 4 Non Blondes), Outkast's André 3000, and hip-hop artist-producers Dr. Dre and the Neptunes. Blending the hip-hop attitude with 1980s-style dance music, *Love.Angel.Music.Baby* featured the hit singles "Rich Girl,"

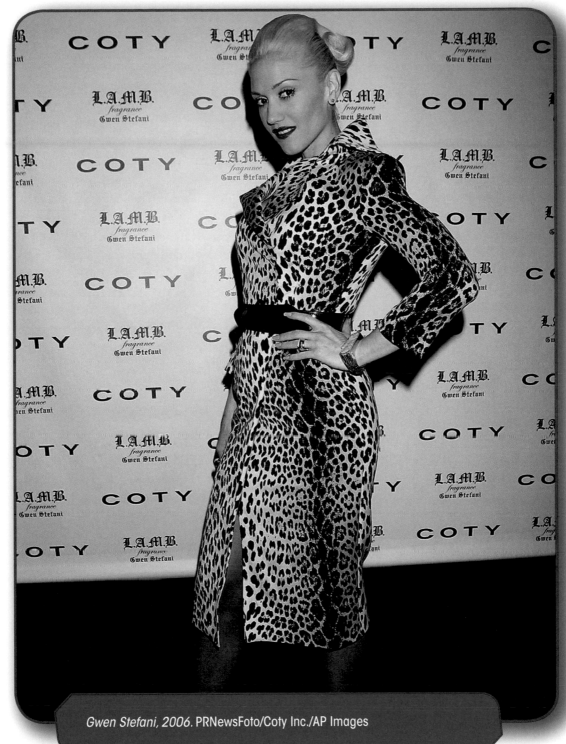

*Gwen Stefani, 2006.* PRNewsFoto/Coty Inc./AP Images

"Hollaback Girl," and "What You Waiting For?" It also introduced Stefani's four-woman Asian dance posse, the Harajuku Girls, whose look was inspired by the outré fashion of Tokyo's Harajuku district. Stefani also tried her hand at acting in director Martin Scorsese's *The Aviator* (2004). Increasingly seen as a trendsetter, she also designed a line of clothing, fashion accessories, perfume, and stationery. She released her second full-length album, *The Sweet Escape*, along with a live DVD, *Harajuku Lovers Live*, in December 2006.

## THE LEADERS OF THE CLUB: DISNEY GOES POP

The Disney Channel served as a springboard for an entire generation of pop singers. *The All New Mickey Mouse Club* launched the careers of cast members Britney Spears, Justin Timberlake, and Christina Aguilera, and *Hannah Montana* catapulted Miley Cyrus and the Jonas Brothers to stardom. Tween sensation Selena Gomez represented the House of Mouse's next wave of pop idols.

### BRITNEY SPEARS

Britney Spears (born December 2, 1981, Kentwood, Louisiana, U.S.) began singing and dancing at age two and was soon competing in talent shows. At age eight she auditioned for Disney's television show *The All New Mickey Mouse Club* but was deemed too young for the program. The impressed producers did, however, encourage her to get an agent in New York City, and she began spending her summers there, attending the Professional Performing Arts School. During this period she started making television commercials and in 1991 appeared in *Ruthless*, an Off-Broadway play. At age 11 Spears finally became a cast member of *The All New Mickey Mouse Club*, joining an ensemble of Mouseketeers that included future pop stars Justin Timberlake (with whom she was later romantically linked) and Christina Aguilera.

After the show's cancellation in 1993, Spears returned home, but she was soon eager to resume her career. At age 15 she made a demo tape that earned her a development deal with Jive Records. Two years later she released her first single, "...Baby One More Time." The song soon became the subject of controversy, both for its lyrics ("Hit me baby one more time") as well as for its Lolita-like video, in which Spears appeared as a provocative schoolgirl. The attention, however, only helped the song, and when the album *(...Baby One More Time)* was released in 1999, it quickly went to number one on the charts and eventually sold more than 10 million copies in the

United States. In 2000 she released her second album, *Oops!...I Did It Again*. It sold 1.3 million copies in its first week of release, setting a record for first-week sales by a solo artist. Although Spears drew criticism for her revealing attire—often imitated by her female fans—she was able to convey a wholesomeness that proved highly profitable. In 2001 she signed a multimillion-dollar deal to be a spokesperson for Pepsi and released her third album, *Britney*, which sold more than four million copies domestically. Its follow-up, *In the Zone* (2003), sold nearly three million, partly on the strength of the hit single "Toxic."

Spears's subsequent studio albums suffered diminished sales but remained major events in the pop music world. The electronic-infused *Blackout* (2007) found her in a self-reflective mood; *Circus* (2008) featured her first Billboard number-one single ("Womanizer") since her debut; and *Femme Fatale* (2011) was her most up-tempo dance-oriented offering to date. Spears also dabbled in acting, making her big-screen debut in 2002 with the lead role in the coming-of-age film *Crossroads*.

Spears often found herself in the spotlight less for her music than for events in her personal life, most notably her tumultuous marriage (2004–07) to dancer Kevin Federline. For many, she came to epitomize the

*Britney Spears.* PRNewsFoto/Iconix Brand Group, Inc./AP Images

endemic growth in the public's fascination with celebrities, catered to by paparazzi and tabloid journalism and fueled by gossip and scandal.

## JUSTIN TIMBERLAKE

In 1996 Justin Timberlake (born January 31, 1981, Memphis, Tennessee, U.S.) and J.C. Chasez, yet another one-time member of the cast of *The New*

*Justin Timberlake, 2006.* Gabriel Bouys/AFP/Getty Images

*Mickey Mouse Club*, were recruited for the male pop vocal quintet *NSYNC. The group's self-titled debut, released in 1998, did well commercially after a slow start, and their second effort, *No Strings Attached* (2000), became one of the fastest-selling albums in history, selling more than 14 million copies and featuring a string of hits, including the chart-topping "It's Gonna Be Me." Timberlake began his solo recording career in 2001 after the release of *NSYNC's third album.

During his tenure with *NSYNC, Timberlake had cultivated his role as a songwriter, and his breakup with longtime love interest Spears provided the inspiration for a number of songs on his Grammy Award-winning (best pop vocal album) solo debut, *Justified* (2002), most notably "Cry Me a River" (best male pop vocal performance). In 2003 Timberlake was a guest performer on the Black Eyed Peas' hit "Where Is the Love?" During the halftime performance of the 2004 Super Bowl, Timberlake was involved in a notorious "wardrobe malfunction" when by design he pulled off part of costar Janet Jackson's top. His second solo release, the Prince-influenced *FutureSex/LoveSounds* (2006), featured production work by Timbaland and Rick Rubin and earned four Grammy Awards, including best dance recording for "SexyBack." Timberlake was not always treated kindly by critics, but few would argue that his solo work, solidly in the vein of rhythm-and-blues and blue-eyed soul, had not transcended his bubblegum dance-pop origins, and he sold millions of recordings in the process.

In addition to his music career, Timberlake acted in films. His first substantial roles were in *Alpha Dog* (2006) and *Black Snake Moan* (2006). In 2010 he portrayed Internet entrepreneur Sean Parker, the cofounder of Napster and the founding president of Facebook, in *The Social Network*, a fictionalized account of Facebook's origins. The same year, he provided the voice of Yogi Bear's diminutive sidekick Boo Boo in *Yogi Bear*, a movie adaptation of the classic TV cartoon. In the comedy *Bad Teacher* (2011), Timberlake appeared as a preppy substitute teacher romantically pursued by Cameron Diaz's title character. He later starred in the racy romantic comedy *Friends with Benefits* (2011) and the sci-fi thriller *In Time* (2011).

In June 2011 News Corporation sold the bulk of its holdings in the social networking site Myspace to advertising group Specific Media, and Timberlake took a minority stake in the company. Timberlake stated that he would try to repurpose Myspace, which had conceded the majority of its former market to Facebook, as a community for musicians and their fans.

## CHRISTINA AGUILERA

After recording the song "Reflection" for the Disney movie *Mulan* (1998), *The New Mickey Mouse Club* alum Christina Aguilera (born December 18, 1980, Staten Island, New York, U.S.) signed a recording deal and released a self-titled debut album of dance-oriented pop music in 1999. Both the album and Aguilera's first single, "Genie in a Bottle," quickly climbed to the top of the Billboard pop charts.

Aguilera's next albums took varying paths but revolved around her powerful voice and exploited her looks and charisma. Emphasizing her Ecuadoran ethnic heritage, she capitalized on the Latin pop music boom by mastering enough Spanish to release *Mi Reflejo* (2000). *My Kind of Christmas* (2000) followed. In 2001

*Christina Aguilera, 2006.* PRNewsFoto/RCA Records/AP Images

Aguilera collaborated with fellow singers Pink, Mya, and Lil' Kim on a popular cover version of LaBelle's 1974 funk classic "Lady Marmalade." Soon after, Aguilera released *Stripped* (2002), on which she cast off her ingenue image and took on a more provocative sexualized persona, epitomized by her hit single "Dirrty." Reminiscent of the work of Etta James and Billie Holiday, *Back to Basics* (2006) pays tribute to Aguilera's jazz and blues influences. She returned to dance pop with *Bionic* (2010), though the album was considered a commercial disappointment. Aguilera received numerous accolades and awards for her music, including several Grammy Awards.

In 2010, after appearing in various cameo roles on film, Aguilera starred opposite Cher in the musical drama *Burlesque*, as a young small-town woman with dreams of becoming an entertainer. The following year she became a judge on the television singing competition *The Voice*.

## MILEY CYRUS

The daughter of country singer and actor Billy Ray Cyrus, Miley Cyrus (born Destiny Hope Cyrus, November 23, 1992, Franklin, Tennessee, U.S.) grew up on her family's farm outside Nashville. Her sunny disposition as a child earned her the nickname "Smiley Miley." She had her name legally changed to Miley Ray Cyrus in May 2008. Though her father was initially reluctant to let her follow in his show business footsteps, at the age of nine she landed a role in an episode of his TV series *Doc*. Another role, in the film *Big Fish* (2003), followed.

In 2005 Cyrus auditioned for the lead role in *Hannah Montana*, a Disney Channel series about a girl who leads a double life as a normal middle-school student and, with the help of a blonde wig, as a glamorous pop singer. Though initially deemed by executives to be too small and young for the character, she persisted and won the part. The show debuted the following year (featuring Billy Ray as her TV dad) and became an immediate sensation, scoring record ratings for cable television and turning the 13-year-old into a bona fide star. Aiming to capitalize on the show's obvious youth-market appeal, a soundtrack album featuring the music of *Hannah Montana* was released in 2006 and eventually sold more than three million copies. It was followed by the equally successful *Hannah Montana 2: Meet Miley Cyrus* (2007), which was packaged as a double CD, with half of the material under Cyrus's own name.

In late 2007 Cyrus embarked on a national tour called "Best of Both Worlds" in support of her latest album. Two concerts from the tour were filmed and presented as a 3-D

Miley Cyrus performing with her father, Billy Ray Cyrus, at the Kids Inaugural: We Are the Future concert in Washington, D.C., January 2009. MC1 Mark O'Donald, U.S. Navy/U.S. Department of Defense

movie; it made more than $30 million in its opening weekend despite having been released only to select theatres. Although already well known to the preteen demographic, she gained wider exposure in early 2008 as her song "See You Again" crossed over to the pop charts. Later that year she released the album *Breakout* and voiced one of the leading roles in the

animated film *Bolt*. For the latter, Cyrus cowrote the single "I Thought I Lost You," which was nominated for a Golden Globe.

Though her celebrity status had increased, Cyrus continued to perform as Hannah Montana in various media. In early 2009 she starred in *Hannah Montana: The Movie* and sang on its soundtrack, and she later issued two additional soundtrack albums (2009, 2010) for the TV show. Later recordings as Miley Cyrus include the EP *The Time of Our Lives* (2009), featuring the hit "Party in the U.S.A.," and Can't Be Tamed (2010).

In 2010 Cyrus starred in the movie *The Last Song*, a romantic drama. After the final episode of *Hannah Montana* aired the following year, she shifted focus to her film career, which included the lead role in the low-budget coming-of-age tale *LOL* (2012).

## JONAS BROTHERS

The Jonas Brothers combined optimistic lyrics, catchy tunes, and cover-boy good looks to become the darlings of the tween set. The members are Paul Kevin Jonas II (born November 5, 1987, Teaneck, New Jersey), Joseph Adam Jonas (born August 15, 1989, Casa Grande, Arizona), and Nicholas Jerry Jonas (born September 16, 1992, Dallas, Texas).

The three brothers were raised in a musical family and imbued with a strong sense of Christian values, notably by their father, an Assembly of God minister. Family sing-alongs in their New Jersey home set the stage for Nick's precocious performances on Broadway beginning at the age of six. In 2004 he released a Christian-themed solo album. The pleasure of making music together prompted the brothers to form a band, with Kevin and Nick on guitar (with keyboard work mixed in) while Nick and Joe shared the lead vocal chores. Their first album, *It's About Time* (2006), featured songs cowritten by Desmond Child and pop star Adam Schlesinger of the band Fountains of Wayne. Although it was given only a limited marketing push, the album sold 62,000 copies; still, the label dropped the band.

Early in 2007 the Jonas Brothers signed with Disney's Hollywood Records, releasing a self-titled album that entered the charts at number five and, propelled by hits such as "S.O.S.," went platinum. The brothers also began appearing regularly on the Disney Channel, most notably in a highly watched 2007 episode of the Miley Cyrus vehicle *Hannah Montana*. The Jonas Brothers then opened for Cyrus on her "Best of Both Worlds" tour. Their music videos became Disney Channel staples, and they starred in a reality program, *Jonas Brothers: Living the Dream*, but their real breakthrough followed their appearance in the Disney movie musical *Camp Rock*, in which Joe played the romantic lead. The brothers were the darlings of "tweenage" (preteen and young teenage) consumers, and in 2008 they became a pop-culture phenomenon with the release of *A Little Bit Longer*, which featured many songs written by Nick.

*The Jonas Brothers* (left to right): *Nick, Joe, and Kevin Jonas, 2009.* Jason Merritt/Getty Images

The album debuted at number one on the Billboard 200 chart, and that year the brothers undertook their own tour, which was filmed for the documentary *Jonas Brothers: The 3D Concert Experience* (2009). In July 2008 they appeared on the cover of *Rolling Stone* magazine as rock critics began acknowledging that the brothers' brand of romantic pop rock was more treat than treacle.

Less than a year after *A Little Bit Longer*, the group released the album *Lines, Vines and Trying Times* (2009), which offered a more mature sound. Nick then recorded a soul-influenced solo effort, *Who I Am* (2010), under the name Nick Jonas and the Administration. In 2009–10 the Jonas brothers starred in a new Disney series, *JONAS* (later *JONAS L.A.*). The half-hour show (in the vein of the Monkees' eponymous television series) featured Kevin, Nick, and Joe as the fictional Lucas brothers, pop stars who are also high school students. They also appeared in *Camp Rock 2: The Final Jam* (2010).

## SELENA GOMEZ

American actress and singer Selena Gomez (born July 22, 1992, Grand Prairie, Texas, U.S.) won legions of young fans as the winsome star of the Disney television series *Wizards of Waverly Place* (2007–12) and as the lead vocalist of the pop act Selena Gomez & the Scene. Gomez, who was named after the popular Tejano singer Selena Quintanilla-Perez, was raised in suburban Dallas. Inspired by her mother, an amateur actress, Gomez tried out for a role on the PBS children's television series *Barney & Friends* and, as a result, appeared regularly on the program in 2002–04. After making her big-screen debut in the family movie *Spy Kids 3-D: Game Over* (2003), she auditioned for the Disney Channel, which eventually led to a guest spot on the TV series *The Suite Life of Zack and Cody*. In 2007 Gomez was cast as Alex Russo, a mischievous tomboy with magical powers, on a new Disney sitcom, *Wizards of Waverly Place*. The show, for which she also sang the theme song, became an instant hit among the preteen set, and she earned favourable comparisons to the channel's leading ingenue, Miley Cyrus.

While continuing to star in *Wizards of Waverly Place*, Gomez acted in various tween-oriented videos and TV movies and provided a voice for the animated feature *Horton Hears a Who!* (2008). She then landed lead roles in the theatrical films *Ramona and Beezus* (2010), which was based on a children's novel by Beverly Cleary, and the romantic comedy *Monte Carlo* (2011). Gomez also ventured into music as the front woman of Selena Gomez & the Scene, an electronic-influenced pop band that produced several dance hits. The group released the albums *Kiss & Tell* (2009), *A Year Without Rain* (2010), and *When the Sun Goes Down* (2011) before announcing its separation in 2012.

Gomez's growing fame was undoubtedly magnified by her romantic relationship, begun near the end of 2010, with pop singer Justin Bieber. She was also known for her philanthropic work, much of it accomplished through UNICEF, which in 2009 appointed her a goodwill ambassador.

## RIHANNA

Robyn Rihanna Fenty (February 20, 1988, St. Michael parish, Barbados) grew up in Barbados with a Barbadian father and a Guyanese mother. As a child she listened to Caribbean music, such as reggae, as well as American hip-hop and R&B. She especially enjoyed singing and won a high-school talent show with a rendition of a Mariah Carey song. About the same time, she started a girl group with two friends, and in 2004 she attracted the attention of Evan Rogers, an American record producer. He helped Fenty record a demo that led to an audition with the rapper Jay-Z, who at the time headed the Def Jam record label, and he soon signed the budding vocalist. For her professional career, she adopted her middle name, Rihanna.

With the effervescent dancehall-inflected single "Pon de Replay" (2005), Rihanna immediately captured an international audience. The song's success buoyed sales for her debut full-length recording, *Music of the Sun* (2005), on which conventional R&B ballads shared space with Caribbean-flavoured dance-pop that showcased her melodious Barbadian lilt. Rihanna soon followed with the album *A Girl like Me* (2006), featuring the up-tempo club-oriented "S.O.S." The song, which was built around a sample of Soft Cell's 1981 new-wave hit "Tainted Love," became Rihanna's first to top the Billboard singles chart.

For *Good Girl Gone Bad* (2007), Rihanna sought to transform her youthful image. With the assistance of such high-profile collaborators as Timbaland and Justin Timberlake, she abandoned the tropical rhythms that had adorned her first two albums and recorded a collection of sleek R&B that presented her as a fiercely independent and rebellious woman.

(She also unveiled a spiky asymmetrical hairstyle.) The gambit paid off, as the album sold several million copies worldwide, and its anthemic lead single, "Umbrella," featuring an introductory rap from Jay-Z, became one of the year's biggest hits and earned Rihanna a Grammy Award.

In early 2009 Rihanna was beaten by her boyfriend, fellow R&B star Chris Brown, in an incident that was widely covered by tabloid news and gossip blogs. (He was subsequently convicted of assault.) The album that followed later that year, *Rated R*, much of which she cowrote, was marked by icily stark production and brooding lyrics that touched on revenge. Although her sales declined somewhat, she scored another major hit with "Rude Boy." Rihanna returned to less-portentous fare on the dance-friendly *Loud* (2010). In early 2011 the album's sexually provocative single "S&M" became her 10th number one Billboard hit—which made her, at age 23, the youngest artist ever to reach that milestone. Included in the total were prominent collaborations with hip-hop artists T.I. and Eminem that appeared on albums of theirs; many felt her vocals on the latter's "Love the Way You Lie" (2010) lent resonance to the song's depiction of an abusive relationship.

Rihanna's sixth album, *Talk That Talk* (2011), produced the infectious international hit "We Found Love."

In 2012 she made her acting debut as a scrappy sailor in the big-budget action movie *Battleship*.

# KATY PERRY

American pop singer Katy Perry (born Katheryn Elizabeth Hudson, October 25, 1984, Santa Barbara, California, U.S.) gained fame for a string of anthemic and often sexually suggestive hit songs, as well as for a playfully cartoonish sense of style. Katy Hudson was raised in southern California, the middle child of two itinerant born-again Christian ministers. Nonreligious music was forbidden in the Hudson household, and she grew up singing church hymns and gospel tunes. As a teenager, she learned to play the guitar and sought a musical career in Nashville with a Christian record label, but her debut album, the gospel-influenced *Katy Hudson* (2001), sold poorly. By then, however, Hudson had found new musical models in such rock artists as Freddie Mercury and Alanis Morissette, whom she had discovered through friends. She soon moved to Los Angeles to pursue success in the secular music realm, adopting her mother's maiden name, Perry, to avoid confusion with the actress Kate Hudson.

Perry's initial efforts at mainstream stardom were fruitless, with two separate record labels signing and subsequently dropping her before any material was released. In 2007, however, Capitol Records put out Perry's EP *Ur So Gay*, which attracted modest attention for its cheerfully flippant title track. She made a greater splash several months later with the single "I Kissed a Girl," an assertive ode to sexual curiosity backed by a hard-edged electro-pop beat. The song quickly stirred controversy, as some critics derided it for promoting same-sex relations and others charged that the racy scenario it depicted catered to male fantasies of female sexuality. Nevertheless, the combination of titillation and polished melodicism helped "I Kissed a Girl" become a number one hit in multiple countries, powering sales for her album *One of the Boys* (2008). With its bouncy, sharp-tongued second single, "Hot N Cold," also proving popular, the album—much of which Perry wrote herself—eventually registered sales of more than one million copies in the United States.

By late 2009 Perry had become frequent tabloid fodder, largely because of her quirky, vividly coloured fashions—which borrowed variously from 1940s pinup models, burlesque performers, and the kawaii ("cute") cultural aesthetic of Japan—as well as her high-profile relationship with English comedian Russell Brand. (The couple married in 2010, but Brand filed for divorce the following

Katy Perry performing in Petaling Jaya, Malaysia, 2010. AFP/Getty Images

frivolity "California Gurls" (featuring rapper Snoop Dogg) and the inspirational "Firework." When "Last Friday Night (T.G.I.F.)" reached the top of the Billboard Hot 100 chart in mid-2011, Perry tied Michael Jackson's record of five number one songs from a single album.

While critics often disparaged Perry's songs as vapid, the music industry was generally kinder, rewarding her with several Grammy Award nominations, including album of the year for *Teenage Dream*. In 2011 she made her big-screen acting debut, providing the voice of Smurfette in the film *The Smurfs*.

## LADY GAGA

Stefani Joanne Angelina Germanotta (born March 28, 1986, New York, New York, U.S.) grew up in an Italian American family in New York City. She learned music at an early age and was performing onstage in New York City clubs by the time she was a teenager. She attended an all-girls school, Convent of the Sacred Heart, in Manhattan before going on to study music at the Tisch School of the Arts at New York University. She studied at Tisch for two years before dropping out to manage her own career.

After dropping out, she began transforming herself from Germanotta into Lady Gaga, whose style combined glam rock and over-the-top fashion

year.) After recording the stripped-down live album *MTV Unplugged* (2009), Perry returned to the studio. The resulting release, *Teenage Dream* (2010), which provided a broader showcase for her full-throated voice, was even more commercially successful than *One of the Boys*, spawning such hits as the warm-weather

design. In 2007 she and performance artist Lady Starlight formed a revue called the Ultimate Pop Burlesque Rockshow. That same year Lady Gaga, who also wrote songs for other pop artists such as Fergie, the Pussycat Dolls, and Britney Spears, was signed by the singer Akon and Interscope Records and began preparing her debut album, *The Fame*, which was released in 2008.

Although she modeled herself on such theatrical performers as David Bowie during his Ziggy Stardust period, the New York Dolls, Grace Slick, and Freddie Mercury—her adopted stage name was derived from Queen's song "Radio Ga Ga"—she created a character that came to occupy a unique space in the music world. Her fashion combined with her up-tempo, synthetic dance music and her edgy, theatrical performance to create stunning sounds and visuals. Indeed, while producing music, Lady Gaga also created her own sexually charged fashions—replete with dazzling wigs and space-age bodysuits—through her creative team Haus of Gaga.

Her first single, "Just Dance," became popular in clubs throughout the United States and Europe and eventually landed at number one on the Billboard Pop Songs chart (also called the radio chart). Three other singles off *The Fame*—"Poker Face," "LoveGame," and "Paparazzi"—also reached number one on the radio chart, making Lady Gaga the first artist in the 17-year history of that chart to have four number ones from a debut album. *The Fame* was well received critically and proved enormously successful commercially, selling more than eight million copies worldwide by the end of 2009. The album also yielded Lady Gaga five Grammy nominations, including for album of the year and song of the year ("Poker Face"); she captured two Grammys—best dance recording ("Poker Face") and best electronic/dance album (*The Fame*)—and her opening duet with Sir Elton John was among the most talked-about elements of the 2010 Grammys telecast. In February 2010 she also picked up three Brit Awards (the British equivalent of the Grammys)—for best international female, best album, and breakthrough act.

Her second album, *The Fame Monster*, was released in November 2009 (it was originally conceived as a bonus disc) and almost instantly produced another hit, "Bad Romance." Other popular singles from the album followed, including "Telephone" (which featured Beyoncé, as did a nine-minute video produced by Jonas Åkerlund starring the pair and referencing Quentin Tarantino's film *Kill Bill: Vol. 1* [2003]) and "Alejandro."

During 2010 Lady Gaga proved to be one of the most commercially

*Lady Gaga, wearing a meat dress, accepting the award for video of the year for "Bad Romance" at the MTV Video Music Awards in Los Angeles, September 2010.* Kevin Winter/Getty Images

successful artists, with a sold-out concert tour (which had been launched to coincide with the release of *The Fame Monster*), while she also headlined Chicago's Lollapalooza music festival and played in front of a record 20,000 people at NBC's *Today* show. She was named one of *Time* magazine's 100 Most Influential People and was named by *Forbes* magazine as one of the world's most powerful women, and she capped off 2010 by being named *Billboard* magazine's artist of the year. After arriving at the 2011 Grammy Awards ceremony encased in a giant egg, Lady Gaga went on to claim honours for best pop vocal album (for *The Fame Monster*) and best female pop vocal performance and best short form video (for "Bad Romance").

Lady Gaga's third album, *Born This Way* (2011), found the entertainer reaching back to earlier musical eras for inspiration. As a blonde dance-pop performer with a penchant for provocation, Lady Gaga had often earned comparisons to the singer Madonna, and on the album's first two singles the similarities were especially pronounced. The title track was a self-empowerment anthem in the style of Madonna's 1989 single "Express Yourself," while "Judas" brazenly mixed sexual and religious imagery. Both songs quickly became hits. Other tracks on the album featured guest appearances from guitarist Brian May of Queen and saxophonist Clarence Clemons of Bruce Springsteen's E Street Band.

Lady Gaga cultivated a devoted following, particularly among gay men (she acknowledged her own bisexuality), who became some of her most loyal fans. She became particularly outspoken on gay rights, especially same-sex marriage, and was a featured speaker at the 2009 National Equality March in Washington, D.C.

## JUSTIN BIEBER

Possessing fresh-faced good looks and a stage presence that belied his years, Justin Bieber (born March 1, 1994, Stratford, Ontario, Canada) emerged as one of the biggest pop sensations of the YouTube generation. He was raised by a single mother in Stratford, and as a child he learned to play the drums, the piano, the guitar, and the trumpet.

In 2007 he participated in a local singing competition, placing second, and his mother posted a video of his performance on the Web site YouTube for friends and family who were unable to attend. She later uploaded other homemade videos, in which Bieber sang popular rhythm-and-blues (R&B) songs and occasionally accompanied himself on acoustic guitar, and they soon attracted attention beyond their originally intended audience. Among those who saw

*Justin Bieber.* Pamela Littky—HarperCollins/AP Images

Bieber's videos was Scott ("Scooter") Braun, a music promoter and talent agent, who invited the 13-year-old Bieber to record demos at a studio in Atlanta. While there, Bieber happened to encounter R&B singer Usher and arranged an informal audition with him. Impressed by Bieber's natural confidence and vocal talent, Usher helped sign him to a recording contract in late 2008.

In May 2009 Bieber unveiled his first single, the buoyant puppy-love song "One Time," and six months later he released the seven-track EP *My World*, composed mainly of glossy R&B-influenced pop. By this time his audience had dramatically expanded to include countless preadolescent girls who considered him a heartthrob, and the recording sold more than one million copies. He replicated the feat with the full-length album *My World 2.0* (2010), which debuted at number one on the Billboard album chart. Its lead single, the yearningly heartfelt "Baby"— featuring a guest appearance from rapper Ludacris—reached the top five of Billboard's singles chart, and several other tracks landed in the Top 40. The official video for "Baby" also became the first to amass more than 500 million views on YouTube.

Later in 2010 Bieber released the album *My Worlds Acoustic*, featuring stripped-down versions of his songs, and published an autobiographical book, *Justin Bieber: First Step 2 Forever: My Story*. *Justin Bieber: Never Say Never*, a documentary film interspersed with 3-D concert footage, opened the following year. Bieber maintained his visibility with the albums *Never Say Never: The Remixes* (2011), a companion to the film, and the Christmas-themed *Under the Mistletoe* (2011), both of which hit number one in the United States and Canada. His enormous popularity was boosted by his allegiance to social media such as Twitter and by his frequent television appearances. On his 2012 release *Believe*, Bieber demonstrated maturing vocal range, but he kept the tone light, returning to the familiar themes of teenage love and longing.

# CHAPTER 8

# The Second British Invasion

At the turn of the 21st century, a succession of British acts exerted an outsize influence on the global music scene. From the tabloid antics of Oasis's Gallagher brothers to Radiohead's next generation art rock; from the Spice Girls' "girl powered" dance tunes to Coldplay's arena-friendly pop anthems, British artists dominated both the headlines and the sales charts.

## BRITPOP

Britpop emerged in the 1990s as a movement that drew consciously on the tradition of melodic, guitar-based British pop music established by the Beatles. Like nearly all musical youth trends, Britpop was about songs, guitars, jackets, and attitudes—though not necessarily in that order. It was perhaps not so much a movement as a simultaneous emergence of fairly like minds, given shape and direction by the determined boosting of the English music weekly the *New Musical Express* (*NME*)—which referred to Paul Weller of the Jam as "the Modfather of Britpop." Indeed, many of those most associated with the term resisted the pigeonhole it offered.

Various peripheral bands were involved in Britpop—most enjoyably, Pulp, from Sheffield, which was fronted by the lanky veteran rocker Jarvis Cocker (born September 19, 1963, Sheffield, England) and had its biggest hit with the single

"Common People"—but it was essentially about Oasis and Blur. What the two bands had in common was a belief in the classic guitar-based pop song with a sing-along chorus—and a love of fashionable sportswear. Their attitudes were quite different, though. While both reached back to British pop's golden age of the 1960s, each had a different take on the inheritance.

Oasis stood for authenticity. At heart the band was two brothers from Manchester, guitarist-songwriter Noel Gallagher (born May 29, 1967, Manchester) and singer Liam Gallagher (born William John Paul Gallagher, September 21, 1972, Manchester). They were northern, working-class, and swimming in illegal drugs and the same kind of romantic aggressiveness as their hero John Lennon. Founded in 1992, Oasis released its first single, "Supersonic," in 1994. Their biggest hit was the album *(What's the Story) Morning Glory?* (1995) and its best-known track, "Wonderwall." Oasis toured the United States; they fought; they entered into disastrous marriages, bought big houses, and took more drugs; and by the late 1990s they had faded into a rut of same-sounding songs.

Blur's take on the pop past borrowed from its reservoir of irony and art school camp—the Rolling Stones' Mick Jagger's makeup and Lennon's whimsies. They were from Essex, the exurban flatlands that separate London from the North Sea. Formed in 1989 and driven by singer Damon Albarn (born May 23, 1968, London, England) and bassist Alex James (born November 21, 1968, Bourneouth, England), Blur had minor success as an "indie" band before finding its place with its third album, *Parklife* (1994), a collection of witty, seemingly light pop songs that held echoes of the Kinks, the Small Faces, and Squeeze. Outgunned and outsold by Oasis in the great Britpop war of 1996, which was reported on by even Britain's leading newspapers, Blur retreated into the angry art dislocation of their eponymous album (1997) before slowly reemerging via the new popism of *13* (1999). Blur's recorded output was intermittent after this point, as Albarn turned his attention to Gorillaz, a "virtual" band that he had formed with Tank Girl artist Jamie Hewlett. Albarn and a host of guest performers provided the music while Hewlett created the striking animation that served as the group's "live" presence.

## SADE

Helen Folasade Adu (born January 16, 1959, Ibadan, Nigeria), the daughter of a Nigerian economics professor and an English nurse, was never addressed by people in her community by her English first name. Her parents began calling her Sade, a

*Sade on the album cover of* Soldier of Love *(2010).* PRNewsFoto/Epic Records/AP Images

shortened form of her Yoruba middle name. When she was age four, her parents separated, and she moved with her mother and younger brother to Essex, England. At 17 Sade began a three-year program in fashion and design at Central St. Martin's College of Art and Design in London. After graduating, she modeled and worked as a menswear designer. Her foray into music began when she agreed to fill in temporarily as lead singer for Arriva, a funk band that had been put together by her friends. Sade later sang with another funk band, Pride, before breaking away with fellow Pride members Stuart Matthewman, Andrew Hale, and Paul Spencer Denman to form the band that would eventually bear her own name.

Sade's smooth sound, which defied easy categorization, was exemplified by the songs "Your Love Is King" and "Smooth Operator," both tracks from the group's debut album *Diamond Life* (1984), which earned Sade and her bandmates a Grammy Award for best new artist. A second album, *Promise* (1985), enjoyed similar popularity and was followed by a world tour. The album featured the hit song "The Sweetest Taboo," which stayed on the American pop charts for six months. In 1988 Sade embarked on a second world tour to coincide with the release of a third album, *Stronger than Pride*.

In 1992 Sade released *Love Deluxe*, which featured the Grammy-winning single "No Ordinary Love." After a subsequent world tour, Sade enjoyed life away from the limelight. She became a mother, while other members of her band recorded separately as Sweetback. The band reunited to produce the critically acclaimed *Lovers Rock* (2000), which earned a Grammy for best pop vocal album.

In 2001 Sade embarked on a highly successful world tour, excerpts of which were featured on *Lovers Live*

(2002). Sade's first album of original material in a decade found the band wrapping new instrumentation and rhythms around the smooth vocals that had defined it since the 1980s. The Grammy-winning title track of *Soldier of Love* (2010) incorporated martial beats and harsh guitars, and critics praised the trip-hop and reggae influences that coloured Sade's trademark soulful melodies.

# STING

Sting (born Gordon Matthew Sumner, October 2, 1951, Wallsend, Northumberland, England) grew up in Newcastle and, as a self-taught musician, he saw music as a means of getting away from his industrial neighborhood. After graduating from a teacher training college in the early 1970s, he worked as a soccer coach and music instructor at a convent school while playing with various jazz bands in his spare time. A fellow band member supposedly gave him the nickname Sting because of both a yellow and black shirt he was fond of wearing and his biting personality.

Sting became a founding member of the Police in 1977 at the request of drummer Stewart Copeland. Andy Summers replaced another guitarist later in the year to finalize the band. After some moderate success in Europe, the trio decided to do a low-budget tour of the East Coast of the United States and slowly gained a following. Their song "Roxanne" began getting radio play in 1978, and the following year A & M Records released their albums *Outlandos d'Amour* and *Reggatta de Blanc*.

The Police—often classified as a new-wave band—produced three more successful albums and numerous chart-topping songs before disbanding in 1984: *Zenyatta Mondatta* (1980), which contained the hit "Don't Stand So Close to Me" and went platinum in various parts of the world; *The Ghost in the Machine* (1981), for which Sting taught himself to play saxophone; and *Synchronicity* (1983), featuring "Wrapped Around Your Finger," "King of Pain," and "Every Breath You Take." The latter song earned Sting a Grammy for his songwriting and the Police a Grammy as the year's best pop recording by a group; the trio won other Grammy awards in the 1980s in various rock categories.

As a solo artist Sting experimented with various types of music, infusing elements of country, jazz, gospel, and reggae into rock. *Ten Summoner's Tales* (1993) included the popular "If I Ever Lose My Faith in You," while *Brand New Day* (1999) earned him Grammy awards for best pop album and best pop male vocals. His other solo albums include *The Dream of the Blue Turtles* (1985), *The Soul Cages* (1991), and *Mercury Falling* (1996). He continued to record into the 21st century, interpreting the works of 16th-century lutist John Dowland on *Songs from the Labyrinth* (2006) and applying orchestral arrangement to the Police catalog on *Symphonicities* (2010). In 2007 the Police reunited for an appearance at the Grammy Awards and followed with a highly successful world tour.

Sting acted in several motion pictures, including *Quadrophenia* (1979), *Brimstone & Treacle* (1982), *Dune* (1984), and *The Bride* (1985), and wrote music for numerous films. In 1989 he performed on Broadway in *The Threepenny Opera*. Active in many humanitarian and environmental efforts, he founded the Rain Forest Foundation in 1987.

# PJ HARVEY

Polly Jean Harvey (born October 9, 1969, Corscombe, near Yeovil, England), the child of countercultural parents in rural England, seems to have grown up with a sense of rock as simply another elemental force within the landscape. "Sheela-na-gig," for instance, a single from her first album, *Dry* (1992), took as its central image the female exhibitionist carvings with gaping genitals found throughout Ireland and the United Kingdom, whose origins are the subject of debate. The song, like many others by Harvey, treats female sexuality as a ravaging, haunted force,

but, instead of acting the victim, she theatrically embodies her obsessions, equates them with the alluring menace of rock and the blues, and builds herself into an archetype. In other hands—for example, those of the postpunk rocker Nick Cave, one of her major influences—such moves would run the risk of absurdity. But Harvey controls her self-presentation with extraordinary care: a skeletal figure with brightly reddened lips and an enigmatic smile, she uses polished diction even as the narrative takes her from teasing murmur to throttled scream.

Initially, the name PJ Harvey referred not just to Harvey but to the trio she formed with bassist Stephen Vaughan (born June 22, 1962, Wolverhampton) and drummer Robert Ellis (born February 13, 1962, Bristol). Under the engineering supervision of Steve Albini (whose reputation as a sonic extremist was based on his own bands, Big Black and Shellac, and on his production of groups such as the Pixies and Nirvana), they recorded Harvey's most challenging album, *Rid of Me* (1993); a softer version of some of the same material, *4-Track Demos*, came out later the same year. Following the tour in support of these releases, Ellis and Vaughan left PJ Harvey, which became the moniker for Harvey as a solo artist. *To Bring You My Love* (1995) featured an expanded band

and more-accessible arrangements. When Harvey toured with this material, she set aside her rugged guitar playing for a more theatrical presentation and was received with the kinds of cult accolades that Bruce Springsteen had generated two decades earlier. Yet Harvey failed to capitalize on the enthusiasm. On *Dance Hall at Louse Point* (1996), a collaboration with John Parish, who had been her bandmate in Automatic Dlamini when they were teenagers, she gave up control of the music, which, far more than her lyrics, turned out to be her main strength.

The next PJ Harvey album, *Is This Desire?* (1998), was deliberately subdued, an exercise in art song. In 2000, however, Harvey came out with *Stories from the City, Stories from the Sea*, a return to anthemic rock with pop aspirations and an unlikely twist: for the first time, Polly Jean Harvey was singing about love and sex with wholehearted satisfaction. That album earned her the first Mercury Prize ever awarded to a woman. More collaborations with other artists followed—most notably with hard rockers Queens of the Stone Age, on whose side project *Desert Session, Vol. 9–10* (2003) she was a major presence. In 2004 Harvey released the self-produced *Uh Huh Her*, on which she played all the instruments except percussion and continued her unique discourse on love, which from all

indications had again turned bad for her. In 2006 Harvey's live radio performances for renowned disc jockey and alternative tastemaker John Peel were released as *The Peel Sessions, 1991–2004*. Harvey's 2007 album, *White Chalk*, is a return to art song: it is sung almost entirely in falsetto and accompanied by piano (an instrument Harvey barely knows) rather than guitar. Rarely has a rocker so capable of letting go also been so determined to hold back.

She followed *White Chalk* with another collaboration with Parish— the wide-ranging *A Woman a Man Walked By* (2009). From the confrontational growl of the album's title track to the softly spoken lines of "Cracks in the Canvas," Harvey once again demonstrated that her voice was an instrument capable of conveying dramatic emotional range. Harvey later surfaced with *Let England Shake* (2011), a rollicking folk-influenced album that alluded to the battles of World War I as part of a complex portrait of her relationship to her homeland. In 2011 *Let England Shake* earned Harvey her second Mercury Prize, making her the first two-time winner of that award.

## RADIOHEAD

Radiohead was arguably the most accomplished art-rock band of the early 21st century. This revered

*Radiohead, c. 1990.* Photoshot/Hulton Archive/Getty Images

quintet made some of the most majestic—if most angst-saturated—music of the postmodern era. Formed in the mid-1980s at Abingdon School in Oxfordshire, Radiohead comprised singer-guitarist Thom Yorke (born October 7, 1968, Wellingborough, Northamptonshire, England), bassist Colin Greenwood (born June 26, 1969, Oxford, Oxfordshire), guitarist Ed O'Brien (born April 15, 1968, Oxford), drummer Phil Selway (born May 23, 1967, Hemingford Grey, Huntingdon, Cambridgeshire), and guitarist-keyboardist Jonny Greenwood (born November 5, 1971, Oxford).

Strongly influenced by American bands such as R.E.M. and the Pixies, Radiohead paid early dues on the local pub circuit. With their university education completed, the group landed a deal with Parlophone in late 1991. Although its debut album, *Pablo Honey* (1993), barely hinted at the grandeur to come, the startling single "Creep"—a grungy snarl of self-loathing—made major waves in the United States.

*The Bends* (1995) took even the band's most ardent fans by surprise. A soaring, intense mix of the approaches of Nirvana and dramatic vocalist Jeff Buckley, the album's powerful sense of alienation completely transcended the parochial issues of mid-1990s Britpop. Driving rockers such as "Bones" were skillfully offset by forlorn ballads such as "High and Dry." The widely acclaimed *OK Computer* (1997) was nothing short of a premillennial version of Pink Floyd's classic album *Dark Side of the Moon* (1973): huge-sounding and chillingly beautiful, with Yorke's weightless voice enveloped on masterpieces such as "Lucky" by webs of dark, dense textures. In its live performances, Radiohead became one of pop music's most compelling acts.

The pressure to follow up one of the most acclaimed recordings of the 20th century told particularly on Yorke's fragile psyche. The band made false starts in Paris and Copenhagen before settling down back in England. When *Kid A* came out in October 2000, it signaled that Radiohead—and Yorke above all—wanted to leave the wide-screen drama of *OK Computer* behind. The resulting selection of heavily electronic, more or less guitar-free pieces (notably "Kid A" and "Idioteque") confounded many but repaid the patience of fans who stuck with it. Though the album was a commercial success, it met with mixed critical reaction, as would the similar *Amnesiac* (2001), produced during the same sessions as *Kid A*. But if Radiohead had seemingly disavowed its musical past on these two albums—moving away from melody and rock instrumentation to create intricately textured soundscapes—it found a way to meld this approach with its guitar-band roots on the much-anticipated album *Hail to the Thief* (2003), which reached number three on the U.S. album charts. In 2006 Yorke, who had reluctantly become for some the voice of his generation, collaborated with the group's modernist producer, Nigel Godrich, on a solo album, *The Eraser*.

The band, having concluded its six-album contract with the EMI Group in 2003, broke away from major label distribution and initially released its seventh album, *In Rainbows* (2007), via Internet download. An estimated 1.2 million fans downloaded the album within its first week of availability, paying any price they wished to do so. The novel distribution method generated headlines, but it was the album's content—a collection of 10 tracks that served as a confident, almost optimistic, sonic counterpoint to *The Bends*—that led critics to declare it the most approachable Radiohead album in a decade.

*In Rainbows* was released to retailers as a standard CD in 2008, and it immediately hit number one in both the United States and Great Britain. The group won its third Grammy for the album, and the *In Rainbows* box set, which featured CD and vinyl copies of the original tracks, a CD of eight bonus songs, and a booklet of original artwork, received the Grammy for limited edition packaging. In 2009 the group released the single "Harry Patch (In Memory Of)," a tribute to Britain's last known World War I veteran. The song was available for download from Radiohead's Web site for the price of £1, with all proceeds benefiting a veterans' charity.

The group's eighth release, *The King of Limbs* (2011), debuted using the same online distribution model as *In Rainbows*, but it adhered to a standard pricing model rather than a "pay what you wish" system. The album's title was a reference to a 1,000-year-old oak tree in Wiltshire's Savernake Forest, and its eight tracks played on the interaction of technology and the natural world. At only 37 minutes it was the shortest of Radiohead's full-length releases, but the title of the album's final track, "Separator," and its refrain, "If you think this is over, then you're wrong," led critics to speculate that *The King of Limbs* was intended to serve as the first part of a longer work.

## SPICE GIRLS

The Spice Girls dominated the global charts in the late 1990s with a mixture of infectious dance beats and playful sex appeal. Under the banner of "Girl Power," the group offered a feminist alternative to the boy bands of the day. The band's members were Ginger Spice (born Geraldine Estelle

Halliwell, August 6, 1972, Watford, England), Sporty Spice (born Melanie Jayne Chisholm, January 12, 1974, Liverpool, England), Posh Spice (born Victoria Addams [later Victoria Beckham], April 7, 1975, Hertfordshire, England), Scary Spice (born Melanie Janine Brown, May 29, 1975, Yorkshire, England), and Baby Spice (born Emma Lee Bunton, January 21, 1976, London, England).

The group was formed when Halliwell, Brown, Chisholm, Bunton, and Addams responded to a 1993 advertisement in a trade magazine for a "manufactured" female pop group. The five, who had backgrounds in dance and acting, were chosen from the hundreds of women who auditioned, and they worked so well together that they became housemates. Personality conflicts led them to break with their original manager, a decision that united them and signaled the first stirrings of the "Girl Power" ethic. The group was signed to Virgin Records in 1995, but a lack of effective management hampered the band's development. The Spice Girls' first single, "Wannabe," was finally released in July 1996. It soared to the top of the British pop charts, and it held that position for most of the summer. Around this time, an article in *Top of the Pops* magazine anointed the women Ginger, Sporty, Posh, Scary, and Baby, and the names

were embraced by the band, its fans, and the media. "Wannabe" went on to hit number one in some 30 countries, and the music video that accompanied the song made the Spice Girls an international sensation. The follow-up single, "Say You'll Be There," paved the way for the band's debut album, *Spice* (1996), which sold more than 20 million copies worldwide.

In 1997 the Spice Girls made their debut in the United States, quickly establishing dominance over the Billboard singles and album charts. The group's second full-length album, *Spiceworld*, accompanied *Spice World: The Movie* in late 1997. While the film was greeted with a harsh critical reception, fans filled the theatres and made it a minor box-office success.

By the beginning of 1998, however, the Spice Girls' fortunes began to wane. The celebrity power of individual members took precedence over the group's music, a fact that became apparent when Posh announced her engagement to soccer star David Beckham. Ginger left the group in the middle of the *Spiceworld* tour in May 1998, and Posh became a fixture in tabloids and fashion magazines after she married Beckham in 1999. The Spice Girls' final album, ironically titled *Forever*, was released in 2000. It peaked at number two on the British charts, but it barely entered the Billboard Top 40. In February 2001 the band officially broke up, and the individual members pursued solo projects. Rumours of a reunion circulated for some years, and in June 2007 the Spice Girls announced that Ginger, Sporty, Posh, Scary, and Baby would once again take the stage for a world tour. The three-month tour ended in early 2008. The group also reunited for a performance at the closing ceremony of the London 2012 Olympic Games.

## COLDPLAY

Coldplay was formed in 1998 at University College, London, with the pairing of pianist-vocalist Chris Martin (born March 2, 1977, Exeter, England) and guitarist Jon Buckland (born September 11, 1977, London). The band was later filled out with fellow students Guy Berryman (born April 12, 1978, Kirkcaldy, Scotland) on bass and Will Champion (born July 31, 1978, Southampton, England), a guitarist who later switched to drums. Coldplay penetrated the U.K. Top 100 in 1999 with the single "Brothers & Sisters" on the independent Fierce Panda label before signing with major label Parlophone. Later that year the band released the *Blue Room* EP to a flurry of glowing reviews.

Coldplay's full-length debut *Parachutes* (2000) sold millions on the strength of Martin's vocals and such singles as the bittersweet "Yellow." Parachutes earned the band its first Grammy Award, for best alternative album, and paved the way for the more ambitious *A Rush of Blood to the Head* (2002). The latter album earned the group two more Grammy Awards, and singles such as "Clocks" helped drive the band's total album sales over the 20 million mark. Coldplay followed the concert album *Live 2003* (2003) with *X & Y* (2005), a collection of guitar-driven, arena-friendly rock anthems (including the hit single "Speed of Sound") that elevated the group to the rank of such "big bands" as U2 and Radiohead. Meanwhile, Martin's marriage to American actress Gwyneth Paltrow earned him celebrity status independent of his musical achievements.

The band's 2008 release, *Viva la Vida*, produced in part by Brian Eno, topped the charts in the United States and the United Kingdom, and the album's title track, arguably Coldplay's most radio-friendly effort yet, was the number one single on both sides of the Atlantic. That popularity was reflected at the 2009 Grammy Awards ceremony, where the band collected honours for song of the year, best rock album, and best pop performance by a duo or group. Working again with Eno, Coldplay returned with the sleek *Mylo Xyloto* (2011), which notably featured a duet between Martin and pop singer Rihanna.

# AMY WINEHOUSE

British singer-songwriter Amy Winehouse (born September 14, 1983, London, England—died July 23, 2011, London) skyrocketed to fame as a result of the critically acclaimed multiple Grammy Award-winning album *Back to Black* (2006), but her tempestuous love life, erratic behaviour, and substance-abuse problems stalled her recording career even as they made her a favourite subject of tabloid journalism.

Winehouse was born to a Jewish family and was raised primarily by her mother, a pharmacist, who divorced her father, a taxicab driver, when Winehouse was nine. Early on she demonstrated an interest in the arts, but she was expelled from Sylvia Young theatre school for wearing a forbidden nose ring. At the prestigious BRIT School, Winehouse showed ability as an actor as well as a singer, and by age 16 she was performing with jazz groups. On her critically acclaimed debut album, *Frank* (2003), she proved herself to be a shrewd, caustic lyricist, and her smoky, evocative vocals drew comparisons to jazz and rhythm-and-blues legends Sarah Vaughan, Dinah Washington, and Billie Holiday.

A series of tumultuous romances followed for Winehouse, none more fevered than her on-again, off-again relationship with Blake Fielder-Civil,

British pop singer Amy Winehouse. Shaun Curry/AFP/Getty Images

about whom many of the heartbreak songs on her next album, *Back to Black*, were written. Her singing on that album, more in the vein of Motown and 1960s and '70s soul, delighted critics. A very different-looking Winehouse had begun appearing in the tabloids as the new album took off in Britain and broke through in the United States, entering the American charts at number seven, the highest debut position ever for a British woman. Stick-thin and tattooed, Winehouse began piling her jet-black hair in an enormous beehive that, along with heavy Cleopatra-style eye makeup, became her trademark look. After marrying Fielder-Civil in May 2007, Winehouse began behaving increasingly erratically and canceling shows. Her very public slide into personal chaos—marked by dramatic anorexic weight loss, drunken performances, an arrest in Norway for marijuana possession, and the incarceration of Fielder-Civil after a bar fight—culminated in January 2008 in the posting on the Internet by the *Sun* newspaper of a video in which Winehouse appeared to be smoking crack cocaine.

In the wake of the video, Winehouse had difficulty obtaining a visa to appear at the 2008 Grammy Awards ceremony in Los Angeles, and a special satellite performance was arranged in London. At the event, *Back to Black* was honoured with five Grammy Awards, including two (best song and best recording) for the infectious "Rehab," with its sultry "no, no, no" refusal to enter drug and alcohol treatment. In November 2008 she was named Best Selling Pop/Rock Female at the World Music Awards. However, her life seemed to continue to spin out of control. Although she had entered rehab, she

had not remained long, and reports of substance abuse continued to follow her. In July 2009 she and Fielder-Civil divorced. Two years later Winehouse attempted a comeback tour, but it was canceled after the singer appeared to be intoxicated at the opening concert. She died from alcohol poisoning the following month. Her duet with Tony Bennett, "Body and Soul," was released posthumously in 2011, and the song ultimately won a Grammy Award for best pop performance by a duo or group. It was followed later that year by *Lioness: Hidden Treasures*, a collection that included previously unreleased original songs, covers, and demos.

## ADELE

Adele Laurie Blue Adkins (born May 5, 1988, Tottenham, London, England) was raised by a young single mother in various working-class neighbourhoods of London. As a child, she enjoyed singing contemporary pop music and learned to play the guitar and the clarinet. However, it was not until her early teens, when she discovered rhythm-and-blues singer Etta James and other mid-20th-century performers, that she began to consider a musical career. While she honed her talents at a government-funded secondary school for the performing arts, a friend began posting songs Adkins had written and

*Singer Adele posing in the press room at the 54th annual Grammy Awards in Los Angeles, California, Feb. 12, 2012.* Kervork Djansezian/Getty Images

recorded onto the social networking Web site Myspace. Her music eventually caught the attention of record labels, and in 2006, several months after graduating, she signed a contract with XL Recordings.

After building anticipation in Britain with some well-received live performances, Adele (as she now billed herself) released her first album, *19*, in 2008. (The title referred to the age at which she penned most of the tracks.) The recording debuted at number one on the British album chart, and critics praised Adele's supple phrasing, her tasteful arrangements, and her ability to channel her intimate emotional experiences (especially with heartbreak) into songs that had wide resonance. She also earned comparisons to Amy Winehouse, whose style was also conspicuously influenced by soul music. (For many fans, however, Adele's zaftig figure and down-to-earth persona made her the more-relatable star.) A performance on the television program *Saturday Night Live* helped introduce Adele to American audiences, and in early 2009 she won Grammy Awards for best new artist and best female pop vocal performance (for the lush bluesy song "Chasing Pavements").

For her next album, Adele enlisted a number of songwriters and producers, including Rick Rubin, to collaborate with her. The result, *21* (2011), was a bolder and more stylistically diverse set of material, with singles ranging from the earthy gospel- and disco-inflected "Rolling in the Deep" to the affecting breakup ballad "Someone Like You." Both songs hit number one in multiple countries, and, despite a vocal-cord ailment that forced Adele to cancel numerous tour dates in 2011, the album became the biggest-selling release of the year in both the United States and the United Kingdom. Additionally, with worldwide sales of more than 17 million copies by January 2012, it was credited with helping revive the flagging recording industry.

Following successful throat surgery, Adele performed at the 2012 Grammy Awards ceremony. She also collected six Grammy trophies, including those for album, record, and song of the year (the latter two honoured "Rolling in the Deep"). Days later she received two Brit Awards (the British equivalent of the Grammys). The sales spike for *21* after both events further confirmed the singer's emergence as a commercial juggernaut.

# CHAPTER 9

# Urban Contemporary

**U**rban contemporary began as an American radio format designed to appeal to advertisers who felt that "black radio" would not reach a wide enough audience. Responding to disco's waning popularity in the late 1970s, African American-oriented radio created two new, nearly synonymous formats, retronuevo and quiet storm (the latter named after a Smokey Robinson hit); both were characterized by a subtle, smooth musical approach that looked back to the rhythm-and-blues ballad tradition. Among the artists who found the greatest success in these formats were Anita Baker and Luther Vandross, both of whom reached the large crossover pop audience in the early 1980s that gave rise to the urban contemporary radio format.

Although not as light and pop-oriented as the Motown sound, the format eschewed grittier or blues-driven music (such as Southern soul) that was deemed "too black." Targeted at the multicultural diversity of large cities, urban contemporary came to include artists such as Chaka Khan, the Commodores, Earth, Wind and Fire, Janet Jackson, and Jeffrey Osborne, as well as white performers such as Phil Collins and David Bowie. In the late 1980s a number of artists began melding rhythm-and-blues-style vocals and hip-hop rhythms, distancing themselves from urban contemporary (while pushing it toward a rawer sound); called new jack swing, this new style was most notably practiced by producers

Teddy Riley and Babyface, singers Keith Sweat and Bobby Brown, and the vocal group Bell Biv Devoe.

## LUTHER VANDROSS

While growing up in a public housing project on Manhattan's Lower East Side, Luther Vandross (born April 20, 1951, New York, New York, U.S.—died July 1, 2005, Edison, New Jersey) was encouraged to pursue music by his widowed mother. He began his professional career singing commercial jingles and background vocals and worked as a vocal arranger and songwriter, contributing "Everybody Rejoice" to the Broadway musical *The Wiz* in 1972. As a featured vocalist on the album *The Glow of Love* (1980) by the disco group Change, Vandross came to the attention of record executives and signed with Epic, which allowed him to write and produce his own material. In 1981 Vandross's first album for that label, *Never Too Much*, sold more than one million copies, and its title song was a number-one rhythm-and-blues hit.

So began a long string of million-selling albums that featured Vandross's distinctive baritone, precise phrasing, and unabashedly romantic songs, including "Here and Now," for which he won his first Grammy Award in 1990. In the process, Vandross became one of the most

*Luther Vandross.* Hulton Archive/Archive Photos/Getty Images

popular artists in the crossover genre called urban contemporary music. As a producer, Vandross was responsible for successful albums for Dionne Warwick and Aretha Franklin, who, along with the Supremes, influenced his music. In 2003 Vandross suffered a debilitating stroke shortly before the release of what proved to be his last studio album, *Dance with My Father*, which earned four Grammy Awards.

# ANITA BAKER

Anita Baker (born January 26, 1958, Toledo, Ohio, U.S.) was one of the most popular artists in urban contemporary music, a genre that her sophisticated, tradition-oriented soul and rhythm-and-blues singing helped to define. Her talent first became apparent when she sang in church choirs in Detroit, Michigan, where she grew up. Against her family's wishes, she dropped out of community college to pursue a singing career, performing in nightclubs with local bands and joining the funk group Chapter 8, with whom she toured for several years and recorded an album that included the hit "I Just Want to Be Your Girl." Discouraged when the band was dropped by its record company, Baker ceased performing. Lured back into the business by Beverly Glen Records, she recorded *The Songstress* (1983), a solo album that sold more than 300,000 copies and spent more than a year on the charts.

Anita Baker, c. 1988. Hulton Archive/Archive Photos/Getty Images

Moving to Elektra, she served as executive producer of her next album, *Rapture* (1986), which won two Grammy Awards, sold more than five million copies, and spawned two hit singles: "Sweet Love" and "You Bring Me Joy." The album *Giving You the Best That I've Got* and a three-month tour with Luther Vandross followed in 1988, and *Compositions* was released in 1990; both albums won Grammys. Personal issues led Baker to take a four-year hiatus, but in 1994 she returned with the album *Rhythm of Love*. In 1996 she signed with Atlantic Records. She also was the founder of the Bridgforth Foundation, an organization that supported education in Detroit. *My Everything* (2004), Baker's first album of new material in a decade, explored jazz arrangements while retaining the vocal stylings that had brought her success in the 1980s and '90s.

## THE POINTER SISTERS

The Pointer Sisters scored a string of pop, dance, and urban contemporary hits in the 1970s and '80s. The sisters were Ruth Pointer (born March 19, 1946, Oakland, California, U.S.), Anita Pointer (born January 23, 1948, Oakland), Bonnie Pointer (born July 11, 1950, Oakland), and June Pointer (born November 30, 1953, Oakland—died April 11, 2006, Santa Monica, California).

The group, which initially consisted only of Bonnie and June, began with a series of successful appearances at San Francisco nightclubs in the late 1960s. By 1972 sisters Anita and Ruth had made it a quartet, and the group had been signed to a recording contract with Atlantic Records. Their debut album, *The Pointer Sisters* (1973), spawned their first hit song, "Yes We Can Can." The group went on to collect the Grammy Award for best country vocal for the crossover hit "Fairytale" (1974), making them the first African American act to win that category.

Drawing equally from the gospel sound of the Staple Singers and the disco rhythms of Donna Summer, the Pointer Sisters became the model of the post-Motown girl group. Their high point came with the 1983 release *Break Out*. The triple-platinum album produced a string of hits, and the Pointers collected Grammys for the singles "Automatic" and "Jump (for My Love)." While each of the sisters experimented with solo careers, none of them achieved success comparable to that of the group, and they faded from the spotlight in the early 1990s.

## QUINCY JONES

Quincy Jones (born March 14, 1933, Chicago, Illinois, U.S.) was reared in Bremerton, Washington, where he studied the trumpet and worked locally with the then-unknown pianist-singer Ray Charles. In the early 1950s Jones studied briefly at the prestigious Schillinger House (now Berklee College of Music) in Boston before touring with Lionel Hampton as a trumpeter and arranger. He soon became a prolific freelance arranger, working with Clifford Brown, Gigi Gryce, Oscar Pettiford, Cannonball Adderley, Count Basie, Dinah Washington, and many others. He toured with Dizzy Gillespie's big band in 1956, recorded his first album as a leader in the same year, worked in Paris for the Barclay label as an arranger and producer in the late 1950s, and continued to compose. Some of his more successful compositions from this period include "Stockholm Sweetnin'," "For Lena and Lennie," and "Jessica's Day."

# MOTOWN GOES WEST: LOS ANGELES

In the immediate post-World War II period, Los Angeles had a strong, distinctive black music industry. Yet, as the city grew in importance as a music centre, the business became increasingly dominated by whites. Even the city's notable jazz scene was overwhelmingly white. In the 1980s, however, Los Angeles again developed a vital black music business—arguably as a result of the growing confidence of the black middle class and in response to the period's booming economy. Michael Jackson was a key, if not the key, figure. Like Elvis Presley 35 years earlier, Jackson made pop music that was black, white, and neither. The world saluted him as the first African American music megastar, and Los Angeles became the world's black music centre. Central to this development was Jackson's veteran producer, Quincy Jones. Also playing important roles were up-and-coming producers L.A. (Antonio Reid), Babyface (Kenneth Edmonds), and Teddy Riley, whose music was marketed as new jack swing, or swingbeat.

Back in the United States in 1961, Jones became an artists-and-repertoire (or "A&R" in trade jargon) director for Mercury Records. In 1964 he was named a vice president at Mercury, thereby becoming one of the first African Americans to hold a top executive position at a major American record label. In the 1960s Jones recorded occasional jazz dates, arranged albums for many singers (including Frank Sinatra, Peggy Lee, and Billy Eckstine), and composed music for several films, including *The Pawnbroker* (1964), *In the Heat of the Night* (1967), and *In Cold Blood* (1967). Jones next worked for the A&M label from 1969 to 1981 (with a brief hiatus as he recovered from a brain aneurysm in 1974) and moved increasingly away from jazz toward pop music. During this time

series *The Fresh Prince of Bel-Air* (1990–96). In 1993 he founded the magazine *Vibe*, which he sold in 2006. Throughout the years, Jones has worked with a "who's who" of figures from all fields of popular music. He was nominated for more than 75 Grammy Awards (winning more than 25) and seven Academy Awards and received an Emmy Award for the theme music he wrote for the television miniseries *Roots* (1977). *Q: The Autobiography of Quincy Jones* was published in 2001.

## BOYZ II MEN

Boyz II Men emerged in the 1990s and became one of the most successful rhythm-and-blues groups of that decade. The principal members were Nathan Morris (born June 18, 1971, Philadelphia, Pennsylvania, U.S.), Michael McCary (born December 16, 1971, Philadelphia), Shawn Stockman (born September 26, 1972, Philadelphia), and Wanya Morris (born July 29, 1973, Philadelphia).

The members of Boyz II Men grew up in separate neighbourhoods of Philadelphia and came together as high-school friends at the Philadelphia High School for the Performing Arts, where they studied classical music and vocal arts. The name Boyz II Men came from a song that had been recorded by the pop quintet New Edition. In 1989 the

Music producer Quincy Jones and daughter actress Rashida Jones, 2009. Larry Busacca/ Getty Images

he became one of the most famous producers in the world, his success enabling him to start his own record label, Qwest, in 1980.

Jones's best-known work includes producing an all-time best-selling album, Michael Jackson's *Thriller* (1982), organizing the all-star charity recording "We Are the World" (1985), and producing the film *The Color Purple* (1985) and the television

# NEW JACK SWING

New jack swing (also known as swingbeat) was the most pop-oriented rhythm-and-blues music since 1960s Motown. Its performers were unabashed entertainers, free of artistic pretensions; its songwriters and producers were commercial professionals. Eschewing the fashion for sampling (using sounds and music from other recordings), the makers of new jack swing discovered their rhythms on the newly available SP1200 and 808 drum machines (which had already been used by hip-hop producers). They laid an insistent beat under light melody lines and clearly enunciated vocals. In contrast to the sex-and-drugs-and-guns messages of gangsta rap, this was music that the industry preferred to promote as the Sound of Young Black America.

The key producers were L.A., Babyface, and Teddy Riley, who crafted romantic songs for the dance floor. L.A. (Antonio Reid, whose nickname was derived from his allegiance to the Los Angeles Dodgers baseball team) and Babyface (youthful-looking Kenneth Edmonds) had been members of the Deele, a group based in Cincinnati, Ohio, before becoming writer-producers. Their million-selling hits for Bobby Brown in 1988 ("Don't Be Cruel" and "My Prerogative") led to work with Paula Abdul, Whitney Houston, and Boyz II Men. In the early 1990s the duo relocated to Atlanta, Georgia, where their LaFace label launched soul diva Toni Braxton and the female trio TLC. A native of New York City's Harlem district and influenced by the Gap Band, Riley moved from performing with the band Guy to producing for Brown, Michael Jackson, and his own group, Blackstreet, material that was more directly sexual than that by L.A. and Babyface.

quartet managed to meet Michael Bivins—who had been a member of New Edition—and gave him an impromptu audition. Bivins later signed on as their manager and helped define their gentlemanly image.

In 1991 Boyz II Men debuted on Motown records with the album *Cooleyhighharmony*, which went on to sell more than seven million copies. In 1992 their recording of "End of the Road," from the movie soundtrack of *Boomerang*, spent 13 consecutive weeks in the number one slot on Billboard's pop chart, eclipsing by two weeks the previous record set by Elvis Presley—"Don't Be Cruel" backed with "Hound Dog"—in 1956. In 1994 the group helped write and produce the album *II*. After Whitney Houston broke their record by spending 14 weeks at number one with "I Will Always Love You," Boyz II Men came back to tie her with "I'll Make Love to You." The release of their follow-up single, "On Bended Knee," put them with an elite group of artists (Presley and the Beatles) who succeeded themselves at the number one spot.

After a world tour, the band started work on their next album, *Evolution*, which was released in 1997. While it had several hits—notably, "4 Seasons of Loneliness" and "A Song for Mama"—the album failed to sell as well as their previous efforts.

Their next albums, *Nathan Michael Shawn Wanya* (2000) and *Full Circle* (2002), also saw declining sales. In 2003 Michael McCary left the group because of health issues. Boyz II Men continued to tour, and their later albums include *Throwback* (2004), which featured covers of their favourite songs, and *The Remedy* (2007).

# R. KELLY

R. Kelly (born Robert Sylvester Kelly, January 8, 1967?, Chicago, Illinois, U.S.) became one of the best-selling rhythm-and-blues artists of the 1990s and early 2000s. He was raised in public housing projects in Chicago and was taught a powerful sense of Christian faith by his mother. His singing style has been described as "church-trained," and, though faith has been a recurring theme in his lyrics, such early singles as "Sex Me" (1993) established carnality at the centre of his music. The tension between the sacred and the profane, along with the contrast of tough-guy persona and tender vocals, have been constants in his career. Kelly's debut album, *Born Into the '90s* (1992), delivered a smooth and melodic signature sound laced with hip-hop rhythms. Subsequent efforts achieved progressively greater success as Kelly's dominance of the rhythm-and-blues market translated into pop stardom. His ballad "I Believe I Can Fly" (1996) was a massive hit and earned three Grammy Awards, including best rhythm-and-blues song.

Kelly had more Top 40 hits than any other male solo artist in the 1990s, including "Bump n' Grind" (1994), "You Remind Me of Something" (1995), and "I Can't Sleep Baby (If I)" (1996). However, his personal life was dogged by controversy, which came to a head in 2002 when the authorities came into possession of a videotape (first given to the *Chicago Sun-Times* by an anonymous source) that allegedly showed Kelly having sex with an underage girl. Kelly was soon indicted on multiple charges related to child pornography, though, as a result of a variety of circumstances, his trial did not begin until 2008. Over the long pretrial period, Kelly continued to release albums that, if anything, grew even more sexually explicit, though they also included songs of uplift, such as many of those on *Happy People/U Saved Me* (2004). Despite some initial public shock and backlash, most sold as well as his earlier releases (notably, *Chocolate Factory* achieved double-platinum status in 2003), and he remained one of the world's foremost rhythm-and-blues stars. On June 13, 2008, a three-week trial concluded with a jury's acquittal of Kelly on all charges.

# AALIYAH

Aaliyah Dana Haughton (born January 16, 1979, Brooklyn, New York—died August 25, 2001, Abaco Islands, The Bahamas) was considered on the verge of superstardom at the time of her death at age 22. Her first two albums—*Age Ain't Nothing but a Number* (1994), with its hit singles "Back and Forth" and "At Your Best (You Are Love)," and *One in a Million* (1996)—established her as an emerging R&B talent. She scored Grammy nominations for her singles "Are You That Somebody?" (1998) and "Try Again" (2000) and had embarked on a promising career as an actress. In addition to her starring role in the movie *Romeo Must Die* (2000), she portrayed the title character in the film adaptation of Anne Rice's *Queen of the Damned* and was beginning two sequels to the movie The Matrix (1999). She had just released a third album, *Aaliyah* (2001), when she was killed in a plane crash as she was leaving The Bahamas after filming a music video.

# USHER

As a youngster, Usher (born Usher Raymond IV, October 14, 1978, Chattanooga, Tennessee, U.S.) sang in church choirs but sought entry into the mainstream music industry by entering talent shows. At age 12 he moved with his mother and brother to Atlanta, and two years later he secured a recording contract with LaFace Records. Usher was released in 1994, with the 15-year-old singer moving beyond his choirboy background by proclaiming that "it's only a sexual thing" on the slow-groove single "Can U Get wit It." The album was not a commercial success, and Usher spent the next few years working on a follow-up, *My Way* (1997), which marked him as a major R&B star. His singles "You Make Me Wanna" and "Nice & Slow" topped the R&B charts (the latter was also a number one pop song), and the performer reached greater audiences through appearances on television shows (he had a recurring role on UPN's *Moesha* series). In onstage performances, he showed prowess as a dancer that was as notable as his fluid singing voice.

His third studio album, *8701* (2001), further cemented Usher's reputation as a smooth, seductive, and bankable artist. Music from *8701* gave Usher two number one pop hits, "U Remind Me" and "U Got It Bad," and his first two Grammy Awards. He continued to make appearances in various television shows, including the period drama *American Dreams* (2002) in the role of Marvin Gaye, before releasing his fourth album,

*Confessions*, in 2004. The album, which sold more than one million copies during its first week of release, featured Usher extending his range beyond ballads, collaborating most famously with Atlanta rappers Lil Jon and Ludacris. At the 2004 Billboard Music Awards, he collected 11 trophies and was named overall artist of the year.

The awards continued to accumulate in 2005. Usher won two prizes at the People's Choice Awards and three more at the Grammys—for best contemporary R&B album, best R&B performance by a duo or group (with Alicia Keys for "My Boo"), and best rap/sung collaboration (with Ludacris and Lil Jon for "Yeah!"). In 2005 Usher also starred as a disc jockey who protects a mobster's daughter in the film *In the Mix*, though his acting, and the film as a whole, received unfavourable reviews. The following year he portrayed Billy Flynn in the long-running Broadway musical *Chicago*.

After a four-year break, Usher returned to recording with *Here I Stand* (2008), a soulful album that saw the brash lothario of *8701* and *Confessions* settle into the routine of family life. The follow-up album, *Raymond v. Raymond* (2010), continued to serve as a window into Usher's private life, but it was a dark reflection of *Here I Stand*, as it traced the disintegration of his marriage. In 2011 *Raymond v. Raymond* won a Grammy for best contemporary R&B album, and the single "There Goes My Baby" won best male R&B performance.

In addition to performing, Usher became a part owner of the National Basketball Association's Cleveland Cavaliers in 2005. His charity work included New Look Foundation, an organization he established to help educate youths from lower-class backgrounds about the business of entertainment management. The organization was also involved in the efforts to rebuild New Orleans after Hurricane Katrina (2005).

# ALICIA KEYS

Alicia Keys (born Alicia Augello Cook, January 25, 1981, New York, New York, U.S.) began performing at age four and playing piano at age seven, concentrating on classical music and jazz. At age 14 she began composing, and two years later she graduated as valedictorian from the Professional Performing Arts School in Manhattan. Keys's compositions showed modern influences but were rooted in the sounds of earlier soul artists, including Marvin Gaye and Stevie Wonder. After attracting the attention of record mogul Clive Davis, she signed to his Arista Records in 1998, and, when Davis formed J Records in 2000, she was one of the first artists to sign with the new label. In 2001 Keys released *Songs in A Minor*, a hugely successful debut album that featured a number one hit with "Fallin'" and that went on to sell more than 10 million copies worldwide. She won five Grammy Awards in 2002, including those for song of the year and best new artist.

The following year Keys released a second album, *The Diary of Alicia Keys*. She also recorded a duet with Usher called "My Boo," which for six weeks was the number one song on Billboard's Hot 100 chart. In 2005 Keys cemented her status as one of pop music's leading artists by winning four Grammy Awards: best album, song, female vocal performance, and performance by a duo or group with vocals. That same year she recorded and released *Unplugged*, an album from the MTV special on which she performed stripped-down versions of past hits, new songs, and covers of songs popularized by Aretha Franklin and by the Rolling Stones.

In 2007 Keys released the soul-infused *As I Am*, which featured the Grammy-winning single "No One." The following year she teamed with Jack White of the White Stripes on "Another Way to Die," the lead single on the soundtrack to the James Bond film *Quantum of Solace*. *As I*

*Alicia Keys, 2005.* Scott Gries/Getty Images

*Am* continued to post strong sales throughout 2008, and the single "Superwoman" earned Keys a Grammy for best female rhythm and blues vocal performance in 2009. Later that year she collaborated with Jay-Z on the chart-topping single "Empire State of Mind," and in December she released her fourth studio album, *The Element of Freedom*.

In addition to her music-related activities, Keys acted in several films, including *Smokin' Aces* (2006), *The Nanny Diaries* (2007), and *The Secret Life of Bees* (2008). She also directed one of five segments that made up the cable TV movie *Five* (2011), about women living with breast cancer.

## BEYONCÉ

Beyoncé (born Beyoncé Giselle Knowles, September 4, 1981, Houston, Texas, U.S.) was nine years old when she formed the singing-rapping girl group Destiny's Child (originally called Girl's Tyme) in 1990 with childhood friends. In 1992 the group lost on the *Star Search* television talent show, and three years later it was dropped from a recording contract before an album had been released. In 1997 Destiny's Child's fortunes reversed with a Columbia recording contract and then an eponymous debut album that yielded three hit singles, including the Top Ten hit "No, No, No Part 2." Their follow-up album, *The Writing's on the Wall* (1999), earned the group two Grammy Awards and sold more than eight million copies in the United States. *Survivor* (2001), the group's third album, reached the number one spot on the Billboard 200 chart.

Beyoncé was clearly the leader of the group and wrote hit songs for Destiny's Child such as "Bootylicious." Eventually, the group parted ways to pursue individual projects. Beyoncé used her songwriting talents to pen her first solo album, *Dangerously in Love* (2003). The album debuted to rave reviews, and it eventually topped the charts. In 2004 Beyoncé won five Grammy Awards, including best contemporary R&B album and best female R&B vocal performance.

Destiny's Child reunited in 2004 to release a fourth studio album, *Destiny Fulfilled*. The album, as successful as the group's previous efforts, sold more than seven million copies worldwide and spawned several hit singles. The trio embarked on a world tour in 2005, during which they announced that the group would officially disband. That same year they released their final album, *#1's*, a collection of well-known songs and number one hits.

In 2006 Beyoncé released her second solo studio album, *B'Day*, which featured several coproducers,

*Destiny's Child (from left to right): Beyoncé, Michelle Williams, and Kelly Rowland, 2005.* PRNewsFoto/McDonald's/AP Images

including the Neptunes. The album's first single, "Déjà Vu," was a number one hit. In 2008 she married rapper Jay-Z, and the union made them one of the top-earning couples in the entertainment industry. Later that year Beyoncé released the double album *I Am...Sasha Fierce*. While *I Am* was a collection of introspective ballads, *Sasha Fierce* contained dance tracks familiar to most of her fans. The album generated five Billboard Top 20 singles, including the number one "Single Ladies (Put a Ring on It)," and it contributed to Beyoncé's dominance of the 2010 Grammy Awards. Her six awards, which included those for song of the year, best female pop vocal performance, and best contemporary R&B album, amounted to the most Grammys collected by a female artist in a single night. Days after a triumphant headlining performance at England's Glastonbury Festival,

Beyoncé released *4* (2011), a genre-bending mix of ballads and dance tracks that evoked influences ranging from Motown-era torch songs to the audio collages of rapper M.I.A.

In 2001 Beyoncé made her acting debut in the television movie *Carmen: A Hip Hopera*, which aired on MTV. Her role as Foxxy Cleopatra in *Austin Powers in Goldmember* (2002) made her a film star and led to parts in *The Fighting Temptations* (2003) and *The Pink Panther* (2006). In 2006 she played Deena Jones in *Dreamgirls*, the film adaptation of the 1981 Broadway musical about a 1960s singing group. Beyoncé's performance was nominated for a Golden Globe and her song "Listen" for an Academy Award. She later starred in *Cadillac Records* (2008), in which she portrayed singer Etta James, and the thriller *Obsessed* (2009).

# CHRIS BROWN

Chris Brown (born May 5, 1989, Tappahannock, Virginia, U.S.) grew up in small-town Virginia. As a child, he discovered a love for dancing and singing, and, when he was 15 years old, he was signed to Jive Records. His first album, a self-titled release, debuted in 2005. Sales climbed steadily on the strength of the chart-topping single "Run It!" and the quality Brown displayed both in vocals and in dancing earned him early comparisons to stars such as Usher and Michael Jackson.

In 2006 Brown was nominated for two Grammy Awards, including best new artist, and in 2007 he expanded his entertainment career with roles in the dance drama film *Stomp the Yard*, the popular TV melodrama *The O.C.*, and the holiday comedy-drama film *This Christmas*. In late 2007 he also released his second album, *Exclusive*, which was lauded for showcasing Brown's growing maturity while still appealing to his target teen demographic. Exclusive featured collaborations with such big names as Lil Wayne and Kanye West, and its single "Kiss Kiss," featuring singer-rapper T-Pain, reached the top of the Billboard Hot 100.

In 2009 Brown's professional image was tarnished in the wake of his felony assault of fellow R&B star Rihanna, who was then his girlfriend, for which he was later sentenced to 180 days of community labour and five years of supervised probation. The highly publicized incident sparked controversy and remained in the media for months. Brown's third album, *Graffiti*, debuted in December that year. Reviews seemed somewhat polarized over his musical expression of his turbulent relationship with Rihanna and its aftermath, and the album did not sell as well as his first two releases. However, two years later Brown rebounded with the album *F.A.M.E.*, which became his first number one album on the Billboard 200 chart and won him his first Grammy Award, for best R&B album.

In 2012 Brown and Rihanna again made headlines, this time for releasing remixes of each other's songs via social networking site Twitter; the incident sparked rumours of reconciliation between the two.

# CHAPTER 10

# Adult Contemporary

**P**op balladeers, torch singers, and latter-day crooners can all be found under the diverse "adult contemporary" banner. Drawing upon soul, jazz, Broadway, and pop traditions, adult contemporary artists achieved a broad commercial appeal. Indeed, the power of the pop ballad to articulate private feeling as public emotion was dramatically illustrated by Elton John's performance of "Candle in the Wind" at the funeral of Diana, princess of Wales, in 1997. The recorded version of that song remains one of the best-selling singles of all time.

## DIONNE WARWICK

Dionne Warwick (born Marie Dionne Warrick, December 12, 1940, East Orange, New Jersey, U.S.) earned widespread appeal with a soulful sound that appealed to multiple generations of listeners. She is perhaps best known for her collaborations with such high-profile artists as Burt Bacharach and Barry Manilow.

Warrick was raised in a middle-class, racially integrated community in East Orange, New Jersey. Her family was both spiritually and musically inclined—her mother managed a renowned gospel choir, the Drinkard Singers, and her father became a gospel record promoter—and Dionne, as everyone called her, began singing in church at a young age. She often played piano or organ for the Drinkard Singers, and she sometimes sang in place of absent adult members. As a teen, she formed a group called the Gospelaires with her sister, Dee Dee. The group enjoyed relative success, singing backup for a number of musicians in local venues and on recordings. Warrick continued to perform with the Gospelaires after enrolling at the Hartt School of the University of Hartford, Connecticut, in 1959. She often made trips to New York to record with the group, and during one of these sessions she met composer and producer Burt Bacharach, who invited her to sing on some demos he was recording with lyricist Hal David. Her singing caught the attention of an executive at Scepter Records, and Warrick was soon signed to the label. In 1962 she released her first single—"I Smiled Yesterday," with the more popular B side "Don't Make Me Over"—written and produced by Bacharach and David. Warrick's surname was misspelled as "Warwick" on the record, and she adopted the mistake as her name thereafter.

The single proved relatively successful, and Warwick subsequently began touring worldwide. In the mid-1960s she began appearing in popular nightclubs and theatres and also on television, including appearances on *Hullabaloo* and *The Red Skelton Hour*. Warwick continued to release hit singles and albums throughout the 1960s, largely collaborations with Bacharach and David. Top 10 singles from this period included "Walk On By" (1964), "I Say a Little Prayer" (1967), and "(Theme from) *Valley of the Dolls*" (1968), the latter of which, by reaching number two on the Billboard pop chart, pushed Warwick further into the spotlight. In 1969 she earned her first Grammy Award, for best female contemporary pop vocal performance, for "Do You Know the Way to San Jose?" (1968). A second Grammy, for best female contemporary vocal performance, followed two years later for "I'll Never Fall in Love Again."

After a decade of successful collaborations, Bacharach, David, and Warwick quarreled and parted ways. From 1971 Warwick rendered her surname "Warwicke" on the advice of astrologer friend Linda Goodman but reverted the spelling to "Warwick" some five years later. She had few hits for the majority of the 1970s, with the notable exception of "Then Came You" (1974), a collaboration with the Spinners that topped the charts. Her popularity increased once more in 1979 with the songs "Deja Vu" and "I'll Never Love This Way Again," which garnered her Grammy Awards for best female R&B vocal performance and best female pop vocal performance, respectively. She maintained this popularity through the 1980s, and during that time she eventually reconciled with Bacharach, performing on his "That's What Friends Are For" (1985), which also featured Gladys Knight, Elton John, and Stevie Wonder. The song, the proceeds of which went to funding AIDS research, earned Warwick her fifth Grammy.

Warwick's commercial success dwindled in the 1990s, and she instead gained attention as the spokesperson for the Psychic Friends Network, hosting their infomercials. In addition to her music, Warwick devoted much of her time to entrepreneurial endeavours—including a skin care and fragrance line and an interior design group—and to charity projects. In 2010 she published an autobiography, *My Life, as I See It* (cowritten with David Freeman Wooley).

*Diana Ross, 2006.* PRNewsFoto/Manhattan Records/EMI Music Marketing/AP Images

## DIANA ROSS

Diana Ross (born Diane Earle, March 26, 1944, Detroit, Mich., U.S) began her music career in 1959, when she joined several neighbourhood friends to form the pop-soul vocal group the Primettes. The group was renamed the Supremes after signing a recording contract with Motown late the following year. Consisting of Ross, Mary Wilson, and Florence Ballard (replaced in 1967 by Cindy Birdsong), the Supremes achieved 12 number one hits on the pop charts, including "Baby Love" (1964), "Stop! In the Name of Love" (1965), and "Someday We'll Be Together" (1969). In 1967 the group was renamed Diana Ross and the Supremes, foreshadowing Ross's solo career, which she launched in 1970.

Beginning with "Ain't No Mountain High Enough," from her debut album *Diana Ross* (1970),

Ross enjoyed more than a decade of chart-topping success in multiple categories. "Love Hangover" (1976) and "Upside Down" (1980) were among her pop hits, while her duet with the Commodores' Lionel Richie, "Endless Love" (1981), topped Billboard magazine's pop, rhythm and blues (R&B), and adult contemporary charts. Ross also developed a film-acting career in the 1970s, beginning with a starring role as blues singer Billie Holiday in *Lady Sings the Blues* (1972) and continuing with *Mahogany* (1975), for which she also recorded the hit theme song "Do You Know Where You're Going To," and *The Wiz* (1978).

After riding a wave of hits into the mid-1980s, Ross saw her commercial fortunes begin to wane. Much of her work showed a stylistic shift from pop and R&B toward disco, and the bulk of her albums were either rereleases or rerecordings of earlier material. In 2006, however, she issued *I Love You*, a compilation of her own interpretations of love songs by various artists, and she embarked on a vigorous concert tour the following year to promote the album. Despite her virtual absence from the charts, Ross remained a popular concert draw into the early 21st century, propelled by her enduring status as one of the preeminent musical performers of her time. With the Supremes, she was inducted into the Rock and Roll Hall of Fame in 1988.

# NATALIE COLE

The daughter of legendary crooner Nat King Cole, Natalie Cole (born February 6, 1950, Los Angeles, California, U.S.) earned a degree in child psychology from the University of Massachusetts in 1972. Although uncertain about pursuing a career in entertainment, she accepted a summer job singing with a band and was soon performing regularly. In 1974 she met Chuck Jackson and Marvin Yancy, songwriters and record producers who became frequent collaborators and helped her sign with Capitol Records. A string of rhythm-and-blues albums followed, beginning with her debut album, *Inseparable* (1975), which earned Cole two Grammy Awards, including one for best new artist. The following year *Natalie* was released, which went gold and received a Grammy for the hit single "Sophisticated Lady." Her success continued with *Unpredictable* (1977) and *Thankful* (1977), both of which went platinum.

In the early 1980s Cole's career stalled because of drug problems and a serious throat ailment. She eventually overcame her difficulties, and by the end of the decade she had begun singing more jazz-inspired pop. Her comeback was completed in 1991 with the release of *Unforgettable with Love*, a double album that featured her father's classics, including

"Smile," "The Very Thought of You," and "Mona Lisa." A commercial and critical success, it was Cole's first album to reach number one and earned three Grammy Awards. The title track was digitally engineered to simulate a father-and-daughter duet. Later albums include *Take a Look* (1993), *Snowfall on the Sahara* (1999), and *Ask a Woman Who Knows* (2002). She returned to her father's songbook for *Still Unforgettable* (2008), a collection of romantic standards that won the Grammy Award for best traditional pop vocal album in 2009. In 2000 her autobiography, *Angel on My Shoulder* (written with Digby Diehl), was published.

# HARRY CONNICK, JR.

Harry Connick, Jr., (born September 11, 1967, New Orleans, Louisiana) grew up in New Orleans, where his father, a longtime district attorney (1973–2003), and his mother, a judge, also owned a record store. Connick began performing when he was five years old. He subsequently studied with Ellis Marsalis and James Booker at the New Orleans Center for Creative Arts. After high school he moved to New York City to attend Hunter College and the Manhattan School of Music. He signed a contract with Columbia Records and in 1987 released his first album, *Harry Connick, Jr.*, on which he played the piano. On his second effort, *20* (1988), he also sang.

In 1989 Connick co-produced the soundtrack for Rob Reiner's film *When Harry Met Sally…*, which included performances by his jazz trio and his own rendering of such classic songs as "But Not for Me" and "I Could Write a Book." The album went multiplatinum and earned Connick his first Grammy Award for best jazz vocal performance. In 1990 he tackled his first acting role, in the movie *Memphis Belle*, and released two albums, *We Are in Love*, a big-band sound with vocals, and *Lofty's Roach Soufflé*, showcasing instrumental jazz. Connick won a second Grammy Award for best jazz vocal performance for *We Are in Love*.

Connick's later albums include *Blue Light, Red Light* (1991), *25* (1992), *She* (1994), the big-band album *Come by Me* (1999), the Grammy Award-winning pop album *Songs I Heard* (2001), *30* (2001), *Only You* (2004), *Your Songs* (2009), and *In Concert on Broadway* (2011). In 2007 he released two tributes to his hometown, *Oh, My Nola* and *Chanson du Vieux Carré* ("Song of the French Quarter").

Simultaneously, Connick pursued an acting career, portraying a lonely little boy's grown-up friend in *Little Man Tate* (1991), a serial killer in *Copycat* (1995), a hotshot fighter pilot in *Independence Day* (1996), the doomed Lieutenant Cable in a TV version of the musical *South Pacific* (2001), and a doctor in *Dolphin Tale* (2011). He scored as a leading man in the romantic comedies *Hope Floats* (1998) and *New in Town* (2009) and in a recurring role on the TV sitcom *Will & Grace* (2002–06). Connick received Tony Award nominations for his score for the musical *Thou Shalt Not* (2001) and for his Broadway acting debut in *The Pajama Game* (2006). He returned to Broadway in late 2011 in a reimagining of the musical *On a Clear Day You Can See Forever*.

Connick is also involved in cultural and philanthropic endeavours, particularly those centered on his home town. In 1993 he was the cofounder of the Krewe of Orpheus, the first multiracial group to participate in annual Mardi Gras parades. He participated in numerous benefits to assist with the rebuilding of post-Hurricane Katrina New Orleans, and he and Branford Marsalis sponsored the Musicians' Village for displaced New Orleans musicians. In 2011 he helped the U.S. Library of Congress launch the National Jukebox Web site (www.loc.gov/jukebox), featuring a huge collection of pre-1925 recordings.

## CÉLINE DION

The youngest of 14 children raised in a small town near Montreal, Céline Dion (born March 30, 1968, Charlemagne, Quebec, Canada) began singing with her musically inclined family when she was five years old. At age 12 she came to the attention of impresario René Angélil—whom she eventually married in 1994—and he launched her career with the album *La Voix du bon Dieu* (1981; "The Voice of God"). Dion subsequently won an award at the World Popular Song Festival in Tokyo in 1982, and the following year she received the first of many Félix awards (for musicians from Quebec). Also in 1983 she became the first Canadian recipient of a gold record in France. Invited to represent Switzerland at the Eurovision Song Contest in 1988, Dion won with her performance of "Ne partez pas sans moi" ("Do Not Leave Without Me"). By the end of the 1980s, she had recorded eight studio albums in French. As she transitioned into adulthood, she shed her image as a winsome naïf in favour of a more worldly look and sound.

In 1990 Dion released her first English-language album, *Unison*, and the romantic ballad "Where Does My Heart Beat Now" became her first top-10 single in the United States. She attracted further international attention for her Grammy Award-winning duet with Peabo Bryson on "Beauty and the Beast" (1991), from the Disney animated feature of the same name. Before long, Dion's evident vocal talent and emotionally driven songs had made her a worldwide phenomenon, even as some critics dismissed her music as schmaltzy and overly polished. With *The Colour of My Love* (1993), she scored another hit single (the soaring "The Power of Love"), and *Falling into You* (1996) earned two Grammys, including album of the year.

Perhaps Dion's greatest renown, however, came from her recording of "My Heart Will Go On," the theme of the blockbuster motion picture *Titanic* (1997). The song won an Academy Award, topped charts in multiple countries, and helped propel sales of her album *Let's Talk About Love* (1997)—which also featured duets with Barbra Streisand and Luciano Pavarotti—into the tens of millions. Throughout the 1990s Dion continued to record in French, with *D'eux* (1995; "About Them," also released as *The French Album*) becoming the best-selling Francophone album of all time.

At the beginning of the 21st century, Dion took a hiatus from her career to focus on her family. She returned with the albums *A New Day Has Come* (2002) and *One Heart* (2003), which flirted with dance pop in addition to her usual adult contemporary fare. While the releases were commercially successful by most standards, their sales did not reach Dion's previous heights. In 2003 she began performing a live show in Las Vegas, which ran for more than four years, and she launched a second residency there in 2011. Dion's later recordings include the English-language *Miracle* (2004) and *Taking Chances* (2007) and the French-language *1 fille & 4 types* (2003; "1 Girl & 4 Guys") and *D'elles* (2007; "About Them"). Despite the fact that Dion was no longer the dominant cultural force that she had been a decade earlier, it was reported in 2007 that worldwide sales of her albums had surpassed 200 million.

Dion was invested as an Officer of the Order of Canada in 1998 and was appointed Companion in 2008. A memoir, *Ma vie, mon rêve* (*My Story, My Dream*; with Georges-Hébert Germain), was published in 2000.

# MARIAH CAREY

Mariah Carey (born March 27, 1970, Huntington, New York, U.S.), whose mother was a vocal coach and former opera singer, began performing as a child. After graduating (1987) from high school in Greenlawn, New York, she moved to New York City to pursue a singing career. She made a demo tape that led Tommy Mottola, an executive at Columbia Records, to sign her in 1988; the couple married in 1993. Her debut album, *Mariah Carey* (1990), showcased her incredible vocal range and blended several musical genres, including gospel,

*Mariah Carey, 2001.* PRNewsFoto/Virgin Records/AP Images

pop, and rhythm and blues (R&B). It was a huge success, and in 1991 Carey won Grammy Awards for best new artist and best female pop vocalist. That same year she made history when the title track from her follow-up album, *Emotions*, became her fifth consecutive chart-topping single. Later hit albums include *Music Box* (1993) and *Daydream* (1995), both of which sold some 10 million copies in the United States. All the recordings were accompanied by music videos that helped make Carey a fixture on MTV.

Despite such success, Carey grew tired of the sweet and wholesome image that her label had developed for her. After announcing her separation from Mottola in 1997 (they divorced in 1998), she made *Butterfly* (1997), which reflected her new independence. The album was heavily influenced by hip-hop and rap, and the related music videos revealed a more sexual Carey. The single "Heartbreaker" topped the charts in 1999, making Carey the only artist to have a number one song in each year of the 1990s. The achievement underscored her position as the decade's top-selling female vocalist.

In 2001 Carey signed an $80 million contract with Virgin Records that made her the highest-paid recording artist. Her career quickly took a downturn, however, as she suffered a breakdown and was hospitalized following erratic behaviour. She starred in *Glitter* (2001), but both the semiautobiographical film and its accompanying album fared poorly. In 2002 Virgin terminated its contract with Carey. Later that year she signed with Island/Def Jam, but her first album for the label, *Charmbracelet* (2002), was a disappointment. However, her follow-up, *The Emancipation of Mimi* (2005), was a critical and commercial success, becoming the top-selling album of the year, with more than six million copies sold in the United States. It also earned three Grammy Awards, including best contemporary R&B album. "Touch My Body," from the 2008 release E=MC2, became Carey's 18th number one song, moving her past Elvis Presley on the list of career chart-topping hits and leaving her just two short of the Beatles' record. In 2009 Carey released her 12th studio album, *Memoirs of an Imperfect Angel*.

In addition to her recording career, Carey continued to act. After appearing in the drama *Tennessee* (2008), she earned praise as a social worker in the critically acclaimed *Precious* (2009).

## JOSH GROBAN

Josh Groban (born February 27, 1981, Los Angeles, California, U.S.) did not study voice seriously until his teens, when he became active in musical theatre at the Los Angeles

County High School for the Arts. In late 1998 he was introduced to Grammy-winning producer David Foster, who hired Groban to sing at a number of events, and Groban soon received a recording contract from Warner Brothers.

Concerned that Groban's singing—often in Italian—defied easy categorization, his promoters organized a series of performances on TV news and talk shows, as well as two guest spots on the popular series *Ally McBeal*. The appearances, which capitalized on the singer's onstage magnetism, fueled sales of his first album, *Josh Groban* (2001). Produced by Foster, the album blended pop with classical songs, showcasing Groban's rich baritone voice and romantic sensibility. His continuing performances at high-profile media events, including the closing ceremony of the 2002 Winter Olympic Games in Salt Lake City, Utah, extended Groban's international appeal.

Groban's subsequent albums include *Josh Groban in Concert* (2002), which was recorded live during an appearance on the public TV series *Great Performances*; *Closer* (2003), which featured more original compositions, as well as performances by such guest artists as classical violinist Joshua Bell; and *Awake* (2006), which included collaborations with the South African group Ladysmith Black Mambazo and jazz pianist Herbie Hancock. In 2007 Groban's *Noël*, a collection of Christmas songs, became the top-selling album of the year in the United States. For his next studio album, *Illuminations* (2010), he worked with rock and hip-hop producer Rick Rubin.

Groban headlined concert versions of the 1980s musical *Chess on Broadway* (2003) and at London's Royal Albert Hall (2008). In 2011 he made his film debut with a role as a sleazy lawyer in the comedy *Crazy, Stupid, Love*.

## MICHAEL BUBLÉ

As a child, Michael Bublé (born September 9, 1975, Burnaby, British Columbia, Canada) enjoyed a particularly close relationship with his grandfather, who introduced him to the crooners of the 1930s and '40s. He began performing in his teens, with the assistance of his grandfather, who bartered his services as a plumber to buy stage time for Bublé. His break came in 2000 when he sang at the wedding of the daughter of former Canadian prime minister Brian Mulroney, who introduced him to the Grammy-winning producer and arranger David Foster. Foster signed him to his 143 Records label in 2001, and two years later Bublé released his first album, *Michael Bublé*. It earned him the 2004 Juno Award for new artist of the year. His Christmas album, *Let It Snow!* (2003), was followed by two live CD/DVDs, *Come Fly with Me* (2004) and *Caught in the Act* (2005).

Bublé's breakthrough album, *It's Time* (2005), was named both album and pop album of the year at Canada's 2006 Juno Awards. Alongside standards by the Gershwins and Cole Porter and pop tunes from the 1950s and '60s, it included a single cowritten by Bublé, "Home," which was awarded the Juno for single of the year. *It's Time* topped the charts in Canada, Australia, Italy, and Japan and sold strongly in Britain and the United States, where it received two Grammy nominations. His 2007 release, *Call Me Irresponsible*, earned Bublé a Grammy Award for best traditional pop vocal album, and its success pushed his lifetime album sales over the 15 million mark. Bublé collected a second Grammy for the live album *Michael Bublé Meets Madison Square Garden* (2009). He followed with *Crazy Love* (2009), a collection of pop standards that won the Grammy for best traditional pop vocal album in 2011.

# CHAPTER 11

# Latin Popular Music

Since the 1930s, Latino musicians had flirted with mainstream acceptance in the U.S., beginning with the "king of rhumba," Xavier Cugat. In the late 1940s, New Yorkers flocked to dance halls to hear Tito Puente and Eddie Palmieri. In 1959 Ritchie Valens had a Spanish-language rock-and-roll hit with "La Bamba," and in the 1960s the group Santana infused its propulsive rock with Latin rhythms. Those rhythms were also pivotal to hits by non-Latinos, notably Jerry Leiber and Mike Stoller's work with the Drifters in the early '60s and the Philadelphia soul of writer-producers Kenny Gamble and Leon Huff in the 1970s. In the 1980s, Cuban-born Gloria Estefan broke through with a string of Latin-flavoured pop hits, Spaniard Julio Iglesias became an international star, and Panamanian salsa singer Rubén Blades and Los Angeles's roots rockers Los Lobos became critics' darlings. None of these inroads, however, was as deep as the wave of Latin pop that emerged at the end of the century. Modern Latin popular music was a hybrid that drew on a variety of cultures and styles, from tango to Tejano ballads, Afro-Cuban polyrhythms to Brazilian bossa nova. By incorporating these diverse elements, Latin American recording artists achieved widespread crossover success in the late 20th and early 21st centuries. In 2000 the National Academy of Recording Arts & Sciences launched the Latin Grammys, an annual awards show dedicated to one of the music industry's fastest growing markets.

# JULIO IGLESIAS

Julio Iglesias (born Julio José Iglesias de la Cueva, September 23, 1943, Madrid, Spain) was raised in an upper-middle-class neighbourhood of Madrid. After finishing his secondary education, Iglesias went on to study law at the urging of his father. At the same time he played on the junior reserve squad of the popular Real Madrid professional soccer club. However, his aspirations of becoming a professional football player ended when he became partially paralyzed in his early twenties because of a benign spinal tumour. During his lengthy recovery, Iglesias was given a guitar by one of his nurses, and he taught himself to play by accompanying songs on the radio. After he had sufficiently recovered mobility, Iglesias was sent to study English in the United Kingdom. During that time he penned his first single, "La vida sigue igual" ("Life Goes on as Usual"), with which he won a Spanish song competition in 1968.

After the competition Iglesias continued to write and perform music, releasing his first album, *Yo canto* ("I Sing"), in 1969. This marked the beginning of a steady stream of albums and LPs over the following decades. In 1970 he won the honour of representing Spain in the Eurovision Song Contest with his song "Gwendolyne." Though Iglesias did not win that competition, his song became a major hit in Europe and rocketed him to stardom. By 1973 he had sold 10 million albums, including albums in German, Portuguese, French, and Italian. In 1981 Iglesias's Spanish version of "Begin the Beguine" by Cole Porter became the first all-Spanish song to reach number one on the British music charts.

His English-speaking audience grew over the next few years, and in 1984 he released his breakout hit English-language album, *1100 Bel Air Place*. The album, which went on to sell some four million copies in the U.S. alone, was an eclectic mix of styles that included duets with popular American artists such as Willie Nelson and Diana Ross. His song with Nelson, "To All the Girls I've Loved Before," reached the top 10 on the Billboard charts. Subsequent collaborations included duets with Dolly Parton, Art Garfunkel, Stevie Wonder, Luciano Pavarotti, and Frank Sinatra. Though his touring schedule slowed during the 1990s, Iglesias remained popular into the 21st century, continuing to perform at sold-out stadiums around the world. By 2011 he had released more than 75 albums in more than a dozen languages, and his career sales figures totaled in the hundreds of millions.

Iglesias was the recipient of numerous honours and awards, including a Grammy Award for best

Latin pop performance in 1987. In 2001 Iglesias completed his law degree at Complutense University in Madrid. His autobiography, *Entre el cielo y el infierno* (*Between Heaven and Hell*), was published in 1981. Two of Iglesias's sons, Julio, Jr., and Enrique, followed their father into pop music stardom, the latter earning a Grammy Award in 1996.

## TEJANO

The evolution of Tejano began in northern Mexico (a variation known as norteño) and Texas in the mid-19th century with the introduction of the accordion by German, Polish, and Czech immigrants. Distinguished primarily by instrumentation and orchestration, three forms of Tejano (Spanish: "Texan") music developed.

The original form, conjunto, which was seen as more déclassé than mariachi music, featured the accordion as the melodic lead instrument backed rhythmically by the bajo sexto (a 12-string guitar) and an acoustic bass guitar. Its initial repertoire included waltzes, polkas, mazurkas, and rancheros. In modern conjunto, a drum kit was added and the acoustic bass replaced by an electric one. Conjunto's best-known performers in the 1920s and '30s, accordionists Pedro Ayala and Narciso Martínez, were succeeded by Tony de la Rose and Leonardo ("Flaco") Jiménez in

Oscar Martínez, 1960. © Iris Martinez-Simmons

conjunto's "golden age" in the late 1940s and early '50s.

In the 1930s Tejano's second major form, banda, or orquesta, emerged. Tejano big bands, most notably La Orquesta de Beto Villa, building upon the big band lineup popularized by swing bands, quickly incorporated Mexican folk music and conjunto traditions. By the mid-1950s bandleader and vocalist Isidro López had made crooning a staple of banda; however, his addition of the bajo sexto and the accordion to the orchestral lineup was reversed by Oscar Martínez, whose band featured a brass-oriented instrumentation that would remain the template for banda (two trumpets, alto and tenor saxophones, guitar, bass, and drums), which peaked in the 1970s.

Rejecting horns, saxophones, and the accordion even as it embraced a largely conjunto repertoire, Tejano's third musical form, grupo, originated in the 1960s with keyboard instruments and synthesizers as its foundation. Grupo's most famous performer, Selena, became an international celebrity before being killed in 1995. A reflection of the growing Mexican American cultural pride in the last half of the 20th century, all three forms of Tejano have continued their popularity into the 21st century.

## LYDIA MENDOZA

American Tejano singer Lydia Mendoza (born May 21, 1916, Houston, Texas—died December 20, 2007, San Antonio, Texas) captivated audiences with her interpretations of such songs as "Mal hombre," "La valentina," and "Angel de mis anhelos." The queen of Tejano was also dubbed the "lark of the border" and the "songstress of the poor" and was noted for her mastery of the 12-string guitar. In 1999 Mendoza was the recipient of a National Medal of Arts.

## SELENA

American singer Selena (born Selena Quintanilla Perez, April 16, 1971, Lake Jackson, Texas—died March 31, 1995, Corpus Christi, Texas) started performing at age nine with her family band. A vivacious entertainer whose fluid voice celebrated the sound of Tejano, Selena's Tex-Mex popularity earned her laurels as the queen of Tejano, and she won a 1994 Grammy Award for best Mexican American album for *Selena Live*. Another album, *Amor Prohibido*, sold more than 400,000 copies and was nominated for a 1995 Grammy award. She was dubbed the Latin Madonna and was poised to achieve crossover success with the release of her first English-language album before being murdered by the founder of her fan club, who was suspected of embezzlement. At the time of Selena's shooting death, her song "Fotos y Recuerdos" was number four on Billboard's Latin chart.

## JENNIFER LOPEZ

Jennifer Lopez (born July 24, 1969, Bronx, New York, U.S.), who was born into a family of Puerto Rican descent, took dance lessons throughout her childhood and from an early age had aspirations of fame. She performed internationally with stage musicals, and at age 16 she made

Jennifer Lopez and Marc Anthony, 2010.
John Shearer—Kohl's Department Stores/
PRNewsFoto/AP Images

and Jack Nicholson (*Blood and Wine*, 1997). Lopez still remained somewhat in the periphery of the public vision, however, until she landed the lead role in *Selena* (1997), a biopic of the murdered Tejana singer. She went on to star in a number of thrillers and action dramas, including *Anaconda* (1997), *U Turn* (1997), *Out of Sight* (1998), and *The Cell* (2000), and she gained widespread praise for *The Wedding Planner* (2001), her successful first attempt at romantic comedy. That release was quickly followed by the romantic drama *Angel Eyes* in the middle of the year.

In 1999 Lopez added pop artist to her list of titles with the release of her debut album, *On the 6*. To the surprise of many critics, the album quickly went platinum and subsequently sold more than eight million copies worldwide. Taking its title from Lopez's well-known nickname, her second album, *J.Lo* (2001), sold more than 270,000 copies in its first week. Lopez was involved in a series of high-profile relationships—first with rapper and producer Sean ("Puff Daddy") Combs (later known as Diddy) and later with actor Ben Affleck—that subjected her to heavy scrutiny by the entertainment media. In 2003 she starred opposite Affleck in *Gigli*, which was widely panned by critics, and a number of her subsequent films were box-office disappointments. In 2004 Lopez married singer Marc

her film debut with a small role in *My Little Girl* (1986). Her television break came in 1990 when she was cast as one of the "Fly Girls," dancers who appeared on the comedy show *In Living Color*.

After she left the show, she turned her focus to acting, first in several short-lived television series and then in movie roles. Film success came quickly, and by the mid-1990s she was appearing with such notable actors as Robin Williams (*Jack*, 1996)

# RY COODER

Introduced to the guitar at age three, adept at the instrument by age eight, and a teenage habitué of the Los Angeles blues scene, Ry Cooder (born Ryland Peter Cooder, March 15, 1947, Los Angeles, California, U.S.) formed the Rising Sons with Taj Mahal and played in Captain Beefheart's Magic Band before setting off on one of the most interesting career journeys of his generation. Having worked occasionally as a session musician in the 1960s, contributing to albums by the Rolling Stones and Randy Newman, he commenced a series of albums under his own name in 1970 for Reprise that amounted to an exploration of American roots music, starting with country, gospel, and blues and moving through jazz and rhythm and blues to Tex-Mex and Hawaiian music. In an era of virtuoso instrumentalists and self-sufficient singer-songwriters, Cooder was preoccupied with subtleties of tone, texture, and feel and mostly recorded other people's material. Rarely content simply to re-create a past recording, he restlessly searched for new rhythmic arrangements to showcase the emotion, wit, or pathos of each lyric.

His most noteworthy albums were *Paradise and Lunch* (1974) and *Chicken Skin Music* (1976), the latter of which helped to introduce the Texas accordion player Flaco Jiménez to an international audience. Despite performing live in support of each album, Cooder never reached beyond a cult audience, and in the 1980s he switched his attention to soundtracks. He composed scores for several Walter Hill films but made the greatest impact in Wim Wenders's *Paris, Texas* (1984), the vast panoramas of which provided the perfect visual counterpoint to Cooder's moody, reverberating slide guitar.

In 1992 he resumed his recording career via collaborations with musicians from other countries. *A Meeting by the River* with Indian guitarist V.M. Bhatt won a Grammy Award for best world music album of 1993 and was the recording debut of Cooder's son

Joachim as a percussionist. Two years later father and son took part in the Los Angeles recording sessions by Malian guitarist Ali Farka Touré, and the resultant album, *Talking Timbuktu*, became one of the best-selling world music albums of 1994 and won that year's Grammy. By that point a substantial audience trusted Cooder's judgment and skill, and they followed him in even greater numbers when he joined a group of veteran Cuban musicians convened by the British label World Circuit for a week in Havana recording *The Buena Vista Social Club* (1997). That album and the subsequent Buena Vista releases *Buenos Hermanos* (2003) and *Mambo Sinuendo* (2003) earned Cooder a trio of Grammy Awards. His later works included the concept album *Chavez Ravine* (2005) and the folk-fusion recording *My Name Is Buddy* (2007).

Anthony, and the couple appeared in *El Cantante* (2006), the biopic of salsa musician Hector Lavoe. Her later albums include *Rebirth* (2005); the Spanish-language *Como ama una mujer* (2007), which reached the number one spot on Billboard's Latin album chart; *Brave* (2007); and *Love?* (2011), which featured the up-tempo hit "On the Floor."

In February 2008 Lopez gave birth to twins, her first children and Anthony's fourth and fifth. She returned to the big screen in *The Back-up Plan* (2010), a romantic comedy in which she starred as a single woman who finds Mr. Right after becoming pregnant through artificial insemination. In January 2011 Lopez joined the television talent show *American Idol* as a judge. Later that year it was announced that Lopez and Anthony were divorcing, although in 2012 they began working together as producers and hosts of the TV program *¡Q'Viva!: The Chosen*, a talent competition for Latin American performers. Lopez subsequently appeared in *What to Expect When You're Expecting* (2012), an ensemble comedy about parenting.

## SHAKIRA

Shakira (born Shakira Isabel Mebarak Ripoll, February 2, 1977, Barranquilla,

*Singer Shakira performs her "Hips Don't Lie."* KMazur/WireImage/Getty Images

Colombia), who has a Lebanese father and a native Colombian mother, started belly dancing at an early age and by age 10 had begun writing songs and taking part in talent competitions. A local theatre producer helped her land an audition with a Sony Corp. executive in 1990, and Shakira was subsequently signed to a record deal. Her first two albums, *Magia* (1991) and *Peligro* (1993), were only moderately successful, however. After taking a break from recording to act in the Latin soap opera *El oasis*, Shakira resumed her music career in impressive fashion with *Pies descalzos* (1995). The album produced several hits, including "Estoy aquí," "Pienso en ti," and "Un poco de amor."

After releasing *¿Dónde están los ladrones?* in 1998, Shakira focused her efforts on establishing herself in the American market. In 2001 her album *MTV Unplugged* (2000) won the Grammy Award for best Latin pop album, and she released her first English-language album, *Laundry Service*, that same year. Although her English-language songwriting skills were questioned by some (Shakira wrote all her own lyrics), *Laundry Service* sold more than 13 million copies worldwide.

Shakira continued her crossover success in 2005 with the release of the Spanish-language *Fijación oral, vol. 1* in June and the English-language *Oral Fixation, Vol. 2* in November.

Both albums debuted in the top five in the United States, and her single "Hips Don't Lie" (featuring Wyclef Jean) topped charts around the world in 2006. At that year's Latin Grammy Awards, she captured song-of-the-year and record-of-the-year awards for the single "La tortura," and *Fijación oral, vol. 1* was named album of the year as well as best female pop vocal album. A live recording, *Oral Fixation Tour*, followed in 2007. Also that year Shakira performed in Hamburg as part of Live Earth, a worldwide concert series organized to bring attention to climate change and environmental sustainability.

For her next English-language album, *She Wolf* (2009), Shakira adopted an electro-pop sound. The following year she scored another international hit with "Waka Waka (This Time for Africa)," a collaboration with a South African band, after it was chosen as the official anthem of the 2010 World Cup. The track later appeared on her breezily eclectic *Sale el sol* (2010), which earned a Latin Grammy for best female pop vocal album.

Shakira devoted considerable time and energy to social causes. In 2003 she became a UNICEF goodwill ambassador, traveling internationally to raise awareness of the struggles of children in less-developed countries. She also created the Pies Descalzos

Foundation, which focused on helping children displaced by violence in Colombia.

## ALEJANDRO SANZ

Spanish guitarist and singer-songwriter Alejandro Sanz (born Alejandro Sánchez Pizarro, December 18, 1968, Madrid, Spain) soared to international stardom in the late 20th century with his flamenco-influenced popular music. Sanz was raised in Cádiz, a city in the Andalusia region of Spain. His father was a professional guitarist who had worked with the likes of Spanish stars Manolo Escobar and Lola Flores. Sanz took up guitar when he was seven years old and began composing songs a few years later. He left trade school at age 16 in order to pursue music as a career and recorded his first solo work, *Los chulos son pa' cuidarlos* ("Pimps Are for Nurturing"), in 1989.

Veritable pop-star status came in 1991 with the release of Sanz's first album, *Viviendo deprisa* ("Living Fast"), and continued with *Si tú me miras* (1993; "If You Look at Me") and 3 (1995). His next album was the record-breaking *Más* (1997; "More"), which showcased a maturity in lyrical content and sensibility that appealed to a broader audience. *Básico* ("Basic"), which had previously been released in a limited edition and featured selected songs from his past albums, followed a year later. The eagerly anticipated *El alma al aire* (2000; "The Soul in the Air") was tremendously successful; it won Latin Grammy Awards in 2001 for best album, best song, best male pop vocal album, and best record of the year. Sanz's popularity in the world of Latin music was reaffirmed with the release of *MTV Unplugged* (2001), which again garnered multiple Latin Grammys.

Sanz ventured into new stylistic terrain on his later albums, collaborating with an array of international artists, including Colombian vocalists Shakira and Juanes, among others, on the Grammy-winning *El tren de los momentos* (2006; "The Train of Moments"). Although he consciously allowed his style to evolve, Sanz remained a specialist in flamenco-infused ballads and love songs, which he performed in a distinctly gravelly voice. Such songs made up the bulk of his eighth studio release, *Paraíso Express* (2009). It won the Grammy for best Latin pop album in 2011 and spawned the crossover hit "Looking for Paradise," a duet with American rhythm-and-blues singer Alicia Keys.

## JUANES

When Juanes (born Juan Esteban Aristizábal Vásquez, August 9, 1972,

Medellín, Colombia) was seven years old, his father and brothers taught him to play guitar, and he quickly became immersed in the musical traditions of his Colombian homeland. Later he became infatuated with rock and roll, and for 11 years he was a singer and guitarist for Ekhymosis, a heavy metal band that enjoyed a strong following in his country. Juanes grew restless with the artistic limitations of the band, however, and in 1999 he moved to Los Angeles to pursue a solo career.

In 2000 Juanes debuted with *Fíjate bien* ("Take a Good Look"), a brooding album that produced a handful of hits and earned the singer three Latin Grammy Awards, including best new artist. Juanes's major breakthrough came in 2002 with the release of his second album, the bright and energetic *Un día normal* ("A Normal Day"), which included the chart-topping songs "A Dios le pido" ("I Ask God"), an anthem for peace, and "Fotografia" ("Photograph"), a duet with Canadian pop singer Nelly Furtado. *Un día normal* won five awards at the 2003 Latin Grammys, including album of the year, record of the year, and song of the year. In 2004 he released *Mi sangre* ("My Blood"), which also received multiple Grammys.

Juanes's passion for music was matched by his concern with the problems that plagued Colombia. Through his songs—which remained firmly rooted in cumbia, tango, and the regional music of his native country—as well as through his ongoing philanthropic work, he condemned the world's violence while projecting hope for a better future. In 2006 Juanes started the Mi Sangre Foundation, an organization dedicated to eradicating Colombia's land mines and supporting victims of land mine accidents. The Juanes Peace Park, with special facilities for people with disabilities, opened in his hometown of Medellín in 2008. Juanes's 2007 album *La vida…es un ratico* ("Life…Is a Moment") continued his call for peace, love, and social change. His own record label, 4Js, named after his father and siblings (whose names start with the letter J), was launched in 2007 as well. In 2009 Juanes organized and headlined a peace concert in Havana despite criticism from opponents of Cuba's government. The well-attended event featured some 15 other performers.

## CALLE 13

The Puerto Rican popular music duo Calle 13 (English: "13th Street") was known for intelligent, poetic, and sharply pointed social and political commentary—all delivered through a distinctive blend of hip-hop with a broad range of Latin American music styles. René Pérez Joglar (also known as "Residente," born February 23, 1978, San Juan, Puerto Rico) was the master of language, while his stepbrother, Eduardo José Cabra Martínez (also known as "Visitante," born September 10, 1978, San Juan, Puerto Rico), masterminded the music. The duo was one of the most popular and influential groups on the Latin popular music scene in the early 21st century.

Pérez and Cabra met in a middle-class neighbourhood in San Juan, Puerto Rico, and became brothers when Pérez's mother married Cabra's father. Although the stepparents eventually divorced, the boys' bond remained strong, and they continued to visit each other throughout their youth. Whenever Cabra went to the gated community on 13th Street ("Calle 13") in the San Juan suburb of Trujillo Alto where his brother lived, he'd announce himself to the guard as a "Visitor" ("Visitante") coming to see a "Resident" ("Residente"). That recurring experience ultimately formed the foundation of the duo's professional personae.

Both boys were involved in the arts from a young age. Cabra began formal music lessons when he was six years old and eventually studied piano, saxophone, and flute, before teaching himself guitar and experimenting with computer-generated sounds. He maintained his interest in music—particularly in production and composition—while studying accounting and information systems at the University of Puerto Rico. Pérez, meanwhile, was absorbed in literature as a youth, pursued undergraduate study at the School of Visual Arts (Escuela de Artes Plásticas) of Puerto Rico, and later received a master's degree in animation from Georgia's Savannah College of Art and Design.

Calle 13 started recording music in 2004, with Residente writing and rapping and Visitante supporting the vocals with a mixture of hip-hop and other types of electronic music. In 2005 the brothers signed a contract with the White Lion label in Puerto Rico and subsequently created a stir with "Querido FBI" ("Dear FBI"), a poignant criticism of the U.S. government aired in the wake of the FBI's killing that September of Puerto Rican pro-independence leader Filiberto Ojeda Ríos. Toward the end of 2005 the brothers released their first album, *Calle 13*, which included "Atrévete-te-te" ("I Dare You-You-You"), the group's first major hit. With engaging lyrics and imagery that spoke to the middle-class fear of the urban poor, the song effectively elevated the album to best-seller status and propelled the brothers to celebrity.

During the next several years Calle 13's popularity skyrocketed, as the brothers gained audiences elsewhere in Latin America as well as in Spain and on the U.S. mainland. The brothers traveled widely, absorbing influences from an array of artists. Residente was inspired most notably by Panamanian salsa musician, actor, and political activist Rubén Blades. The duo eventually collaborated with Blades, as well as with Mexican rock band Café Tacuba, Nigerian Afro-beat musician Seun Kuti (son of Afro-beat founder Fela Anikulapo-Kuti), Puerto Rican experimental-rock musician Omar Rodriguez Lopez, and Peruvian singer-songwriter Susana Baca, among others. Although Calle 13's music has often been classified as reggaeton (a type of Spanish-language rap), the brothers rejected the label, citing the genre as only one of many influences in their music. While reggaeton

lyrics were typically vulgar, sexist, and replete with clichés, Residente's poetry—although often raunchy—was notably cerebral; it was colourful, provocative, witty, and somewhat surreal.

In the first five years of their professional career, Calle 13 was showered with Latin Grammy Awards. In 2006 the duo won best new artist, and *Calle 13* won best urban music album. The brothers' next three albums—*Residente o Visitante* (2007), *Los de atrás vienen conmigo* (2008; "Those from Behind Are Coming with Me"), and *Entren los que quieran* (2010; "Everybody Is Welcome")—also received awards in various categories. In 2011 Calle 13 made Latin Grammy history by receiving a record-breaking nine awards in a single night.

# CHAPTER 12

# Modern Country

**T**he definition of "country" is a slippery one, and the genre's relationship with rock and pop has traditionally been somewhat fluid. Indeed, in the golden age of rockabilly, performers might have shifted between country and rock idioms in the space of a single song. The lush production values and formulaic constraints of the later "Nashville Sound" led to a rebellion of sorts, and outlaw music was born. By openly embracing rock rhythms, outlaw once again narrowed the distance between rock and country. Over time, electric guitars replaced more traditional instruments and country music became more acceptable to a national urban audience. Despite its embrace of other popular styles, country music retained an unmistakable character as one of the few truly indigenous American musical styles.

## DOLLY PARTON

Dolly Parton (born January 19, 1946, Locust Ridge, Tennessee, U.S.) was born into a poor farming family, the fourth of 12 children. She displayed an aptitude and passion for music at an early age, and as a child she was a featured singer and guitarist on local radio and television shows in Knoxville, Tennessee. In 1964, immediately following her high school graduation, she set out for Nashville to pursue a career in music.

Dolly Parton rehearsing with country music singer-songwriter Kenny Rogers, 2005. PRNewsFoto/CMT/AP Images

In Nashville Parton became the protégée of country music singer and Grand Ole Opry star Porter Wagoner. Through repeated appearances on Wagoner's syndicated television show, Parton gained coast-to-coast recognition. She soon attracted the attention of the music industry moguls at RCA Records and subsequently recorded more than a dozen hit songs—together with Wagoner—on the RCA label. Owing much to her association with Wagoner, Parton rapidly emerged as one of country music's most popular singers.

In 1974 Parton discontinued her work with Wagoner to launch a solo career, in which she enjoyed immediate success: in both 1975 and '76 she was chosen female singer of the year by the Country Music Association (CMA). About the same time, Parton began to cross over to the pop music market, and in 1978 she won a Grammy Award for her song "Here You Come Again" and was named entertainer of the year by the CMA. As her career developed, Parton received more Grammys, both for her songs, including "9 to 5" (1980) and "Shine" (2001), and for her albums, including *Trio* (1987; with Linda Ronstadt and Emmylou Harris) and *The Grass Is Blue* (1999).

In the 1980s Parton appeared in several successful films, most notably *Nine to Five* (1980; also known as *9 to 5*) and *The Best Little Whorehouse in Texas* (1982), for which she revived one of her most popular songs, "I Will Always Love You" (1974). (Whitney Houston later recorded the song for the film *The Bodyguard* [1992], and it went on to sell millions of copies.) In 1989 Parton played a principal role in *Steel Magnolias*. In the 1990s and 2000s she guest-starred in many television series and appeared in several made-for-television movies. In 2009 Parton wrote the music and lyrics for a Broadway musical adaptation of the film *9 to 5*. Three years later she starred in the film *Joyful Noise*.

Aside from her stage and screen activities, Parton was involved in a broad array of other projects. In 1986 she opened Dollywood—a theme park centred on Appalachian traditions—in the Great Smoky Mountains of eastern Tennessee. Two years later she created the Dollywood Foundation, an organization with the aim of providing inspiration and educational resources to children.

In 1994 Parton published her autobiography, *Dolly: My Life and Other Unfinished Business*, which was a best seller in the United States.

Parton's contributions to the arts and culture of the United States earned her numerous awards from organizations beyond the music and film industry. She was named a Living Legend by the Library of Congress in 2004 for her enrichment of the American cultural heritage. In 2005 she received the U.S. government's National Medal of Arts, and in 2006 she was recognized at the Kennedy Center for the Performing Arts in Washington, D.C., for her lifetime artistic achievement.

## WILLIE NELSON

Willie Nelson (born April 30, 1933, Fort Worth, Texas, U.S.) learned to play guitar from his grandfather and at the age of 10 was performing at local dances. He served in the U.S. Air Force before becoming a disc jockey in Texas, Oregon, and California during the 1950s. He also was performing in public and writing songs then; by 1961 he was based in Nashville, Tennessee, and playing bass in Ray Price's band. Price was among the first of dozens of country, rhythm and blues, and popular singers to achieve hit records with Nelson's 1960s tunes, which included the standards "Hello Walls," "Night

*Willie Nelson performing at a USO concert at Ramstein Air Base in Germany, 2005.* Mike Theiler—USO/PRNewsFoto/AP Images

Life," "Funny How Time Slips Away," and "Crazy." By contrast, Nelson achieved only modest success as a singer in that decade.

Nelson moved back to Texas in the 1970s and, beginning with his 1975 album *Red Headed Stranger*, with its hit song "Blue Eyes Crying in the Rain," became one of the most popular country music performers.

His performances featured a unique sound, of which his relaxed, behind-the-beat singing style and gut-string guitar were the most distinctive elements. Unusual for a country music album, songs by Hoagy Carmichael, Irving Berlin, and other mainstream popular songwriters made up his 1978 *Stardust*, which sold four million copies. The next year he made

# OUTLAW MUSIC

Outlaw music was a movement of American country music in the 1970s spearheaded by Willie Nelson and Waylon Jennings. Sometimes called progressive country, outlaw music was an attempt to escape the formulaic constraints of the Nashville Sound (simple songs, the use of studio musicians, and lush production), country's dominant style in the 1960s. An outgrowth of the honky-tonk style pioneered by Hank Williams, it mixed folk's introspective lyrics, rock's rhythms, and country's instrumentation. Like Southern rock and the country rock that developed in Los Angeles, outlaw music was a rock and roots music hybrid that had a local flavour.

In 1971 Nelson left Nashville, Tennessee, and returned to his native Texas. Cultivating a long-haired image that violated country's social conservatism, he restarted his career in Austin, where hippies and rednecks mingled in clubs such as the Armadillo World Headquarters. The movement spawned by this scene took its name from *Ladies Love Outlaws* (1972), an album by Jennings (a one-time disc jockey who had played bass in Buddy Holly's band before eventually going to Nashville in the mid-1960s to write and record). Nelson's Wild West concept album, *Red Headed Stranger* (1975), had production so spare that Columbia fought against its release. Yet that album, featuring "Blue Eyes Crying in the Rain," captivated a large crossover audience with its Western storytelling and lean artiness, as did *Wanted: The Outlaws* (1976), recorded by Jennings; his wife, Jessi Colter; Nelson; and Tompall Glaser. The movement risked falling into its own formula as other outlaws appeared, but Jennings remained an eclectic, if inconsistent, performer, while Nelson branched out in other musical directions.

his film-acting debut in *The Electric Horseman*; his later films included *Honeysuckle Rose* (1980) *Red Headed Stranger* (1987), *Wag the Dog* (1997), and *The Dukes of Hazzard* (2005). In the mid-1970s he had produced annual Fourth of July country music festivals in Dripping Springs, Texas; in the 1980s he organized annual Farm Aid festivals to raise money for farmers. Apart from continuing to record country and popular songs on his own, he recorded with at least 75 other singers, most notably Waylon Jennings. In 1990 the Internal Revenue Service, claiming he owed $16.7 million in unpaid taxes, seized his assets; to raise money he recorded the two-CD album *The IRS Tapes: Who'll Buy My Memories* (1991).

Nelson was inducted into the Country Music Hall of Fame in 1993. He remained a prolific recording artist and maintained a relentless touring schedule into the 21st century. Long an advocate of marijuana legalization, Nelson became something of an elder statesman within that movement, serving as a board member for the National Organization for the Reform of Marijuana Laws.

## WAYLON JENNINGS

Waylon Jennings (born June 15, 1937, Littlefield, Texas, U.S.—died February 13, 2002, Chandler, Arizona) recorded some 60 albums and 16 number one country hits and sold more than 40 million records worldwide.

Jennings, who performed professionally from the age of 12, first toured as a bassist for Buddy Holly and only narrowly missed getting on the plane that in 1959 crashed with Holly, Ritchie Valens, and the Big Bopper (J.P. Richardson) aboard. Chet Atkins eventually signed Jennings to a contract with RCA Records and took him to Nashville in 1964. Four years later Jennings recorded his first number one song, "Only Daddy That'll Walk the Line." Other hits included "Good Hearted Woman" (1972) and "(I'm a) Ramblin' Man" (1974).

Frustrated by what he saw as the increasingly bland sound of country music, Jennings teamed with Nelson in 1976 to produce their own album, *Wanted: The Outlaws*, which launched the outlaw music movement and became the first Nashville album to sell a million copies. A later duet with Nelson, "Mammas Don't Let Your Babies Grow Up to Be Cowboys," earned the two a Grammy Award in 1978. Jennings wrote the theme song and provided narration for the popular 1980s television series *The Dukes of Hazzard*. In the 1980s, with Nelson, Johnny Cash, and Kris Kristofferson, he formed the Highwaymen, and the group recorded three best-selling albums. Jennings was inducted into the Country Music Hall of Fame in 2001.

# RICKY SKAGGS

American mandolin and fiddle virtuoso Ricky Skaggs (born Rickie Lee Skaggs, July 18, 1954, Cordell, Kentucky, U.S.) played a leading role in the New Traditionalist movement of the 1980s by adapting bluegrass music's instrumentation and historically conscious sensibility to mainstream country music. Skaggs was a child prodigy on the mandolin, and by age seven he had already played onstage with bluegrass founder Bill Monroe and appeared on the Grand Ole Opry and on the television show of bluegrass legends (Lester) Flatt & (Earl) Scruggs. Within just a few more years he had also become extraordinarily proficient on guitar and fiddle. Skaggs's professional career began in 1970, when as teenagers he and singing partner Keith Whitley joined the band of another bluegrass pioneer, Ralph Stanley.

Skaggs left Stanley's group in 1973 and went on to play with a succession of inventive bluegrass bands, including the Country Gentlemen, J.D. Crowe and the New South, and his own Boone Creek. As they increasingly incorporated the drive and harmonies of rock and pop music into their sound, these groups helped to define the "Newgrass" genre. Skaggs, meanwhile, continued to develop a reputation as a string virtuoso with a taste for musical innovation. In 1975 he launched his solo bluegrass career with the album *That's It!*, on the Rebel Records label.

A stint with singer and songwriter Emmylou Harris's Hot Band in 1977–80 brought him to the attention of both country and rock music audiences, and he subsequently signed a contract with Epic Records as a solo Nashville country act. The result was a series of hit albums and some one dozen number one singles on the Billboard country music charts. The Epic releases accelerated the emergent New Traditionalist trend in mainstream country music, which popularized relatively stripped down, leanly produced bluegrass and honky-tonk sounds as well as traditional "home, hearth, and heartbreak" themes at a time when country music was dominated by a highly polished, pop-inspired "urban cowboy" style.

In 1982 Skaggs became a cast member of the Grand Ole Opry, and through the early 1990s he won a series of major awards for his New Traditionalist work. Among his most notable honours were multiple Grammy Awards—for both his instrumental work (1984, 1986) and his tenor vocals (1991)—and numerous Country Music Association awards, including Entertainer of the Year (1985). He also won acclaim for his music video "Country Boy" (1985), which featured Bill Monroe (playing Skaggs's "Uncle Pen") buck dancing (similar to clog dancing) in a New York City subway car.

As the "down home" country style of the New Traditionalists gave way in the 1990s to the arena-ready, rock-influenced theatricality of performers such as Garth Brooks, Skaggs returned to some of his earlier, roots-focused projects, including his influential collaboration with guitarist Tony Rice on older country tunes (inaugurated in 1980 with the album Skaggs & Rice). In the realm of bluegrass, Skaggs shifted his focus to the traditional sound of the genre's founding generation. He established Skaggs Family Records and formed the band Kentucky Thunder. Renowned for their driving tempos and clean, fast instrumental technique, Ricky Skaggs and Kentucky Thunder became and remained a celebrated force in the field, winning seven Grammy Awards—including five awards for best bluegrass album (1998, 1999, 2004, 2006, 2008)—by the end of the first decade of the 21st century. During that period Skaggs also became an outspoken advocate of hard-core bluegrass. Through concert tours and television broadcasts, release of the multi-artist salute album *Big Mon: The Songs of Bill Monroe* (2000), and promotion of bluegrass and bluegrass-gospel bands through his record label, he worked to expand the genre's fan base.

Although Skaggs was widely viewed as the public face of traditional bluegrass, he was a highly versatile musician with broad musical interests who displayed experimentalist as well as preservationist tendencies. Among his most adventurous projects in the early 21st century were a duet album with pop pianist Bruce Hornsby in 2007 and, in the same year, *Salt of the Earth*, a gospel collaboration with his wife Sharon White and family (i.e., the Texan Grand Ole Opry stalwarts the Whites). He also performed with a diverse array of musicians including rock artists Phish and Jack White, jazz trombonist Wycliffe Gordon, and klezmer mandolinist Andy Statman, among others. In 2010 Skaggs returned to a fuller ensemble sound with *Mosaic*, a country music album with a gospel music flavour.

## GARTH BROOKS

Garth Brooks (born Troyal Garth Brooks, February 7, 1962, Tulsa, Oklahoma, U.S.) was born into a musical family; his mother had a brief recording career with Capitol Records in the 1950s. He initially exhibited little interest in music, however, preferring to concentrate on athletics. A track-and-field scholarship brought Brooks to Oklahoma State University, and it was there that he met guitarist

Ty England, with whom he began performing at area nightclubs. Brooks graduated with a degree in advertising in 1984 and moved to Nashville the following year, hoping to break into the music business. This initial foray into the heart of country music was short-lived, however, and Brooks returned to Oklahoma after only a day. In 1986 he married Sandy Mahl, his college girlfriend, and a year later she accompanied him back to Nashville, where he was signed to Capitol Records in 1988.

Brooks released his eponymous debut album in 1989, and he was joined by England in a partnership that became one of the most lucrative in country music. Touring in support of the debut album, the two established an easy onstage banter that became a trademark of Brooks's live shows. While Garth Brooks sold well, listeners and critics could not have anticipated what was to come. In 1990 Brooks released *No Fences*, a blockbuster that sold more than 17 million copies on the strength of singles such as "Friends in Low Places." While his music blurred the line between pop and country, his live performances eschewed country traditions altogether, embracing instead the spectacle of 1970s arena rock. Concerts incorporated pyrotechnics and light shows, and Brooks used a wireless hands-free microphone that allowed him to roam the stage.

Brooks followed his breakthrough release with *Ropin' the Wind* (1991), another genre-bending album that was equal parts honky-tonk and classic rock. It debuted at the top of the Billboard pop chart and went on to sell more than 14 million copies. Brooks turned away from the pop sound of his previous works to deliver the holiday album *Beyond the Season* (1992) and the introspective *The Chase* (1992). Although both releases posted sales figures in the millions, *The Chase* was regarded as somewhat of a disappointment, and Brooks returned to playful rock-influenced tunes on *In Pieces* (1993). Later releases included *Fresh Horses* (1995) and *Sevens* (1997), as well as the concert album *Double Live* (1998).

In 1999 Brooks took the unusual step of recording a straightforward pop album under the pseudonym Chris Gaines. The Gaines character, portrayed by Brooks as a goateed rocker dressed in black leather, came complete with a fictional backstory as well as an assortment of "greatest hits" that were collected on *In the Life of Chris Gaines* (1999). While the album featured impeccable production from the likes of Babyface and Don Was, its content was overshadowed by questions about why Brooks would take his career in such an unexpected direction.

The following year Brooks and his wife divorced, and he announced that he would put music on hold until his youngest daughter's 18th birthday. His next record, *Scarecrow* (2001), would be his last studio effort released before his extended break, and it sold briskly to fans who welcomed Brooks's return to country pop. In 2005 Brooks married fellow country star and frequent duet partner Trisha Yearwood. While he remained committed to his "retirement," Brooks occasionally performed live shows—most notably at a series of nine sold-out concerts in Kansas City, Missouri, in 2007 and a five-show benefit for Los Angeles firefighters and wildfire victims in 2008. These brief engagements seemed to reveal a performer eager to return to the stage, and in October 2009 Brooks officially confirmed the end of his retirement and an extended run at a Las Vegas casino.

## REBA MCENTIRE

As the daughter of a world champion steer roper, Reba McEntire (born March 28, 1955, McAlester, Oklahoma, U.S.) spent time during her childhood traveling between rodeo performances. On the trips, her mother helped nurture her musical abilities, and McEntire formed a band with her siblings while in the ninth grade. She scored her first big break when she was asked to sing the national anthem at the 1974 National Finals Rodeo. Her performance impressed country music star Red Steagall, who helped McEntire record a demo that led to a contract with Mercury Records.

Six years after her first single, "I Don't Want to Be a One Night Stand" (1976), she topped the charts with "Can't Even Get the Blues" (1982). Other hits followed, but McEntire longed to have more control of her own career and to recapture a more traditional country music sound. She moved to the MCA label in 1984, started coproducing her albums, and topped the country charts seven times by the end of 1986. She was the first woman to win six Country Music Association award nominations in one year and was crowned CMA's best female vocalist in an unprecedented four consecutive years (1984–87).

With her musical success established, McEntire expanded into business and acting. Along with second husband and manager Narvel Blackstock, McEntire built an empire that included a talent-management firm, a construction company, a horse farm, and a jet charter service. She made her film debut in the 1990 science-fiction thriller *Tremors*. The following March, a plane carrying her tour manager and seven band members crashed near San Diego, California. McEntire paid tribute to the victims on the album *For My Broken Heart* (1991).

In 1994 McEntire recorded the album *Read My Mind*; published her best-selling autobiography, *Reba: My Story*; appeared in the films *North* and *The Little Rascals*; and won both a Grammy Award and a CMA award for her collaboration with Linda Davis on "Does He Love You." She starred in a number of made-for-television movies over the next few years before landing her own television sitcom, *Reba*, which she also coproduced, in 2001. The show, about a single mother and her family in suburban Texas, ran until early 2007. McEntire continued to tour. Her later albums include *Room to Breathe* (2003).

## THE JUDDS

The Judds, a duo consisting of Naomi Judd (born Diana Ellen Judd, January 11, 1946, Ashland, Kentucky, U.S.) and her daughter Wynonna Judd (born Christina Claire Ciminella, May 30, 1964, Ashland, Kentucky), produced a string of hits in the 1980s and early 1990s. Their effective vocal harmonies, melding of traditional country sounds with popular music styles, and mother-daughter chemistry made them one of country's most enduring acts.

Naomi Judd—known as Diana prior to embarking on her music career—grew up in a small town in Kentucky. Although her musical activities there were largely limited to listening to pop music broadcasts on the radio, she was enamoured with the prospect of a career in performance. Her aspirations were postponed at age 17, however, when she became pregnant by a high-school classmate who rejected any further relationship. During her pregnancy she married Michael Ciminella, who was long identified publicly as the biological father of her first daughter, Christina—later known professionally as Wynonna Judd. In 1968 the Ciminellas relocated to the Los Angeles area, where Naomi's second daughter, Ashley, was born that year. As an adult, Ashley emerged as the screen actress Ashley Judd.

The Ciminella marriage ended in practical terms in 1972, when Naomi filed for divorce, although the separation was not official until 1977. Naomi supported her young family through various jobs, including secretarial work in the Hollywood film industry and waitressing. She also attended nursing school (first at Eastern Kentucky University and then at the College of Marin, California) while living alternately in California and Kentucky. Meanwhile, Wynonna learned to play the guitar during her teen years and showed a strong inclination toward music. She shared with Naomi a growing interest in the work of the tradition-minded female bluegrass duo Hazel Dickens and Alice Gerrard and the blues-influenced pop singer Bonnie Raitt, among others. When mother and daughter began singing together in the late 1970s, they forged a sound that reflected the influence of those artists. They adopted their profes-sional names—Naomi and Wynonna Judd, or, together, the Judds—in 1976, while in Kentucky.

While Naomi was completing nursing school, the fledgling act made appearances in the San Francisco area as the Hillbilly Women, before they moved to Nashville in 1979. Ashley, meanwhile, went to Kentucky in summer 1978, first to live with her paternal grandparents, then with her father, before she reunited with her mother and sister shortly after they settled in Tennessee. Naomi and Wynonna pursued a musical career in Nashville.

For the next few years Naomi worked as a nurse and a model, while she and Wynonna occasionally appeared on Nashville radio and tele-vision. A turning point came in 1982, however, when record producer Brent Maher listened to a Judds audition tape and was stunned by the sound—Wynonna's powerful lead singing complemented by Naomi's delicate har-monizing. By 1983 the Judds had been signed by RCA Victor Records. Their first single release, "Had a Dream (For the Heart)" (1983), made the Billboard

Country Singles chart. The next two, "Mama He's Crazy" and "Why Not Me" (both 1984), were number one hits and Grammy Award winners (best coun-try performance by a duo or group with vocal) that later became country music standards. While her mother and half sister pursued musical inter-ests, Ashley sometimes stayed with her father in Louisville, Kentucky, and sometimes traveled with the Judds. In 1986 she enrolled in the University of Kentucky (Lexington), from which she graduated in 1990.

Through the remainder of the 1980s, the Judds were among the most prominent faces in the field, win-ning the Country Music Association's vocal group of the year award every year from 1985 to 1991. They not only served as role models for up-and-coming female country music artists but also entertained their audiences with their look-alike, often feisty mother-daughter relationship. Indeed, in their own words, the Judds put the fun in dysfunctional.

The duo was forced to dissolve in 1991, after Naomi was diagnosed with debilitating chronic hepatitis C. Wynonna subsequently pursued a solo career with considerable success. Her 1992 singles "She Is His Only Need," "I Saw the Light," and "No One Else on Earth" reached number one on the Billboard country music charts, as did her 1996 release "To Be Loved by You"; her albums, moreover, were effectively marketed in both the pop and country music categories. Wynonna's memoir, *Coming Home to Myself*, was published in 2005. Naomi became an author of children's books and self-help manuals—notably *The Transparent Life: 30 Proven Ways to Live Your Best* (2005) and *Naomi's Guide to Aging Gratefully: Facts, Myths, and Good News for Boomers* (2007)—as well as a motivational speaker and television actress. The Judds reunited briefly in 1999, before touring in 2000. In 2010–11 they staged another full-fledged reunion tour, documented on the cable television series *The Judds*.

# ALAN JACKSON

Alan Jackson (born October 17, 1958, Newnan, Georgia, U.S.) grew up in rural Georgia singing gospel music and performing, as a teenager, in a country duo. After dropping out of school and wedding his high-school sweetheart, Denise, Jackson worked odd jobs while playing with his band, Dixie Steel. After Denise, an airline stewardess, happened upon country artist Glen Campbell in an airport in 1985, Jackson's demo tape landed him a songwriting contract with Campbell's music-publishing company. The couple subsequently moved to Nashville.

In 1989 Jackson became the first artist signed to the country division of Arista Records. His first hit, "Here in the Real World," cowritten in 1990 by Jackson with Mark Irwin, established the singer as a composer of songs that speak directly about the virtues of rural and small-town life, the vagaries of love, and the value of the country music traditions inherited from predecessors such as George Jones and Hank Williams.

A traditionalist in his musical approach, Jackson became a member of the Grand Ole Opry in 1991, and he acknowledged his roots in 1999 on *Under the Influence*, an album featuring his interpretations of songs by artists such as Merle Haggard, Charley Pride, and Gene Watson. Jackson also recorded with George Jones, George Strait, Randy Travis, and Jimmy Buffett, among others.

In response to the tragedy of the September 11 attacks in 2001, Jackson wrote a song that describes the range of reactions to the day's events. "Where Were You (When the World Stopped Turning)" went on to win song of the year awards from the Country Music Association (CMA) and the Academy of Country Music (ACM) as well as the Grammy Award for best country song in 2002.

Jackson's many industry awards include the CMA entertainer of the year award in 1995 and 2002. His 11th album, *Drive* (2002), includes "Where Were You" and the song "Drive (For Daddy Gene)," which paid tribute to Jackson's father. In 2003 Jackson won two ACM awards: album of the year and video of the year for "Drive." That same year his two-disc *Greatest Hits Volume II* entered the Billboard pop and country charts at number one. In 2006 Jackson released two studio albums—*Precious Memories*, a collection of 15 hymns, and *Like Red on a Rose*—both of which reached number one on the country charts.

## SHANIA TWAIN

Shania Twain (born Eilleen Regina Edwards, August 28, 1965, Windsor, Ontario, Canada) took the surname of her stepfather, Jerry Twain, at a young age. After the family moved north to Timmins, Ontario, she developed an exceptional singing voice and by age eight was performing in clubs to help supplement her parents' irregular income. During high school she sang with a Top 40 cover band called Longshot. At age 21 she moved to Toronto, where she worked during the day while singing in clubs at night. Less than a year later, however, her parents were killed in a traffic accident, and she returned home to raise her sister and two brothers.

Twain continued to sing in clubs, and in 1991 she attracted the attention of producer Norro Wilson, who took her to Nashville, Tennessee, to record her first album. She changed her name to Shania, meaning "I'm on my way," a nod to her stepfather's Ojibwa heritage. Her first album, *Shania Twain*, sold only 100,000 copies, but her talent caught the eye of another producer, Robert John ("Mutt") Lange, who had a highly successful career producing albums for Def Leppard, Bryan Adams, and Michael Bolton. Twain and Lange, who immediately began writing songs together, also became romantically involved and married in 1993 (they divorced in 2010). Two years later Twain released her second album, *The Woman in Me*. It was a critical and commercial success, selling more than 18 million copies and winning a Grammy Award for country album of the year.

For her third album, *Come On Over* (1997), Twain produced chart-topping hits on both the country and pop charts, and the following year she embarked on her first tour of North America. By 1999 *Come On Over* had sold more than 10 million copies, which made Twain the best-selling female country musician and the first female recording artist in any genre to have two consecutive albums top the 10 million mark in copies sold. In 2000 she became a face of the cosmetics company Revlon, appearing in advertisements alongside supermodel Cindy Crawford.

Twain released the highly anticipated *Up!* in 2002. The double album contained both country and pop versions of the songs. Her *Greatest Hits* collection, featuring a duet with country artist Billy Currington, appeared in 2004. The following year Twain debuted a fragrance line. In 2011 she launched the reality television series *Why Not? with Shania Twain* and published the autobiography *From This Moment On*. In the same year, she was inducted into the Canadian Music Hall of Fame and received a star on the Hollywood Walk of Fame.

# BROOKS & DUNN

The American country music duo Brooks & Dunn became a fixture on the music sales charts beginning in the early 1990s. The band comprised Leon Eric ("Kix") Brooks (born May 12, 1955, Shreveport, Louisiana, U.S.) and Ronnie Gene Dunn (born June 1, 1953, Coleman, Texas).

By age six Brooks was playing the ukulele; by the time he was a student at Louisiana State University, he was performing regularly in nightclubs. He moved around the United States, working on the Alaska oil pipeline and at an advertising job in Maine. Finally he went to Nashville, where he took a position on the staff of Tree Publishing, writing hit songs for acts such as Sawyer Brown and the Oak Ridge Boys. He also recorded two solo albums before teaming with Dunn in 1990.

Dunn's father was a musician who also worked on oil rigs; his father's musicianship and his mother's devout Baptist faith were strong influences on him. When he was a student at Abilene (Texas) Christian College, planning to be a preacher, a dean gave him an ultimatum: quit playing music in bars or leave school. Dunn chose music. After winning the Marlboro Country Music Talent Search, he moved to Nashville and signed with Tree Publishing.

Arista Records executive Tim DuBois was familiar with the songwriting talents of both men and introduced them in 1990, suggesting that they write songs together. Both artists had set their sights on solo careers but agreed to give the partnership a try. Their first effort became the title track of the album *Brand New Man* (1991), which also included the hit single "Boot Scootin' Boogie." Their second album, *Hard Workin' Man* (1993), confirmed their popularity, immediately reaching number three on the country music charts. With the laid-back Dunn singing and the wildly energetic Brooks playing guitar, the duo also had strong appeal in concert.

Several times they won the entertainer of the year award, once from the Country Music Association and three times from the Academy of Country Music. From the string of good-time honky-tonk hits of their early years to the slick musicianship of their 2007 album, *Cowboy Town*, Brooks & Dunn parlayed their partnership into extraordinarily consistent success. By 2007, with two Grammy Awards and a host of CMA and ACM awards to their credit, Brooks & Dunn had expanded their musical repertoire, incorporating some straight-ahead rock and roll, covering the occasional classic country hit, and even composing a few sombre ballads. Brooks & Dunn disbanded after their 2010 concert tour, and Dunn released his debut solo album, *Ronnie Dunn*, in 2011.

## FAITH HILL

Faith Hill (born Audrey Faith Perry, September 21, 1967, Jackson, Mississippi, U.S.) grew up in Star, Mississippi, where she began singing at an early age. Her first public performance was at a 4-H luncheon at age seven. Influenced by Elvis Presley, Reba McEntire, and Tammy Wynette, Hill formed a band that played at local rodeos while in high school. At 19 she dropped out of college and moved to Nashville, Tennessee, to pursue a career as a professional singer.

In 1993 Hill released her first album, *Take Me As I Am*, which included two country chart-topping singles, "Wild One" and "Piece of My Heart." Her second album, *It Matters to Me*, appeared in 1995 and

*Faith Hill, 2003.* Airman 1st Class Jason Neal—U.S. Air Force

produced a number one single of the same title. The following year, Hill embarked on the Spontaneous Combustion Tour with fellow country singer Tim McGraw. The two were married within months.

It was Hill's third album—*Faith*—issued in 1998, that propelled her to major stardom. Helped by the crossover success of "This Kiss," a romantic up-tempo song, the album sold five million copies. In the fall of 1998 Hill began appearing as a headliner, and in April 1999 she launched her first major tour as a solo artist.

Hill's fourth album, *Breathe*, appeared in 1999. It debuted at the number one spot on the Billboard country album chart and on the Billboard 200 chart, which measured all music genres. In 2000 Hill sang the national anthem at Super Bowl XXXIV, and she later performed at the Academy Awards. When Hill and McGraw combined talents for a tour that same year, more than one million fans turned out for more than 60 shows. Both the Academy of Country Music and the Country Music Association named Hill top female vocalist for 2000.

After the success of *Breathe*, Hill released *Cry* in 2002 and *Fireflies* in 2005—her fifth and sixth studio albums. Both debuted at the number one spot on the Billboard country album chart. Continuing her crossover success, *Cry* also debuted at the number one spot on the pop chart. To promote *Fireflies*, Hill teamed up with McGraw for another tour in 2006, which became the highest-grossing country music tour to that date.

## TIM MCGRAW

Raised by a single mother, Tim McGraw (born Samuel Timothy Smith, May 1, 1967, Delhi, Louisiana, U.S.) was 11 years old before he discovered that his father was famed

*Tim McGraw, 2007.* PRNewsFoto/Stratosphere Casino Hotel and Tower/AP Images

professional baseball pitcher Tug McGraw. After dropping out of college in 1989 to move to Nashville, he found work as a club performer and signed a record contract with Curb Records in 1990. McGraw's 1993 debut recording was unsuccessful, but his follow-up, *Not a Moment Too Soon*, became the biggest-selling country album of 1994 (and the sixth best-selling album of the year in any genre). His celebrity spread with the release of *All I Want* (1995) and with his high-profile marriage in 1996 to country star Faith Hill. By 2000 he was well-established enough to release a 15-song greatest hits package, and 2001 found McGraw and Hill accepting a Grammy Award for their duet "Let's Make Love."

In 2002 McGraw broke with Nashville convention by recording with his touring band, the Dancehall Doctors (most artists employed session musicians in the studio and road musicians in concert), and by releasing the controversial single "Red Ragtop"; a few country radio stations refused to play the song because its story line involved an abortion. In August 2004 McGraw released the album *Live Like You Were Dying.* Its title song, penned by Nashville songwriters Craig Wiseman and Tim Nichols, was a tribute to McGraw's father, who had died of brain cancer in January 2004. That same year, in a rare collaboration between a contemporary country singer and a hip-hop artist, McGraw lent vocals to rapper Nelly's song "Over and Over," which became a mainstream hit. In 2007 McGraw released the album *Let It Go,* and he followed it two years later with *Southern Voice.*

In addition to his music career, McGraw also acted in several films, including *Friday Night Lights* (2004), *The Blind Side* (2009), and *Country Strong* (2010).

# LEANN RIMES

Lee Ann Rimes (born August 28, 1982, Jackson, Mississippi, U.S.) began singing at age two and won her first competition when she was five. Rimes first gained national exposure on a television talent show, appearing as champion for two weeks on *Star Search* when she was eight. She recorded her first full-length album three years later for a local independent label and was soon signed to Curb Records.

It was with Curb that her career took off, and she topped the charts at age 14 with her rendition of "Blue," a song originally written for country legend Patsy Cline. Her debut album, *Blue* (1996), brought the teenager a pair of Grammy Awards. Her label was quick to capitalize on this success, releasing two albums of cover versions (previously recorded material)—*Unchained Melody: The Early Years* and *You Light Up My Life: Inspirational Songs*—in 1997 before *Sittin' on Top of the World* reached the market the following year. Subsequent albums include the eponymous *LeAnn Rimes* (1999), the pop-tinged *Twisted Angel* (2002), and the European exclusive *Whatever We Wanna* (2006). Rimes's 2007 release *Family* showcased her talents as a songwriter and pushed her total album sales over the 37 million

*LeAnn Rimes performing in 2004.* SrA Jonathan Pomeroy, USAF—U.S. Department of Defense

mark. *Lady & Gentlemen* (2011) deviated from the standard cover album formula by reinterpreting traditionally masculine country songs from a female perspective.

## DIXIE CHICKS

The Dixie Chicks achieved crossover success in the pop and country markets, in spite of controversial political statements made by its members. The group's principal members include Martie Maguire (born October 12, 1969, York, Pennsylvania, U.S.), Emily Robison (born August 16, 1972, Pittsfield, Massachusetts), and Natalie Maines (born October 14, 1974, Lubbock, Texas). Early members of the group included guitarist Robin Lynn Macy, who left in 1992, and vocalist Laura Lynch, who was replaced in 1995 by Maines.

The group released three albums with its original lineup—*Thank Heavens for Dale Evans* (1990), *Little*

*Ol' Cowgirl* (1992), and *Shouldn't a Told You That* (1993). With Martie playing the fiddle and mandolin and her sister Emily on the banjo, guitar, dobro, and bass, the Dixie Chicks became known for their instrumental prowess. Following the arrival of Natalie, the group signed with Monument Records and began to revamp its cowgirl image and sound, eventually emerging as sophisticated performers with a hit country single, "I Can Love You Better" (1997). The trio's debut album, *Wide Open Spaces* (1998), sold more than 12 million copies and was named best country album at the 1998 Grammy Awards. "There's Your Trouble" won the Grammy for best country group vocal performance.

The Dixie Chicks' genre-spanning versatility quickly attracted fans from outside country music. In 1999 they received Grammys for their second album, *Fly* (best country album), and the single "Ready to Run." *Home* (2002), a return to the Chicks' acoustic roots, was named best country album at the 2002 Grammy Awards, where the singles "Long Time Gone" and "L'il Jack Slade" also received awards.

In March 2003, Maines ignited a firestorm by declaring onstage in London that she was ashamed that U.S. Pres. George W. Bush was from her native Texas. Many country music radio stations and radio networks banned the group's music, and Maines received death threats. The Dixie Chicks maintained a relatively low profile until 2006, when they returned with a world tour and the release of *Taking the Long Way*. Several tracks, notably "Not Ready to Make Nice," responded defiantly to the group's detractors, and the album's sound, decidedly more rock than country, clearly signaled the Chicks' desire to move on to new musical possibilities and new audiences. The documentary film *Dixie Chicks: Shut Up & Sing*, released later that year, provided an intimate portrait of the group in the aftermath of Maines's controversial remarks. At the 2007 Grammy Awards, the Dixie Chicks became the first all-female group to win the top three honours: album of the year, song of the year, and record of the year.

## RASCAL FLATTS

American country music trio Rascal Flatts achieved success with a crossover sound that appealed to the pop market. The members are lead vocalist Gary LeVox (born Gary Wayne Vernon, Jr., July 10, 1970, Columbus, Ohio, U.S.), bassist Jay DeMarcus (in full Stanley Wayne DeMarcus, Jr., April 26, 1971, Columbus), and guitarist Joe Don Rooney (born September 13, 1975, Baxter Springs, Kansas).

Cousins LeVox and DeMarcus moved from Columbus, Ohio, to Nashville to pursue musical careers in the mid-1990s. DeMarcus played in the backing band of country vocalist Chely Wright, and he and LeVox performed regularly in the Nashville club scene. When their regular guitarist was unable to appear at a session, DeMarcus recruited Rooney, whom he knew from Wright's band, to join them. The trio had an easy chemistry, and they decided to form Rascal Flatts in 1999. They signed to Disney's Lyric Street Records imprint and released the self-titled *Rascal Flatts* in 2000. The album went platinum on the strength of the group's breakout single "Prayin' for Daylight," which reached number three on the Billboard country chart and broke into the Top 40 on the mainstream pop chart.

The band followed with *Melt* (2002), a ballad-heavy collection that featured "These Days," a single that dominated the country charts and gave the group its first number one hit. *Melt* fared equally well on the country album chart, reaching number one and spending two years in the top 100. This success was surpassed with the trio's subsequent releases—*Feels like Today* (2004), *Me and My Gang* (2006), *Still Feels Good* (2007), and *Unstoppable* (2009)—each of which reached the top of Billboard's all-genre album chart. The hit singles

"What Hurts the Most" (2006), a rueful ballad, and "Life Is a Highway" (2006), a rollicking tune featured on the soundtrack to the animated film *Cars*, contributed to the act's growing mainstream popularity. During this time, Rascal Flatts also won accolades from its peers, collecting the Country Music Association award for best new artist in 2002 and dominating the vocal group category from 2003 to 2008.

After Disney shuttered the Lyric Street label, Rascal Flatts in July 2010 signed with Big Machine Records, best known as the home of country superstar Taylor Swift. The band then released the studio albums *Nothing Like This* (2010) and *Changed* (2012), both of which debuted at number one on the Billboard country album chart.

## BRAD PAISLEY

Brad Paisley (born October 28, 1972, Glen Dale, West Virginia, U.S.) was raised in a small town in West Virginia. At age eight he received a guitar from his grandfather, who had introduced him to country music. After performing in church and at various local events, he formed a band with his guitar teacher. When Paisley was age 12, he caught the attention of the program director of a radio station in nearby Wheeling, who invited him to perform on *Jamboree USA*, the station's long-running live country-music program. For the next eight years he polished his act as a regular on the show. In 1991 Paisley enrolled at West Liberty State College in West Liberty, W.Va.; he later transferred to Belmont University in Nashville, where he earned (1995) a bachelor's degree in music business.

After graduation Paisley worked as a songwriter in Nashville before releasing his debut record, *Who Needs Pictures*, in 1999. The album sold more than one million copies, fueled in part by the ballad "He Didn't Have to Be," an affectionate tribute to stepfathers that was Paisley's first number one hit on the Billboard country singles chart. That same year he made the first of dozens of appearances at Nashville's legendary Grand Ole Opry, into which he was later inducted (2001). In 2001, after being nominated for a Grammy Award for best new artist, Paisley returned with the album *Part II*. The hit single "I'm Gonna Miss Her (The Fishin' Song)" established Paisley's reputation as a playfully witty lyricist, and guest spots from Buck Owens and George Jones highlighted his appreciation for traditional country music at a time when many country artists downplayed the genre's roots in a quest for crossover success.

With the release of such albums as *Mud on the Tires* (2003), *Time Well Wasted* (2005), and *5th Gear* (2007), Paisley's popularity steadily grew. His wide-ranging appeal was partially due to the diversity of material he recorded, from lighthearted novelties such as "Alcohol" and "Ticks" to the Grammy-winning instrumental "Throttleneck" and the elegiac "Whiskey Lullaby," a collaboration with bluegrass singer Alison Krauss. (Among his other duet partners during this period were Dolly Parton and Carrie Underwood.) Furthermore, while Paisley remained devoted to traditional styles—gospel standards routinely appeared on his albums—his lyrics were at times strikingly contemporary, focusing on such subjects as reality television and the Internet.

After the mostly instrumental album *Play* (2008), Paisley recorded *American Saturday Night* (2009), which earned critical plaudits for its casual embrace of attitudes not typically associated with country music. The title track, for instance, was a sly paean to multiculturalism, and on "Welcome to the Future," which Paisley claimed was inspired by the election of Pres. Barack Obama, he marveled at cultural and technological progress. By contrast, *This Is Country Music* (2011) was a more conventional celebration of the genre and its values, though no less impressive in its storytelling and musical artistry.

# TAYLOR SWIFT

Taylor Swift (born December 13, 1989, Wyomissing, Pennsylvania, U.S.) showed an interest in music at an early age, and she progressed quickly from roles in children's theatre to her first appearance before a crowd of thousands. She was age 11 when she sang "The Star-Spangled Banner" before a Philadelphia 76ers basketball game, and the following year she picked up the guitar and began to write songs. Taking her inspiration from artists such as Shania Twain and the Dixie Chicks, Swift crafted original material that reflected her experiences of "tween" alienation. When she was 13, Swift's parents sold their farm in Pennsylvania to move to Hendersonville, Tennessee, so that she could devote more of her time to courting country labels in nearby Nashville.

A development deal with RCA Records allowed Swift to make the acquaintance of recording-industry veterans, and in 2004, at age 14, she signed with Sony/ATV as a songwriter. At venues in the Nashville area, she performed many of the songs she had written, and it was at one such performance that she was noticed by record executive Scott Borchetta. Borchetta signed Swift to his fledgling Big Machine label, and her first single, "Tim McGraw" (inspired by and prominently referencing a song by Swift's favourite country artist), was released in the summer of 2006.

The song was an immediate success, spending eight months on the Billboard country singles chart. Now age 16, Swift followed with a self-titled debut album, and she went on tour, opening for Rascal Flatts. Taylor Swift was certified platinum in 2007, having sold more than one million copies, and Swift continued a rigorous touring schedule, opening for artists such as George Strait, Kenny Chesney, Tim McGraw, and Faith Hill. That November Swift received the Horizon Award for best new artist from the Country Music Association, capping the year in which she emerged as country music's most visible young star.

On Swift's second album, *Fearless* (2008), she demonstrated a refined pop sensibility, managing to court the mainstream pop audience without losing sight of her country roots. *Fearless* opened at number one on the Billboard Top 200 chart and sold 592,000 copies in its first week. It ultimately spent more time atop the Billboard chart than had any album released in the previous 10 years. Singles such as "White Horse" and "Love Story" were popular in the digital market as well, the latter accounting for more than four million paid downloads.

*Taylor Swift, 2009.* PRNewsFoto/Procter & Gamble/AP Images

In 2009 Swift embarked on her first tour as a headliner, playing to sold-out venues across North America. That year also saw Swift dominate the industry award circuit. *Fearless* was recognized as album of the year by the Academy of Country Music in April, and she topped the best female video category for "You Belong with Me" at the MTV Video Music Awards (VMAs) in September. During her VMA acceptance speech, Swift was interrupted by rapper Kanye West, who protested that the award should have gone to Beyoncé for what he called "one of the best videos of all time." Later in the program, when Beyoncé was accepting the award for video of the year, she invited Swift onstage to conclude her speech, a move that drew a standing ovation for both performers. At the CMA Awards that November, Swift won all four categories in which she was nominated. Her recognition as CMA entertainer of the year made her the youngest-ever winner of that award, as well as the first female solo artist to win since 1999. She began 2010 with an impressive showing at the Grammy Awards, where she collected four honours, including best country song, best country album, and the top prize of album of the year.

Later that year Swift made her feature-film debut in the romantic comedy *Valentine's Day* and was named the new spokesperson for CoverGirl cosmetics. Although Swift avoided discussing her personal life in interviews, she was surprisingly frank in her music. Her third album, *Speak Now* (2010), was littered with allusions to romantic relationships with John Mayer, Joe Jonas of the Jonas Brothers, and *Twilight* series actor Taylor Lautner. Swift reclaimed the CMA entertainer of the year award in 2011, and the following year she won Grammys for best country solo performance and best country song for "Mean," a single from Speak Now. She continued her acting career with a voice role in the animated *Dr. Seuss' The Lorax* (2012).

# CHAPTER 13

# Singer-Songwriters: The Next Generation

For singer-songwriters in the postpunk era, genre blending was something of a norm. Roots musicians broke into the mainstream as gospel and bluegrass achieved renewed prominence. "Freak folk" artists mixed world and hip-hop influences with acoustic folk sensibilities to create a engaging musical pastiche. Whether its composers worked with a guitar, a piano, or a tablet computer, the singer-songwriter tradition remained alive and well in the 21st century.

## MAVIS STAPLES

Gospel and soul legend Mavis Staples (born July 10, 1939, Chicago, Illinois, U.S.) was an integral part of the Staple Singers, as well as a successful solo artist. At age 11, Staples joined the Staple Singers, a family gospel-singing group led by her father, Roebuck ("Pops") Staples. As a high school graduate in 1957, she had aspirations of becoming a nurse, but her father persuaded her to stay with the group, which recorded several gospel hits by the early 1960s.

The Staple Singers' transition to soul and rhythm and blues began in the late 1960s, when they signed with Stax Records—the same label on which Staples recorded her solo debut, *Mavis Staples*, in 1969. Her second solo effort, *Only for the Lonely* (1970), included the hit "I Have Learned to Do Without You," but it was the Staple Singers' string of Top 40 hits in the 1970s that made Staples and her family true pop stars. Her solo albums of the late 1970s and '80s did not fare well as she experimented unsuccessfully with disco and electro-pop. *Time Waits for No One* (1989) and *The Voice* (1993), despite critics' praise, also failed to prosper, and Staples's struggle to find a suitable outlet for her music continued. In 1996 she recorded *Spirituals and Gospel: Dedicated to Mahalia Jackson* in honour of Jackson, a close friend and role model. Staples curtailed her musical activity as her father's health declined in the late 1990s. Her first recordings after his death in December 2000 were collaborations with other artists, including Bob Dylan and Los Lobos. Her duet with Dylan, "Gonna Change My Way of Thinking" (2003), was nominated for a Grammy Award.

In 2004 Staples returned to the studio to record *Have a Little Faith* as a tribute to her father, whose influence—musical, parental, and spiritual—was everywhere evident on the album. Included on it was Staples's rendition of "Will the Circle Be Unbroken," a favourite of her father's, as well as "Pops Recipe," which incorporated in its lyrics biographical details from the elder Staples's life and cherished examples of his fatherly advice. *Have a Little Faith* was a surprise hit, and it won the W.C. Handy Awards for best blues album and best soul blues album. Staples also received the award for best female soul blues artist in 2005. These awards were her first as a solo performer. In 2005 the smoky-voiced Staples was also nominated for a Grammy Award for best gospel performance for her duet with Dr. John, "Lay My Burden Down" (2004), and she accepted a Lifetime Achievement Award from the Recording Academy on behalf of the Staple Singers.

Her return to form was further confirmed by *We'll Never Turn Back* (2007). Featuring guest performances by Ry Cooder and Ladysmith Black Mambazo, this collection of reinvented gospel classics played brilliantly to the strengths of Staples's voice and Cooder's guitar. Although her live performances were legendary, she had never released a concert album prior to *Hope at the Hideout* (2008), recorded at a small venue in her hometown of Chicago. Staples's set list, grounded in civil rights anthems and freedom songs, could function as a sort of short course in African American history over the previous half century, and the concert album's title, which echoed one of Barack Obama's presidential campaign slogans, and its release date

(November 4, 2008, the day of the presidential election) indicate that Staples considered herself a witness to history. In 2010 she released *You Are Not Alone*, a collection of gospel standards and new songs that was produced by Wilco frontman Jeff Tweedy. It was a critical success, and the following year Staples's long Grammy drought finally came to an end when *You Are Not Alone* was awarded the Grammy Award for best Americana album.

# T BONE BURNETT

T Bone Burnett (born Joseph Henry Burnett, January 14, 1948, St. Louis, Missouri, U.S.) spent his childhood in Fort Worth, Texas, and it was there that he acquired the nickname "T Bone." He became involved in the local music scene, initially as a guitarist with local blues bands and later as the founder of his own recording studio. He moved to Los Angeles in the early 1970s and recorded his debut solo album, *The B-52 Band & the Fabulous Skylarks* (1972), a straightforward collection of bluesy rock tunes. In 1975 he received his major break into the industry, touring as a guitarist on Bob Dylan's Rolling Thunder Revue tour. His second solo album, *Truth Decay* (1980), shows Burnett's maturation as an artist, but he found greater success in

the production booth than he did as a performer.

In 1984 Burnett produced the critically acclaimed major-label debut from Los Lobos, *How Will the Wolf Survive?*, and soon after he worked with Elvis Costello, whose *King of America* (1986) and *Spike* (1989) feature Burnett as both producer and performer. While these and other projects helped to establish Burnett professionally, his work on *The Turning* (1987), an album by Christian pop artist Leslie Phillips, proved significant personally. Burnett and Phillips—who recorded as Sam on later albums—became involved romantically, and the two were married in 1989 (they divorced in 2004).

Burnett continued to record solo material, with the Grammy Award-nominated *The Criminal Under My Own Hat* (1992) providing an excellent window into Burnett's evolving lyrical sensibilities, but he remained outside the mainstream of popular music. That changed dramatically when he selected and composed the music for the Coen brothers' film *O Brother, Where Art Thou?* (2000). Burnett earned four Grammy Awards and was thrust into the public spotlight. He later won Grammys for the Tony Bennett and k.d. lang duet "A Wonderful World" (2002) and for the soundtrack of the Johnny Cash biopic *Walk the Line* (2005). In 2009

Burnett received three Grammys for his work on the Alison Krauss and Robert Plant album *Raising Sand* and one award for B.B. King's *One Kind Favor*.

Although *Raising Sand* boasted impressive sales and near-universal critical acclaim, Burnett was unimpressed with the sound quality of the final recording. In an era in which many producers were mixing music to be louder and denser for the low-fidelity iPod and ringtone markets, Burnett returned to the basics of audio engineering on subsequent albums, using his XOΔE (rendered in English as "CODE") technology. CODE offered a listening experience that replicated the original studio master recording as faithfully as possible, with no additional cost to the consumer. CODE audio DVDs were included in the standard CD package, and listeners could thus compare the two formats side-by-side. CODE was further refined for the 2009 debut album from the psychedelic rock supergroup Moonalice.

That year Burnett also worked with Costello on the album *Secret, Profane & Sugarcane* and produced the Jeff Bridges film *Crazy Heart*, a project for which he also scored the soundtrack. The film's title track, "The Weary Kind (Theme from *Crazy Heart*)," dominated the awards circuit, as Burnett and Ryan Bingham collected an Academy Award, a Golden Globe (2010), and a Grammy (2011). Burnett also won a Grammy in 2011 for his production work on the *Crazy Heart* soundtrack.

Although he spent most of the 1990s and early 2000s involved in producing, Burnett continued to perform. His later albums include *True False Identity* (2006) and *Tooth of Crime* (2008).

# BONNIE RAITT

Bonnie Raitt (born November 8, 1949, Burbank, California, U.S.) embraced a wide musical range that included blues, folk, rhythm and blues, pop, and country rock. Touring and recording with some of the leading session musicians and songwriters of her day, she became a successful recording artist in the 1970s but did not achieve stardom until 1990, when she won four Grammy Awards—three for her 10th album, *Nick of Time* (1989).

Raised in Los Angeles by Quaker parents who were active in music and liberal politics (her father was Broadway musical star John Raitt), Raitt attended Radcliffe College, Cambridge, Massachusetts, from 1967 to 1969 but dropped out to join the East Coast blues and folk music scene. From the start of her career, she played alongside classic blues performers such as Sippie Wallace and Arthur ("Big Boy") Crudup as well as folk rock contemporaries such as Jackson Browne and Little Feat. Her first three albums largely comprised traditional blues material and introduced Raitt's supple phrasing, feminist stance, and keen abilities as a slide guitarist. In 1973 she began recording more-polished pop material, culminating in her first hit single, a 1977 reworking of Del Shannon's "Runaway." Raitt toured extensively and remained politically active, often performing at high-profile charity concerts, such as the 1979 antinuclear benefit sponsored by Musicians United for Safe Energy, an organization she cofounded.

Raitt's career declined somewhat in the 1980s as she struggled with alcoholism but soared again when *Nick of Time* (produced by Don Was) reached the top of the charts in 1990 following its Grammy success. Her popularity continued with the release of a retrospective collection later in 1990 and then *Luck of the Draw* (1991) and *Longing in Their Hearts* (1994), both of which received Grammy Awards. Raitt's other recordings include the double-disc live set *Road Tested* (1995) and the studio albums *Fundamental* (1998), *Souls Alike* (2005), and *Slipstream* (2012). She was inducted into the Rock and Roll Hall of Fame in 2000.

# LUCINDA WILLIAMS

Lucinda Williams (born January 26, 1953, Lake Charles, Louisiana, U.S.), whose father was the poet Miller Williams, began writing songs after borrowing a guitar at age 12. She later studied guitar and then voice, but she never learned to read music. Early musical influences included Joni Mitchell, Joan Baez, and especially Bob Dylan. Miller Williams introduced his daughter to some of his friends, among them the notable writers Allen Ginsberg, Flannery O'Connor, and James Dickey; this exposure strongly influenced her lyrics.

In 1979, having built a solid foundation of live performance, Williams recorded *Ramblin' on My Mind*, an album of folk, country, and blues standards that was reissued in 1991 as *Ramblin'*. She recorded only original songs for her next effort, *Happy Woman Blues* (1980); neither album drew much attention. Williams began working with a series of record labels, none of them for long; major labels proved incompatible with her perfectionism, and several minor labels that she worked with went out of business.

Her big break came in 1988 with the release of *Lucinda Williams*. Widely hailed as a classic, it revealed her growing confidence as a songwriter. The emotional intensity of the songs was underscored by Williams's rough-edged singing, which, though lacking in range, resonated with both vulnerability and power. *Sweet Old World*, a folk-infused collection that included songs of suicide and regret, came out in 1992. That same year, Mary Chapin Carpenter covered Williams's "Passionate Kisses," a single from her self-titled album. Carpenter's version earned Williams a Grammy Award for country song of the year.

Williams's legendary perfectionism was evident during the recording of her fifth album, *Car Wheels on a Gravel Road*. Her initial unhappiness with the work led to a number of delays, and it was not released until 1998. The album brought Williams her first real commercial success. Universally acclaimed, *Car Wheels on a Gravel Road* also won a Grammy for best contemporary folk album. In 2001 she released the understated *Essence*. It featured the song "Get Right with God," which earned Williams a Grammy for best female rock vocal. *World Without Tears* (2003) was her first album to debut in the top 20 of Billboard's Top 200 albums chart.

With the enthusiastic reception in 2007 of the hit album *West*, Williams seemed to have finally earned the high level of commercial success that many believed she deserved. It was followed by *Little Honey* (2008) and *Blessed* (2011), both of which also found acclaim.

# NICK CAVE

Nick Cave (born September 22, 1957, Wangaratta, Australia) played a prominent role in the postpunk movement as front man for the bands the Birthday Party and the Bad Seeds. He is best known for his haunting ballads about life, love, betrayal, and death.

Cave and school friend Mick Harvey formed the Boys Next Door in the mid-1970s in Melbourne with guitarist Rowland Howard, bassist Tracy Pew, and drummer Phil Calvert. The band released several records before relocating to London in 1980 and changing its name to the Birthday Party. Known for its ferocious and intense live shows, the Birthday Party quickly earned a cult following and appeared on John Peel's British Broadcasting Corporation radio program, leading to a record contract with 4AD and the release of their signature album, *Junkyard* (1982).

Following the Birthday Party's breakup in 1983, Cave and Harvey went on to form Nick Cave and the Bad Seeds in Berlin with former Magazine bassist Barry Adamson and Einstürzende Neubauten front man Blixa Bargeld. The Bad Seeds combined the Birthday Party's dark intensity with a passionate exploration of love and the pain it can bring. The band's biggest commercial success was "Where the Wild Roses Grow," a collaboration with the Australian singer Kylie Minogue, from the 1996 album *Murder Ballads*. Bargeld left the Bad Seeds in 2003, but the release of the double album *Abattoir Blues/The Lyre of Orpheus* (2004) signaled that the group was alive and as creatively ambitious as ever. In 2006 Cave formed Grinderman, a Bad Seeds side project that tempered the rage of the Birthday Party with caustic, self-deprecating humour. In between the release of Grinderman's two eponymous albums (2007 and 2010), the Bad Seeds returned to the studio, producing the critically acclaimed *Dig!!! Lazarus Dig!!!* (2008). In 2009 Harvey split with Cave and the Bad Seeds, ending one of the most enduring partnerships in the postpunk era. Cave announced the end of Grinderman two years later.

Cave published the novels *And the Ass Saw the Angel* (1989), a Southern Gothic tale, and *The Death of Bunny Munro* (2009). He also occasionally worked in film. With Bad Seeds member Warren Ellis, he composed scores for such movies as *The Proposition* (2005), *The Assassination of Jesse James by the Coward Robert Ford* (2007), and *The Road* (2009). In addition, he penned the screenplay for *The Proposition*, which earned him a special prize from the 2006 Venice Film Festival. Cave's acting credits include the films *Ghosts...of the Civil Dead* (1988), which he also cowrote, and *Johnny Suede* (1991).

## DAVID BYRNE

While attending the Rhode Island School of Design in the mid-1970s, David Byrne (born May 14, 1952, Dumbarton, Dunbartonshire, Scotland) cofounded the art-rock group Talking Heads, acting as its principal singer and guitarist. Identified with the punk and new wave movements, the band released their debut album, *Talking Heads '77*, in 1977. It was followed by releases that reflected Byrne's interest in experimental pop and African rhythms, including *Speaking in Tongues* (1983), *Stop Making Sense* (soundtrack for film of the same name; 1984), and solo albums such as *Rei Momo* (1989).

Also an ethnomusicologist and producer, Byrne wrote the score for choreographer Twyla Tharp's *The Catherine Wheel* (1980) and directed the film *True Stories* (1986). In 1988 he established Luka Bop Records to introduce U.S. audiences to world music. Later solo releases include *Uh-Oh* (1992), *Grown Backwards* (2004), and *Everything That Happens Will Happen Today* (2008), a collaboration with Brian Eno, who had worked earlier with the Talking Heads and with whom Byrne had released the groundbreaking *My Life in the Bush of Ghosts* (1981). An avid urban cyclist and world traveler, Byrne chronicled his two-wheeled experiences in *Bicycle Diaries* (2009).

# ALANIS MORISSETTE

Alanis Morissette (born June 1, 1974, Ottawa, Ontario, Canada) began studying piano at age six and composing at seven; she wrote her first songs at nine. By age 10 she was acting in *You Can't Do That on Television*, a series on the children's television network Nickelodeon. She used her earnings from that show to cut her first single. At age 14 Morissette signed a song-publishing deal that led to two dance-pop albums, *Alanis* (1991), which sold 100,000 copies and earned her Canada's Juno Award for most promising female vocalist of the year, and *Now Is the Time* (1992), which sold more than 50,000 copies.

Escaping from the pressures of her then-fading teen career, Morissette left home after high school to create a more satisfying and authentic style. She eventually settled in Los Angeles, where she met Glen Ballard, a veteran songwriter-producer. Together the two wrote and recorded *Jagged Little Pill* (1995) in record speed and at negligible cost. The album featured the explosive single "You Oughta Know," a searing fantasy of revenge against an unfaithful lover. She signed with Madonna's label, Maverick, and *Jagged Little Pill*, which Morissette considered to be her real debut, sold more than 14 million copies and remained atop the international billboard charts throughout 1995 and 1996. In 1996 Morissette won Grammy Awards for album of the year, best rock album, best rock song (songwriter), and best female rock performance.

Morissette's follow-up, *Supposed Former Infatuation Junkie*, which she coproduced, appeared in 1998. Featuring Eastern-influenced music, the album was noted for its ballads and catchy pop songs. In 1999 her single "Uninvited" for the film *City of Angels* (1998) won two Grammy Awards, including best rock song. Morissette returned to the recording studio (without producer Ballard) for *Under Rug Swept* (2002), a confessional album that received mixed reviews. *So-Called Chaos* (2004) also failed to re-create the critical and commercial success Morissette had enjoyed in the mid-1990s. In 2005, 10 years after *Jagged Little Pill*'s release, Morissette took it on tour as an acoustic act and released an album version, *Jagged Little Pill Acoustic* (2005).

In addition to working on her music, Morissette continued to act occasionally. In 1993 she made her film debut with an uncredited role in *Anything for Love* (1993). She later portrayed God in Kevin Smith's *Dogma* (1998). Her television work included appearances on the HBO series *Sex and the City* (2000), *Curb Your Enthusiasm* (2002), and *Nip/Tuck* (2006), as well as on the Showtime series *Weeds* (beginning in 2009).

## SINÉAD O'CONNOR

Sinéad O'Connor (born December 8, 1966, Dublin, Ireland) is known for her onstage intensity, shaven head, and alternately searing and soothing voice. She was sent to a succession of boarding schools as a child and quit at age 16 to attend the College of Music in Dublin. She sang with pub-rock band Ton Ton Macoute in 1985 before embarking on a solo career.

Her debut album *The Lion and the Cobra* (1987) won critical praise and received heavy play on college radio. Her sophomore effort, the largely autobiographical *I Do Not Want What I Haven't Got* (1990), shot to the top of the U.S. pop charts. That album produced O'Connor's biggest single, a cover of Prince's "Nothing Compares 2 U." The accompanying video, which featured an arresting extended close-up of O'Connor's face, was honoured numerous times at the 1990 MTV Video Music Awards. She joined Public Enemy in a boycott of the 1991 Grammy Awards ceremony and refused to accept the award for best alternative music performance.

While supporting her torch song collection *Am I Not Your Girl?* (1992), O'Connor appeared on the television show *Saturday Night Live*, concluding her performance by tearing a picture of Pope John Paul II in half. The gesture triggered a massive backlash against the singer. In spite of positive critical reviews of subsequent releases, including *Universal Mother* (1994), *Sean-Nós Nua* (2002), and *How About I Be Me (and You Be You)?* (2012), O'Connor's later work would fail to match the popularity of her early 1990s output.

## SARAH MCLACHLAN

Sarah McLachlan (born January 28, 1968, Halifax, Nova Scotia, Canada) received classical training in guitar, piano, and voice. Rebelling against a conservative upbringing, she focused her musical talents on the popular punk and new-wave music movements of the 1980s. She was discovered by an executive at a Canadian record label when she was 17 and the lead singer of the October Game. After two years at the Nova Scotia College of Art and Design, McLachlan moved to Vancouver, signed a recording contract, and released her debut album, *Touch*, in 1988. The critically acclaimed recording was followed by such other albums as *Solace* (1991), *Fumbling Towards Ecstasy* (1993), and *The Freedom Sessions* (1995), all of which showcased McLachlan's talents as a singer, guitarist, and songwriter. Her fans were immediately drawn to her vocal range and the intense emotion that came to define her music.

These qualities were evident in *Surfacing* (1997), an extremely personal album that was written after months of soul searching. The candidness of such songs as "Sweet Surrender" and "Building a Mystery" earned McLachlan Grammy Awards for best female pop vocal performance and best pop instrumental. She also received Juno (Canadian Music) Awards for best album, best female vocalist, single of the year, and songwriter of the year.

In 1997 McLachlan also helped found Lilith Fair, which brought together some of the most talented and popular women artists in the music industry, including Jewel, Tracy Chapman, and Paula Cole. With the success of the festival, McLachlan proved to wary record executives that women artists were as marketable as their male counterparts. Lilith Fair toured until 1999. Although the festival was revived in 2010, poor ticket sales led to the cancellation of numerous dates, and McLachlan confirmed that Lilith Fair would not return the following year. McLachlan's later albums include *Mirrorball* (1999), which featured live performances; *Afterglow* (2003); and *Wintersong* (2006), a collection of Christmas music.

McLachlan served as a spokesperson for the American Society for the Prevention of Cruelty to Animals (ASPCA), and she appeared in a television commercial that proved to be one of that organization's most effective fund-raising efforts. With narration by McLachlan, and musical accompaniment by her single "Angel," the two-minute spot featured images of dogs and cats in need of a home. The deeply affecting ad generated tens of millions of dollars for the ASPCA.

## BJÖRK

Björk (born Björk Gudmundsdottir, November 21, 1965, Reykjavík, Iceland) recorded her first solo album, a collection of cover versions of popular songs, as an 11-year-old music student in 1977. Throughout her teens she performed with various short-lived bands, ending up at age 18 with Kukl, a punk group that eventually became the Sugarcubes. With Björk as lead vocalist, the Sugarcubes won acclaim in the United Kingdom with their first album, *Life's Too Good* (1986). After recording two more albums over the next five years, *Here Today, Tomorrow, Next Week!* and *Stick Around for Joy*, the band broke up, and Björk embarked on a solo career.

After moving to London, Björk released *Debut*, her first international solo album, in 1993. It was a departure from the harder-edged sound of the Sugarcubes and included a wide variety of musical styles ranging from techno-pop to jazz. *Debut* produced a number of hit singles, including "Big Time Sensuality" and "Venus as a Boy." Her follow-up, *Post* (1995), opened with the single "Army of Me," a characteristically throbbing, synthesized track accompanied by the singer's now-familiar breathy yodel. Never content to conform, Björk in 1997 released her most experimental works to date: *Telegram*, an entire album of *Post* remixes, and *Homogenic*, a studio effort with collaborator Mark Bell. Bell and Björk also worked together on Selmasongs, the score for Lars von Trier's *Dancer in the Dark* (2000), a tragic musical in which she also starred. The film won the Palme d'Or at the Cannes film festival, and Björk was named best actress.

In 2001 Björk released the quiet and hypnotic *Vespertine*. Her first studio album in four years, it refrained from pushing the musical boundaries that had made her a star of the 1990s and instead focused on a more rhythmic, contemplative intimacy. *Medúla* (2004) was an all-vocals and vocal samples-based album that featured beatboxers (vocal-percussion artists), Icelandic and British choirs, and traditional Inuit vocalists, while the similarly eclectic *Volta* (2007) boasted sombre brass arrangements, African rhythms, and guest production from Timbaland. For the ethereal *Biophilia* (2011), Björk used tablet computers to help her compose songs, which were released, in addition to conventional formats, as a series of interactive iPhone and iPad apps. Björk performed "Oceania," a single from *Medúla*, at the 2004 Summer Olympics in Athens. She also composed the soundtrack for her romantic partner Matthew Barney's film *Drawing Restraint 9* (2005).

As a response to the financial turmoil that rocked Iceland in 2008, Björk partnered with an Icelandic venture capital firm to establish a fund that would invest in socially and ecologically responsible businesses. She was awarded the Polar Music Prize for lifetime achievement by the Royal Swedish Academy of Music in 2010.

## JEFF BUCKLEY

Jeff Buckley (born November 17, 1966, Orange county, California—died May 29, 1997, Memphis, Tennessee) created a legacy that far outstripped his tragically brief career.

His multioctave voice was compared to that of his father, the late Tim Buckley, and he attracted a devoted international following. His one full album, *Grace* (1994), featured what is probably his best-known song, a haunting cover of Leonard Cohen's "Hallelujah." He had just begun working on his second album when he drowned in the Mississippi River.

# BECK

Beck (born Beck David Campbell, also called Beck David Hansen, July 8, 1970, Los Angeles, California, U.S.) had art in his genes: his family included a mother (Bibbe Hansen) with ties to Andy Warhol's Factory, a musician father (David Campbell) who would go on to arrange strings for several alternative rockers, and a grandfather (Al Hansen) who was active in the 1960s art movement Fluxus. After a brief excursion into the "anti-folk" scene of New York City's East Village, Beck returned to his native Los Angeles, where he played at coffeehouses in the Silverlake district.

"Loser," recorded as a cheap demo for Bong Load Custom Records, became a radio hit in Los Angeles and eventually, after Beck had signed with major label DGC, a national phenomenon. A rapped lyric performed over a slide-guitar sample, with impressive poetic juxtapositions such as "drive-by body pierce," "Loser" revealed a major talent, though Beck would find himself pigeonholed at first as a Generation X novelty act. The rest of *Mellow Gold*, his 1994 debut album, proved his mastery at a twanged-out meld of folk, rap, 1960s rock, and pop corniness of every vintage.

Beck's unusual contract allowed him to record for other labels: the more traditionally folk *One Foot in the Grave* came out on K and the noisy *Stereopathic Soul Manure* on Flipside (both were released in 1994). But he achieved culture hero status with *Odelay*, his 1996 major label follow-up. Produced by the Dust Brothers, who had helmed the similarly crackpot Beastie Boys album *Paul's Boutique* (1989), *Odelay* stressed hip-hop and sampling even more than *Mellow Gold* had, including the single "Where It's At" (with its memorable chorus, "I've got two turntables and a microphone"). It established Beck as the leading alternative rocker for an audience that had grown weary of the earnestness of grunge. Adding to his palette, Beck explored the sophistication of Brazilian pop on his next album, 1998's *Mutations* (in part named after the psychedelic Brazilian group Os Mutantes). His return to beat-heavy abstract pop, *Midnite Vultures* (1999), which leaned more heavily than ever

*Beck, 2006.* Scott Gries/Getty Images

in a pseudo-rhythm-and-blues direction (Beck at this point was fond of unveiling James Brown-style and break-dance steps in his live show), was a commercial disappointment. Somewhat like David Byrne before him, Beck had so thoroughly conceptualized his art that the results were emotionally desiccated.

Alternately lush and spare, the melancholic follow-up, *Sea Change* (2002), containing some of Beck's most personal lyrics, met with some of the best reviews of his career. The tour in support of the album found the Flaming Lips sharing the bill and the stage (as backing band) with Beck. With his 2005 release, *Guero*, Beck was back to collaborating with the Dust Brothers and back to genre-hopping, as his musical scavenging led to the incorporation of elements of blues, Latin American music, rap-rock, and 1970s rhythm and blues; *Guerolito*, a track-by-track set of deluxe remixes of *Guero* by a host of other producers and performers, was released later in the year. Best known for his work with Radiohead, *Sea Change*'s producer, Nigel Godrich, brought a spacey psychedelic gloss to *The Information* (2006), which came replete with stickers that invited listeners to create a do-it-yourself jewel box cover to mirror Beck's upbeat musical pastiche. Beck teamed with Danger Mouse on *Modern Guilt* (2008), a darkly introspective collection punctuated with '60s guitar riffs.

## SHERYL CROW

Although Sheryl Crow (born February 11, 1962, Kennett, Missouri, U.S.) paid her dues for 10 years, writing songs and singing backup for various big-name artists, her own breakthrough debut album, *Tuesday Night Music Club* (1993), took off quickly once her pop single, "All I Wanna Do," became the anthem of a generation who really did just want to have fun, as the song's lyrics affirmed. Her raspy voice, rock-and-roll rhythm, and country-styled guitar playing reflected the influences of the Rolling Stones, Bessie Smith, Billie Holiday, and Bob Dylan.

Born in a small farming town across the Mississippi River from Memphis, Tennessee, she grew up in a home surrounded by music. Her mother, Bernice, and father, Wendell, a lawyer, played piano and trumpet on weekends for jazz bands. Sheryl began playing piano at 5, and by 6 she could play by ear. She composed her first song at age 13. During high school she learned guitar from playing with local rock bands. She attended the University of Missouri, in Columbia, where she majored in music composition, performance, and teaching. Upon graduation in 1984, she moved to St. Louis, where she taught music to children with special needs. In 1986 she decided to pursue her ambition of making it big in the music industry and moved to Los Angeles.

Crow talked her way into auditions for a tour with Michael Jackson. On the basis of a video audition she was selected by Jackson to accompany his Bad World Tour. For two years she traveled with Jackson and his entourage. She continued writing songs, and her compositions were recorded by artists such as Wynonna Judd and Eric Clapton. As a backup singer she worked with a number of bands, including Foreigner, Stevie Wonder, Rod Stewart, Sting, and Don Henley. It was Henley who encouraged her to perform her own music. For the next three years, she concentrated on her songwriting, but she became disillusioned and suffered a deep depression. After intensive therapy she eventually went back to work.

She signed with A & M Records, who wanted to put out her first album in 1992. The record, however, lacked a strong identity, and A & M decided to scrap the project.

On Tuesday nights she began to meet with a group of songwriters who would gather for creative sessions in a warehouse. The group, which became the Tuesday Night Music Club, attempted to finish a song each night before they went home. The first time she attended one of these sessions they wrote "Leaving Las Vegas," one of the original compositions that would later be part of her debut album, *Tuesday Night Music Club*. The album garnered widespread critical praise, but it was the enormous popularity of "All I Wanna Do" that put her on the charts. At the 1994 Grammy Awards she received three awards: best new artist, best record, and best pop vocal performance by a female for "All I Wanna Do."

Crow toured with John Hiatt and the Eagles, finally achieving national recognition when she performed at festivals such as the H.O.R.D.E. tour and Woodstock '94. Following up on the success of *Tuesday Night Music Club*, she sang with Mick Jagger on the Rolling Stones' concert special and played at the annual White Nights music festival in St. Petersburg, Russia. Released in 1996, Crow's self-titled follow-up album was a massive hit, producing the singles "Everyday Is a Winding Road" and "If It Makes You Happy." It earned her two more Grammy Awards, including a trophy for album of the year. Her later releases included *C'mon, C'mon* (2002), *Wildflower* (2005), and *100 Miles from Memphis* (2010).

## ALISON KRAUSS

Alison Krauss (born July 23, 1971, Champaign, Illinois, U.S.) began studying classical violin at age five but proved to be a bluegrass prodigy. A flamboyant fiddler, she won several contests, led a band when she was 10, won the Illinois State Fiddling Championship two years later, and signed a recording contract at age 14. In 1990 she won a Grammy Award for her third album, *I've Got That Old Feeling*.

The first incarnation of Krauss's backing band, Union Station, included her bass-playing older brother, Viktor, who later joined Lyle Lovett's backing band. As Union Station evolved and changed, Krauss's soprano singing became a primary element in its success. By 1995 the ensemble was a leading bluegrass act with the breakthrough album *Now That I've Found You* and the hit single "When You Say Nothing at All." Each of Krauss's successive efforts became best sellers as well, and her performances on the soundtracks for the films *O Brother, Where Art Thou?* (2000) and *Cold Mountain* (2003) helped to introduce bluegrass to a new audience.

In 2004 the million-selling *Alison Krauss + Union Station Live* was awarded the Grammy for best bluegrass album; "Cluck Old Hen," which showcased Krauss's fiddle, won best country instrumental; and her duet with pop artist James Taylor, "How's the World Treating You," was named best country collaboration with vocals. With those wins, Krauss passed soul legend Aretha Franklin to become the female artist with the most Grammys. She earned an additional three Grammy Awards for *Lonely Runs Both Ways* (2004) and another for the duet "Gone Gone Gone" with Led Zeppelin front man Robert Plant. That single appeared on the album *Raising Sand* (2007), a project that brought together Krauss, Plant, and producer T-Bone Burnett. Burnett, who had worked with Krauss on the *O Brother, Where Art Thou?* and *Cold Mountain* soundtracks, crafted a sound that was equal parts Appalachian roots music, power pop, and guitar-driven rock, tied together by the distinctive vocals of Krauss and Plant. The album was a massive crossover success, hitting number two on the Billboard pop and country charts, and it earned five Grammy Awards for the duo, including record of the year and album of the year. Krauss achieved a Grammy milestone in 2012, when *Paper Airplane* (2011), a work that teamed her with Union Station for the first time since 2004, won best bluegrass album. With 28 total Grammy Awards, Krauss surpassed Quincy Jones to claim the title of living artist with the most Grammys.

## NORAH JONES

Norah Jones (born Geetali Norah Jones Shankar, March 30, 1979, New York, New York, U.S.), the daughter of American concert producer

Sue Jones and Indian sitar virtuoso Ravi Shankar, lived with her mother and grew up in a suburb of Dallas, where her mother's vast collection of music was an early inspiration for her own eclectic taste. She first achieved national recognition by winning three *Down Beat* Student Music Awards as a jazz and vocal novice at Booker T. Washington High School for Performing and Visual Arts. After studying jazz at North Texas State University for two years, Jones dropped out and moved to Manhattan in 1999. There she sang and played in the underground music scene, meeting and collaborating with the musicians who would eventually become known as her band. In 2001 she signed a recording contract with Blue Note Records.

Jones debuted in 2002 with *Come Away with Me*, a mellow, acoustic pop album featuring several recognized jazz musicians. A critical and commercial success, the album eventually sold more than 20 million copies worldwide, and it earned eight Grammy Awards, including album of the year, best new artist, and song of the year ("Don't Know Why," written by her guitarist Jesse Harris). Later in 2003, in the midst of extensive touring and television appearances, Jones issued a concert DVD, Live in New Orleans.

Between working on her first and second albums, Jones formed the side project Little Willies, a band of five friends who shared a taste for classic American music such as that of Willie Nelson and Hank Williams. Little Willies—comprising Jones, Jones's bassist Lee Alexander, Richard Julian, Dan Rieser, and Jim Campilongo—performed mostly cover songs; their eponymous album appeared in 2006.

In 2004 Jones released her second album, *Feels Like Home*. It debuted at number one on the Billboard charts and sold more than one million copies by the end of the first week. Like its predecessor, *Feels Like Home* featured Jones's quiet voice set against intimate, jazz-inspired acoustics. After little promotional touring and few public appearances, Jones released her third album, *Not Too Late*, in 2007. The album, recorded in her home studio, was the first for which Jones was involved in the writing process of every song. In 2007 Jones also made her acting debut, starring in *My Blueberry Nights*; the movie premiered at the Cannes film festival. Her later albums included the indie-flavored *The Fall* (2009) and the breakup-themed *Little Broken Hearts* (2012), which featured production by Danger Mouse.

## ANDREW BIRD

Andrew Bird (born July 11, 1973, Chicago, Illinois, U.S.) was immersed in music from early childhood. He began taking Suzuki-method violin lessons at age four and later earned a degree (1996) in violin performance from Northwestern University, Evanston, Illinois. He chafed at the rigid expectations of the classical music world, however, and after graduation supported himself by playing his instrument everywhere from weddings to Renaissance fairs. Having developed an interest in vintage jazz, he soon fell in with the popular swing-revival band the Squirrel Nut Zippers, appearing on three of their albums in the late 1990s. In the meantime, he landed a recording contract of his own.

Andrew Bird's Bowl of Fire, as his new Chicago-based band became known, won critical notice for its impressive command and fusion of early 20th-century musical idioms, drawing on traditions as varied as swing-era jazz, calypso, German cabaret, and Central European folk songs over the course of three full-length albums, *Thrills* (1998), *Oh! The Grandeur* (1999), and *The Swimming Hour* (2001). The band failed to catch on among audiences, though, and Bird consequently decided to strike out on his own.

After testing the waters with a series of solo gigs, Bird recorded *Weather Systems* (2003) at his family's rural Illinois farm. The album marked a turning point in his songwriting; the idiosyncratic pre-rock-and-roll touches were now filtered through a sound that owed more to contemporary folk and pop-rock music than his previous pastiche-driven work had. (He also, notably, revealed a knack for whistling.) Bird expanded his fan base by frequently opening for more famous musicians (he called the 30-minute performances "guerrilla attacks"), and widespread praise for his next record, *The Mysterious Production of Eggs* (2005), brought him further attention. The success continued with the sprawling *Armchair Apocrypha* (2007), which sold more than 100,000 copies—a considerable number for an independent release. In 2009 Bird released *Noble Beast*, and its debut at number 12 on the Billboard album chart marked a career high. He returned with *Break It Yourself* (2012), which found him partially abandoning the oblique wordplay that distinguished his previous work in favour of greater emotional directness.

## DEVENDRA BANHART

American singer-songwriter Devendra Banhart (born May 30, 1981, Houston, Texas, U.S.) blended acoustic folk, psychedelia, and stream-of-consciousness lyrics into a burgeoning early 21st-century musical aesthetic often termed "freak folk." Banhart tends to write and perform his own music, but he occasionally collaborates with like-minded musical acts, such as CocoRosie and Feathers.

Banhart was born in the United States but spent the first part of his life in Caracas, and this Latin American experience is evident in both his occasional use of Spanish lyrics and the echoes of tropicália in some of his compositions, though that Brazilian musical genre is but one of the many eclectic artforms that have influenced Banhart's music and performance. In addition to employing disparate musical styles, Banhart, who studied for a time at San Francisco Art Institute, also borrows from a variety of literary and visual artforms. His flexible approach to songwriting, coupled with his penchant for the unusual or surreal, has led to several critically acclaimed albums. The first to bring him to wide attention was *Oh Me Oh My...* (2002), an extension of the distinctly personal "lo-fi" recordings he first made on four-track recorders. As his popularity grew (not to mention his beard and hair; the oft-barefooted Banhart is famously hirsute), Banhart's albums became increasingly complex and include *Niño Rojo* and *Rejoicing in the Hands* (both 2004), *Cripple Crow* (2005), and *Smokey Rolls Down Thunder Canyon* (2007). The musical genre that has developed around

him has been variously branded neo-folk, psych-folk, and freak folk, and though those associated with it—including Banhart, Joanna Newsom, Vetvier, Feathers, and the Espers—resist easy categorization, many of them have drawn inspiration from British folk and psychedelic artists from the 1960s and '70s, including the Incredible String Band, Vashti Bunyan, Pentangle, Fairport Convention, Bert Jansch, Nick Drake, and Syd Barrett of Pink Floyd.

## JOHN MAYER

Having taken up guitar playing as a teenager, John Mayer (born October 16, 1977, Bridgeport, Connecticut, U.S.) briefly attended Boston's Berklee College of Music but never completed his studies. Moving to Atlanta, Georgia, he played frequently in local clubs with a band and as a solo act. In 1999 he independently released his debut EP, *Inside Wants Out*. After a 2000 performance at the South by Southwest music festival in Austin, Texas, he signed with the Aware record label, which released the full-length album *Room for Squares* (2001). Columbia Records repackaged the album with additional material for a much higher-profile national release later in 2001. The song "Your Body Is a Wonderland" became a major hit on adult alternative radio stations and earned Mayer

John Mayer, 2008. © Patty Keigan

broaden the scope of his sound. Incorporating his long-standing interest in the blues, he formed the John Mayer Trio, and he also collaborated with rappers Common and Kanye West. *Continuum* (2006), reflecting this new approach, earned Mayer a Grammy for best pop vocal album (to go with one for best male pop vocal performance for "Waiting on the World to Change") and climbed to number two on the Billboard pop chart. He continued to be a Grammy favourite in 2009, picking up awards for best male pop vocal performance (for the single "Say" from *Continuum*) and for best solo rock performance (for "Gravity," from the 2008 live album *Where the Light Is*). During the recording of *Born and Raised* (2012), Mayer was surgically treated for a growth near his vocal cords. Although he was able to complete the album, the recurrence of the growth after the surgery forced him to postpone the resumption of his singing career indefinitely.

a Grammy Award for best male pop vocal performance. Mayer's next studio release, *Heavier Things* (2003), topped the Billboard pop chart and featured the hit "Daughters," which was honoured with two Grammy Awards, including song of the year.

Having established himself as a major presence in the world of adult alternative rock, Mayer sought to

# CHAPTER 14

# Rock in the Age of iTunes

Rock musicians in the first decade of the 21st century found themselves in a paradoxical situation. On the one hand, the business model that had driven (and been driven by) the rise of rock since the late 1960s—the hugely profitable manufacture, promotion, and distribution of albums—seemed to be in terminal crisis. On the other hand, the live music sector, long regarded as uncompetitive commercially and therefore dependent on record company support, flourished. The prices people were prepared to pay for concert tickets rose dramatically from the mid-1990s, and a new kind of multinational music corporation emerged, led by Live Nation, the live-music division of Clear Channel.

If the value of live music rose as the amount of money people were prepared to spend on CDs in the digital age fell, at least part of the live music industry's new profitability was an effect of its own use of digital technology. New Internet-based ticketing companies became significant international businesses in themselves. Clear Channel spun off Live Nation as an independent company in order to avoid accusations of monopoly, but Live Nation's subsequent merger with Ticketmaster, the dominant global ticketing agency, led to new concerns about competitiveness. Though the merger was ultimately approved by the U.S. government in January 2010, Live Nation Entertainment (as the combined corporate entity would be known) was required to license its proprietary ticketing software to its largest competitor, Anschutz Entertainment Group (AEG), and to sell its Paciolan ticketing and event management division to Comcast Spectacor, a subsidiary of media giant Comcast.

Crucial to the shift in the live-music economy was the crowd-drawing power of classic rock acts such as the Rolling Stones and the Police, whose tours topped annual earnings lists. While live shows had once been subsidized by record companies' promotional budgets—live performance being used to sell records—now tours were the source of the major rock groups' continued income, and new recordings were released to promote new tours. David Bowie explained the situation in an interview he gave to the *New York Times* in June 2002:

> *I don't even know why I would want to be on a label in a few years, because I don't think it's going to work by labels and by distribution systems in the same way....I'm fully confident that copyright, for instance, will no longer exist in 10 years, and authorship and intellectual property is in for such a bashing. Music itself is going to become like running water or electricity, so it's like, just take advantage of these last few years because none of this is ever going to happen again. You'd better be prepared for doing a lot of touring because that's really the only unique situation that's going to be left.*

From one perspective, then, rock in the 21st century sounded much as it had in previous decades. The major acts that had emerged since the 1960s, from the Stones to U2, remained the biggest earners, with Coldplay the only new addition to their ranks. From another perspective, however, the digital revolution had the odd consequence of reviving pre-corporate rock methods of musical consumption. The iPod, a portable music player that enabled people to carry around personal libraries of their favourite tracks in a digital format, made the single song (rather than the album) the focus of personal consumption. Rock festivals, which in Europe in particular came to dominate the way new acts and releases were marketed, resembled the kind of package show—a variety of acts on stage—that the Beatles had once played. Moreover, for new bands such as Arctic Monkeys and Kings of Leon, social networking Web sites were crucial to the way in which audiences could be built from the bottom up, initial enthusiasm spreading by word of mouth rather than by top-down media campaigns. The "local" buzz that has always driven youthful

# iTUNES

Created by Apple in 2001, iTunes was at the forefront of the digital music revolution, providing a free, user-friendly means to play and organize digital music and video files. iTunes was developed as a complete work, with nonstandard interfaces that are independent of the host operating system (OS), inverting the typical hardware/OS/application relationship.

Songs stored on iTunes can be organized across a range of detailed information, allowing the user to search under a variety of headings, including artist, album, song, or genre. It also contains functions that allow the user to create various playlists, create CDs, or listen to songs most recently added to the user's library. Additionally, iTunes plays streaming audio from the Internet, connecting listeners to radio stations around the world.

Compatible with both Mac and PC systems, iTunes is an interface to manage Apple Inc.'s popular iPod (MP3 player) and iPhone. Since its beginnings as a digital music library, iTunes has developed many additional features. For instance, in 2003 Apple launched the iTunes Store, which gave users the ability to purchase and download music from the Internet directly to their iTunes library. Within four years the store had sold more than 3 billion songs, and three years after that (in early 2010) it sold its 10 billionth song. In addition to music, the iTunes Store also offers music videos, television shows, electronic games, podcasts (broadcasts transmitted by and through iPods), and feature-length films for download.

For many years Apple had resisted pressure from various record publishers to abandon the company's single price point of $0.99 per song. In April 2009 Apple gave in and began selling some songs, typically new releases by established artists, for a premium price. At the same time, Apple stopped the restrictive practice of including digital rights management (DRM) software in songs downloaded

*A man walks by an outdoor advertisement for the iPod portable media player by Apple along a street in San Francisco, Calif.* Justin Sullivan/Getty Images

from the iTunes Store. This enabled customers to move purchased songs to any equipment or player that supports Apple's AAC encoding format.

In 2011 Apple introduced iCloud, a cloud computing service, in which music recently purchased in iTunes on one device would be placed automatically in iTunes on a user's other devices. Apple also announced iTunes Match, a service in which users could pay to store their music libraries in iCloud and listen to them on any device. Unlike other cloud computing music services, iTunes Match would construct a user's iCloud library from songs already in the iTunes Store, and thus the user would upload only those songs not available in the iTunes Store.

rock and roll now described a sense of musical excitement with an immediate global resonance. The sites for musical discoveries were Myspace and YouTube rather than radio stations or record stores (the most obvious casualties of the consumer shift from CD to MP3 formats). And it was on the Internet, too, that communities of record collectors and musical cultists flourished; for example, the continued interest in vinyl recordings, as both aesthetic and sonic objects, was fuelled by specialist Web sites.

As a musical form, rock had entered middle age, so it was not surprising that it was as much shaped by nostalgia as by youth. In terms of mass cultural impact, the two most significant pop phenomena of the 21st century seemed to have little to do with digital technology. *Mamma Mia!*, the stage show and film based on ABBA songs, was the first great karaoke musical. It may have been a pop rather than rock show, but its appeal was echoed in the vast number of rock tribute bands that could be found playing around the world. The British television program *Pop Idol*, along with its various national versions (such as *American Idol*), was for many rock fans a dispiriting example of "manufactured" music, but it showed the continuing power of television to orchestrate public enthusiasm and, more particularly,

revealed how the conventions of the rock ballad (to which the winners of such shows around the world almost invariably adhered) had become the taken-for-granted means of emotional expression. Fifty years after rock's birth as an alternative to mainstream pop, mainstream pop had become rock. Whatever now happens to the music industry, it is certain that rock will remain the soundscape for most people's lives.

# ROCK FESTIVALS

By the 21st century, annual rock festivals had become a mainstay of the summer concert season. Such massive logistical undertakings—the coordination of dozens of bands, frequently on multiple stages, over an area that dwarfed a standard concert venue—remained a challenge for even the most experienced promoters. In the late 1960s, when festivals first made their appearance, simply securing the event grounds was often too great a task. Unsurprisingly, a good number of these early festivals (and many since then) ended in financial disaster.

## MONTEREY, WOODSTOCK, AND BEYOND

The 1967 Monterey Pop Festival, held at the fairgrounds where the Monterey Jazz Festival was produced, was the first major rock festival, but its logistics, expense, and commercial failure deterred other American promoters from mounting similar events until the Woodstock Music and Art Fair, held in Bethel, New York, in 1969, became the prototype. Like Woodstock, many of the subsequent festivals were commercial disasters, which kept any single rock festival from becoming an annual event as the jazz festivals had become, and the Rolling Stones' unfortunate show at Altamont Speedway in Livermore, California, in 1969 (at which several people were beaten and one man stabbed to death) did nothing to improve their reputation. Another inhibiting factor was expense: because so many bands went unpaid by promoters, most who would be major attractions at a festival priced themselves out of the market. Only a trusted promoter such as Bill Graham, who presented the Watkins Glen (New York) Festival in 1973, could attract big names. In fact, it was Graham who hit on the most workable formula for a rock festival in the mid-1970s with his "Day on the Green" series at the Oakland (California) Coliseum; it was held in an enclosed area, which made it possible for the promoter to minimize gate crashing and the unauthorized sale of alcohol and drugs.

Of the post-Woodstock festivals, the Atlanta (Georgia) Pop Festival in 1969–70 was perhaps the most important to rock history; it packed the lower end of the bill with local groups and thereby invigorated the Southern rock movement of the 1970s. Rock festivals in the United States tapered off after about 1975, only to be revived in 1991 by Perry Farrell, the leader of the alternative rock group Jane's Addiction, who came up with a very successful formula based on the "Day on the Green" concept. Farrell's touring Lollapalooza event endeavoured to bring underground music to middle America by mixing large- and small-stage performances with political and cultural information booths. Genres represented in the Lollapalooza lineup typically included hip-hop, punk, ska, and shoegaze, although the headlining spot was generally reserved for an alternative or hard rock band that had achieved some degree of mainstream success. Canadian singer-songwriter Sarah McLachlan launched Lilith Fair, the all-women festival that followed the Lollapalooza model, and Ozzy Osbourne collected heavy metal artists under the Ozzfest banner.

Woodstock inspired a pair of anniversary concerts in 1994 and 1999, but neither would have been mistaken for the generation-defining event of 1969. While the 1994 festival offered a lineup of classic and contemporary rock acts at a location near the original Woodstock site, the 1999 event was tied to the original by little more than name. Relocated to a decommissioned air force base in Rome, New York, Woodstock '99 featured none of the bands who had performed in 1969, and its musical achievements were overshadowed by the wave of arson and lawlessness that consumed the event's final night. In spite of this, Woodstock '99, which was attended by more than 200,000 people, demonstrated that fans were willing to travel great distances to experience music in a festival setting. Promoters seized upon this knowledge, and the "destination festival" became a fixture of the North American concert scene.

## DESTINATION FESTIVALS

The fires of Woodstock '99 were still fresh in the minds of observers when the Coachella Valley Music and Arts Festival debuted in Indio, California,

*Day one of the Coachella festival in Indio, California, April 13, 2012.* Kevin Winter/Getty Images

in October 1999. Coachella gathered dozens of artists, boasted multiple main stages, and proved that destination festivals could be safe and financially successful. Other destination festivals were soon created: the Bonnaroo Music and Arts Festival in Manchester, Tennessee, in 2001; a reimagined Lollapalooza in Chicago in 2005; and the Pitchfork Music Festival (originally the Intonation Festival) in Chicago in 2006. South by Southwest (SXSW), an independent music conference launched in Austin, Texas, in 1987, had for all practical purposes become a destination festival by the early 21st century. Originally envisioned as a way to connect emerging artists with industry insiders, SXSW grew into a weeklong event that drew tens of thousands of musicians, journalists, label representatives, and fans.

## FESTIVALS IN EUROPE AND JAPAN

In Europe, destination festivals had been an essential part of the summer scene for decades, and good organization and payment of bands had always been part of the agenda. Every country has its important festivals, and rock bands tour the festival circuit each summer, just as jazz performers have done for years. Most European rock festivals are just star-studded, crowd-pleasing events,

but Denmark's Roskilde Festival and France's Trans Musicales in Rennes, with their balance of big names and developing acts, became important career stepping-stones for international performers, and England's Glastonbury Festival became a cornerstone of the British rock scene for established acts and newcomers alike. England's Reading and Leeds festivals achieved new prominence in the 21st century, and the legendary Isle of Wight Pop Festival was resurrected in 2002. Elsewhere in the world, the Fuji Rock Festival, held in the shadow of Japan's Mount Fuji since 1997, showcased a selection of domestic and international acts.

## WOMAD

WOMAD (World of Music, Arts and Dance) was conceived in 1980 by a group of individuals—most notably Peter Gabriel (former leader of the British rock band Genesis)—who shared a love of the world's music traditions. The group aimed to bring a broad international spectrum of music, arts, and dance to new audiences, and in 1982 the first WOMAD music festival was held in Shepton Mallet, Somerset, England. The event failed to break even, however, and consequently Gabriel reunited with former Genesis bandmates, both to pay off debts and to raise money for the cause. A second event, staged the following year, was somewhat more successful and allowed for the establishment of the nonprofit WOMAD Foundation. While continuing to operate on a shoestring budget, the organization's founders soon realized that one festival a year in the United Kingdom was not going to keep WOMAD afloat.

With a number of countries eager to host the WOMAD festival, regular events were subsequently established in the United Kingdom, Australia, Spain, the United Arab Emirates, and New Zealand. Yet other countries—such as Canada, Greece, Japan, and the United States—held WOMAD festivals on a one-time or intermittent basis. The organization grew steadily, and, within 25 years of its founding, it had hosted more than 150 festivals involving thousands of performers worldwide.

WOMAD festivals typically span an entire weekend and showcase music and dance from many regions of the world. Some performers are seasoned international touring artists with spectacular stage shows, whereas others are local favourites with a palpable connection to the audience. Most groups blend various urban popular styles with elements of traditional music, but some performers present traditional forms adjusted minimally for the international concert stage. Festival attendance varies by the size of the venue and length of the festival. At the annual events in Adelaide, S.Aus., for instance, attendance averaged more than 70,000 in the early 21st century; in New Zealand, by contrast, attendees numbered about 14,000. Aside from music and dance performances, WOMAD festivals feature food and craft vendors and offer assorted workshops and other activities for children. Ultimately, the events are intended to offer a family-friendly entertaining and educational experience to people of all ages.

## SOUTH BY SOUTHWEST

South by Southwest (SXSW) began in 1987 as the South by Southwest Music and Media Conference when a promotion company, South by Southwest, Inc., decided to showcase the eclectic Austin music scene for music industry professionals. SXSW invited these insiders to Austin for the inaugural event, which was attended by 700 people.

The conference grew over the years, and it quickly began to attract international attention. Organizers estimated that more than 12,000 attendees had seen some 2,000 musical acts on more than 80 stages in 2010. Private events and parties, sponsored by record labels, music bloggers, and radio stations, are held throughout Austin as showcases for specific artists. Conference goers also attend workshops and discussions, with topics ranging from band promotion to legal issues to artist talks. A trade show is held concurrently in the Austin Convention Center, and people use the opportunity to network and view new products and technology.

In 1994 the SXSW Film Festival and the SXSW Interactive Festival were added. The expanded festival, dubbed "SXSWeek," is held in March and lasts 10 days. The film portion also presents workshops and discussion panels, as well as a juried festival that presents awards to films in such categories as documentary, music video, and experimental short. SXSW Interactive focuses on presentations and networking opportunities for technology professionals.

## BURNING MAN

Burning Man was inaugurated in 1986, when Larry Harvey and Jerry James—two members of the San Francisco arts community—burned an 8-foot- (2-metre-) tall wooden effigy of a man on San Francisco's Baker Beach in celebration of the summer solstice. Twenty people witnessed the event. Over the next four years Harvey and James (and ever-expanding crowds) returned to the site with increasingly taller effigies. In 1990, however, when a 40-foot- (12-metre-) tall effigy was prepared for immolation at the beach location, the police intervened at the last minute and forbade the structure from being set ablaze. Consequently, the event was moved that year to the Black Rock Desert, where the effigy was burned on the Labor Day weekend, in early September. Once it had relocated, the festival never returned to San Francisco or to the solstice; rather, it made the desert its long-term home and Labor Day its calendrical landmark.

The Burning Man festival expanded dramatically over the next two decades. Its duration was extended to span the entire week preceding Labor Day, with ignition of the effigy regularly scheduled for the Saturday before the holiday. Meanwhile, attendance rose exponentially, exceeding 50,000 by 2010. Each year a temporary city—with named streets, villages, and camps—was erected in the desert to accommodate all of the attendees. After the festival was over, however, the city was completely obliterated, in keeping with the "leave no trace" policy of the festival organizers.

Every Burning Man festival has a unique theme, announced well in advance of the event, and virtually all aspects of the festival reflect that theme. For example, in 2000 the theme was "The Body," and the streets of the city were given names such as "Head Way" and "Feet Street." The many camps and villages within the city are founded on relevant sub-themes and may be organized further around particular foods, sports, learning disciplines, or arts. Throughout the festival's history, a shared love of electronic music has been a common thread for many attendees. Although Burning Man's dedicated "rave" camp was discontinued in 1996, the event continued to be popularly perceived as a sort of desert dance party—a characterization that minimized the harsh realities of existence on the playa. While the festival has no central stage, individual camps are welcome to host musicians of all sorts.

Anyone attending Burning Man is expected to be an active participant, particularly through the installation of art projects or by involvement in one of the camps or villages. Unlike most other festivals, Burning Man is virtually vendor-free. With minimal goods for sale, people are expected to bring with them whatever they need for a week's subsistence in the desert and to trade for any items they might lack. Ultimately, Burning Man is an exercise—indeed, a challenge—in balancing cooperation, self-reliance, individual expression, and creative collaboration in the formation of an artistic community.

## LOLLAPALOOZA

Lollapalooza was begun in 1991 by Jane's Addiction leader Perry Farrell as a multicity venue for his band's farewell tour. Farrell claimed that he chose the festival's name—an archaic word meaning "extraordinarily impressive"—after he heard the word used in a Three Stooges film. Acts that played in that tour, which reached 20 cities across the United States and Canada, included the Rollins Band, Nine Inch Nails, and Ice-T. The events were profitable, so a similar tour was planned for 1992 with a second stage added. The festival again visited many cities across North America, establishing the format of Lollapalooza through 1997. The tour began losing money, however, and it was canceled in 1998. Lollapalooza was revived in 2003, but it continued to struggle financially, and the 2004 tour was also canceled.

Abandoning the show's previous touring model, Farrell found new backers, and Lollapalooza was given a third chance in 2005—this time as a destination festival in Chicago. The two-day format was such a success that a third day was added for 2006, and Lollapalooza became an annual event, with the organizers signing a contract to keep the festival in Chicago at least through 2018.

Held each August in Grant Park, Lollapalooza attracts some 200,000 attendees, including many families. The Kidzapalooza area caters to the youngest fans, with concerts, music workshops, and interactive art exhibits. For adults, side stages offer up-and-coming artists an opportunity to perform for a wider audience, and DJs play a varied selection of electronic music in the festival's dance tent. Headlining acts appear on a staggered schedule, allowing attendees time to travel between stages, as well as minimizing the amount of excess noise, or "sound bleed," that could intrude on a given performance.

In 2011 the Lollapalooza brand expanded to South America, with a two-day festival held in April in Santiago, Chile.

## COACHELLA VALLEY FESTIVAL

The Coachella Valley Music and Arts Festival began in October 1999 as a two-day festival at the Empire Polo Club in Indio, California. Beck and Rage Against the Machine headlined, and more than 25,000 people attended, but the festival failed to make money. It was held just months after the disastrous Woodstock '99, and it was unclear if promoters could turn a profit on a weekend-long multistage event. Coachella's organizers took a year off and then brought the festival back as a one-day event in April 2001. (The change in month was also an effort to avoid high temperatures in the desert heat.) Coachella returned to a two-day format the following April and expanded to a third day in 2010.

Although electronic music tends to be better represented at Coachella than at other festivals, lineups have included the top names in rock, pop, and hip-hop, with a blend of emerging artists and established performers. Organizers remained committed to keeping the festival fresh, and very few acts have made repeat appearances. Headlining artists have included Madonna, Jay-Z, Portishead, and Paul McCartney. High-profile reunions are also a fixture of the festival, with groups such as Pavement, Faith No More, the Specials, and Iggy and the Stooges having taken to the stage for the first time in years.

Aside from experiencing music performances, attendees can view art (especially sculpture) and enjoy food and drink. In 2010 organizers angered some attendees by eliminating single-day tickets in favour of full three-day festival passes. Attendance was not hurt, however, and Coachella set a record by attracting about 75,000 people each day.

## BONNAROO MUSIC AND ARTS FESTIVAL

The first Bonnaroo, organized by veteran music promoter Ashley Capps and held in Manchester, Tennessee, in 2002, attracted about 70,000 visitors. The music and arts festival took its name from the 1974 album *Desitively*

*Bonnaroo* by jazz pianist Dr. John. In the Creole slang of New Orleans, *bonnaroo* means, roughly, "best on the street."

The music performed at the festival is not limited to any locale or genre. At the four-day multistage festival, held on a 700-acre (280-hectare) farm in June, attendees can hear a variety of music—from rock and jazz to hip-hop and world music. Musical guests have included Bonnie Raitt, Bruce Springsteen, Bob Dylan, Jay-Z, Emmylou Harris, Pearl Jam, and Radiohead. Many of the attendees camp at the site, and a children's area is provided by a nonprofit organization that promotes family-friendly activities at rock festivals.

A central area of the festival site, called Centeroo, is open 24 hours a day, offering food and craft vending and other activities. Bonnaroo attendees can also view films, sample specialty beers at the Broo'ers Festival, or dance all night at the Silent Disco. At this unique event, DJs play electronic music until the early morning hours, but nearby campers remain undisturbed, as the party is broadcast directly to wireless headsets worn by attendees.

In 2004 attendance topped 90,000, and ticket sales were later capped at 80,000. In 2007 event organizers bought more than 500 acres (200 hectares) of farmland, and they signed an agreement to lease more than 200 additional acres (80 hectares) for campsites, which ensured that Bonnaroo could continue at the Manchester site.

## PITCHFORK MUSIC FESTIVAL

Pitchfork Media, a Chicago-based Internet publisher of music news and reviews, curated the Intonation Music Festival in 2005. The following year the company organized its own Pitchfork Music Festival. It was held over two days in July at Chicago's Union Park and attracted more than 36,000 fans to hear some 40 bands, including Band of Horses, Yo La Tengo, and Mission of Burma, on two main stages. In 2007 the festival expanded to three days and was attended by some 48,000 visitors. Musical guests have included Animal Collective, Pavement, Modest Mouse, Sonic Youth, Public Enemy, and the Flaming Lips. In 2011 the festival expanded to Paris, with a two-day lineup that was organized by Pitchfork and Bon Iver frontman Justin Vernon.

Activism has gone hand in hand with the Pitchfork Music Festival. In 2008 concertgoers could register to vote, for example, and organizers said that more than 1,200 people did so. In 2010 the organizers purchased carbon credits to offset the traveling the musicians would do to reach the festival. The organizers also encouraged festival attendees to recycle, to utilize greener methods of travel to and from the festival, and to purchase their own carbon offsets.

## POP IDOLS

From the earliest days of rock, "manufactured" talent has been an element of the industry. Girl groups with interchangeable lead singers paved the way for the Monkees, an American answer to the Beatles concocted for the purposes of a television program. Even the Sex Pistols, the symbol of punk rebellion, were created by Malcolm McLaren as a promotional tool for his clothing store. As labels looked for a way to reduce costs in an increasingly competitive market, the use of televised talent shows to discover and promote new artists was quite successful.

## EUROVISION SONG CONTEST

The Eurovision Song Contest, organized by the European Broadcasting Union, gathers performers—selected at the national level by each participating country's public broadcasting service—from across Europe and representing virtually every genre of popular music.

*Finnish heavy metal group Lordi celebrating their win at the 2006 Eurovision Song Contest.* Sean Gallup/Getty Images

First held on May 24, 1956, in Lugano, Switzerland, the contest was one of the earliest attempts to broadcast a live televised event to a large international market. The inaugural proceedings featured solo artists (duos were admitted in 1957, but groups would not be allowed to compete until 1971) from just seven countries. That number would more than double by the time the 1961 contest was held in Cannes, France.

Contestants were originally evaluated by a "jury" of representatives from different countries, who awarded points for each performance. The early 21st century saw the addition of a popular vote that allowed viewers to participate via telephone or text message. In addition to a cash prize, the winner earns widespread recognition; moreover, traditionally, the victor's homeland is accorded the right to host the contest the following year. While an appearance in the competition does not guarantee future commercial success, the Eurovision Song Contest was instrumental in launching the careers of Julio Iglesias (Spain, 1970), ABBA (Sweden, 1974), Céline Dion (Switzerland, 1988), and dancer Michael Flatley, whose intermission performance in 1994 stole the show and launched the global phenomenon known as Riverdance.

Eurovision Song Contest winners are listed in the table in the Appendix.

## PUFFY AMIYUMI

Puffy AmiYumi skyrocketed to stardom in Japan in the mid-1990s and later helped to establish Japanese pop (J-pop) in the Western world. The group's two lead singers—Ami Onuki (born September 18, 1973, Tokyo, Japan) and Yumi Yoshimura (born January 30, 1975, Osaka, Japan)—captured their audiences through their well-blended voices, their intelligent lyrics and novel musical arrangements, and their vibrant, youthful stage presence.

Puffy AmiYumi was formed in 1995 when the Sony Corporation began a talent search for two appealing young women to form a pop duo that would be a hit with schoolgirls. Tokyo native Ami Onuki was selected after she submitted a demo tape in response to an advertisement. Yumi Yoshimura of Osaka was discovered by a talent agency. The two had a unique chemistry from the start, both personally and vocally. Both women credited Okuda Tamio, a respected Japanese singer-songwriter and producer, for mentoring them through the early stages of their joint career. In 1996 they released their first single, "Asia no junshin" ("True Asia"), which was a huge hit throughout Asia. The single was soon followed by their debut album, *AmiYumi*.

Their next five albums expanded their audience and the range of their music. They collaborated with other pop musicians to create a jangly sound that freely melded with other styles, including country, hard rock, and bossa nova. In their first five years, they sold more than 14 million CDs in Japan alone. Their albums *Jet CD* (1998) and *Fever Fever* (1999) were regarded as J-pop classics.

Puffy AmiYumi made its first venture into the North American market in 2001 with the album *Spike*. The band got airtime on college radio stations and appeared at popular alternative music venues in big cities. Five years and three albums later, the group was still tremendously popular in Asia and was picking up momentum in the United States. Puffy AmiYumi also saw its musical popularity translate into success on television and in fashion. The *Pa-Pa-Pa-Pa-Puffy* variety show appeared on Japanese television from 1997 to 2002; the animated series *Hi Hi Puffy AmiYumi* debuted on American cable television in 2004; and the *Hi Hi PUFFY Club* debuted on TV in 2006. The group also had a line of merchandise that included toys, shoes, and clothing.

In 2006 Puffy AmiYumi celebrated a decade of success by kicking off an international concert tour and releasing the album *Splurge*. With what seemed an ever-expanding fan base, the duo subsequently recorded several more albums, including *Hit &*

*Yumi and Ami of Puffy AmiYumi.*

*Fun* (2007); *Honeycreeper* (2007); and *Puffy AmiYumi X Puffy* (2009).

## AMERICAN IDOL

Since its debut on the Fox network in 2002, *American Idol* has become one of the most-watched shows in the United States and has produced numerous imitations. The *American Idol* format was imported from England, where it aired as *Pop Idol* and was the creation of music and television executive Simon Fuller. Both shows follow the same premise: judges travel throughout the country in search of its most talented singer. In the U.S. version a series of auditions narrows the candidates to a top few, who compete against each other on a studio set in Hollywood.

Originally, contestants had to be between 16 and 24 years of age; the age rules were later modified, eventually allowing for performers aged 15 to 28. The early auditions tend to focus on the spectacle offered by tone-deaf contestants warbling before the judges. As the field of candidates narrows, the show becomes a more stylized showcase for talented contestants. The performers sing well-known pieces, which usually correspond to a set theme that can vary from season to season, and celebrity guests routinely make appearances on the show. In the contest's final stages, the home audience—rather than the panel of judges—votes via telephone or text message and decides the winner.

The show's original lineup featured host Ryan Seacrest and a panel of judges that included former pop star Paula Abdul, music producer Randy Jackson, and British music executive Simon Cowell. During the auditions the judges critiqued the performers in a predictable manner: Abdul's comments were typically sympathetic, Jackson's humorous, and Cowell's biting. *American Idol*'s eighth season, which aired in 2009, saw a number of changes to the show's formula, most notably the addition of a fourth judge,

songwriter Kara DioGuardi. Judges were also given the power to directly influence the final rounds of competition with the "judges' save rule," which allowed the panel to override the votes of the viewing public once per season to give a deserving contestant a second chance. In August 2009 Abdul left the show when contract negotiations with *American Idol* producers broke down, and she was replaced by Ellen DeGeneres. At the conclusion of the ninth season, in May 2010, Cowell left the program, and both DeGeneres and DioGuardi also departed later that year. For the 10th season, which aired in 2011, Jennifer Lopez and Aerosmith lead singer Steven Tyler joined Jackson as the show returned to its original three-judge format. In July 2012, Lopez and Tyler announced that they were leaving the show. Following the pair's departure, it was announced that they would be replaced by Mariah Carey, rapper-singer Nicki Minaj, and country musician Keith Urban.

Several winners of the contest became recording sensations, most notably Kelly Clarkson, the winner of season one, and Carrie Underwood, the winner of season four. Other winners included Ruben Studdard, Fantasia Barrino, Taylor Hicks, Jordin Sparks, David Cook, Kris Allen, and Lee DeWyze. Proving that success on the show was not necessarily a prerequisite to success in

# SIMON COWELL

After leaving school at age 16, Simon Cowell (born October 7, 1959, Brighton, East Sussex, England) was hired to work in the mail room at EMI Music Publishing and was eventually given the chance, in 1979, to discover performers to sing newly published songs. In 1985 he and a partner formed Fanfare Records, which enjoyed some success before folding in 1989. Later that year BMG Records hired Cowell as an artist and repertoire consultant. In the process of signing a string of successful acts for BMG, Cowell became a shaping influence in popular music.

Having witnessed the success of the British television series *Popstars* (2000), a reality show built around competing musical acts, Cowell and British music and television producer Simon Fuller developed the show's format a step further by allowing viewers to choose the winners in the final rounds of a new show, *Pop Idol* (2001). The Fox Broadcasting Company imported the show, along with Cowell as judge, to the United States, where it premiered in 2002 as *American Idol*. An immediate hit, it became the highest rated American television show. Its popularity was partly due to Cowell's acerbic put-downs of contestants and, on occasion, of his fellow judges.

In 2006 *The X Factor*, a talent competition cojudged by Cowell and coproduced by his company, Syco Productions, won the award for best entertainment program from the British Academy of Film and Television Arts. That same year he became executive producer of three new American shows—*American Inventor*, a competition that promised a million-dollar manufacturing contract for the winner; *America's Got Talent*, a show open to all types of entertainers; and *Celebrity Duets*, a short-run singing competition between pairings of professional singers and celebrities. Cowell also sold the format of *Duets* to Great Britain's ITV. In 2007 he became executive producer of *Grease Is the Word*, a reality show to find the next stars for the British revival of the musical *Grease*. In May 2010 Cowell left *American Idol* in order to work on a U.S. version of *The X Factor*, which debuted in September 2011.

His autobiography, *I Don't Mean to Be Rude, but…*, was published in 2003.

show business, Jennifer Hudson was voted off in season three but went on to win an Academy Award for her performance in *Dreamgirls* (2006), and Chris Daughtry, a finalist in season five, scored multiplatinum success with his hard rock band Daughtry.

## KELLY CLARKSON

Kelly Clarkson (born April 24, 1982, Fort Worth, Texas, U.S.) grew up in Burleson, Texas, a suburb of Fort Worth, where her vocal prowess was first recognized by her school's choir teacher when she was a seventh grader. Upon finishing high school, Clarkson moved to Los Angeles, where she unsuccessfully tried to break into show business. In 2002, after returning to Texas, she became a contestant on the first season of Fox Broadcasting Company's *American Idol*. Viewers were smitten with Clarkson's arresting voice, charisma, and humour. Her prize for winning

the contest was $1 million and a recording contract with RCA.

Just two weeks after her *American Idol* win, Clarkson released her first single, "A Moment Like This," which quickly achieved platinum status. *Thankful*, her debut album of pop songs, followed in 2003. Her second full-length album, *Breakaway* (2004), which moved beyond Clarkson's initial pop sound into a rock vein, sold more than 11 million copies worldwide and featured the hit singles "Because of You," "Behind These Hazel Eyes," and "Since U Been Gone." The album and "Since U Been Gone" also won Grammy Awards for best pop album and best pop vocal performance, respectively. Clarkson's third album, *My December* (2007), marked a new era in her career; even more rock-oriented than her previous releases, it was also more confessional, revealing a more mature side of the prolific songwriter, who cowrote most of her

*Kelly Clarkson, 2006.* Eric A. Clement/U.S. Navy
(Image Number: 060510-N-1328C-178)

material. Clarkson followed with *All I Ever Wanted* (2009), which featured the hit single "My Life Would Suck Without You," and *Stronger* (2011), which returned to the pop sound of *Breakaway*.

## JENNIFER HUDSON

Jennifer Hudson (born September 12, 1981, Chicago, Illinois, U.S.) began singing at age seven in her Chicago church choir. As a teenager, she performed at wedding receptions and in local talent shows and musical theatre. After graduating (1999) from Chicago's Dunbar Vocational Career Academy, Hudson attended Langston (Oklahoma) University. In 2001 she transferred to Kennedy-King College in Chicago to study music and appeared in a local musical production of *Big River*. Hudson then landed her first professional singing job on a Disney cruise ship as Calliope, the head Greek muse, in a 2003 production of *Hercules: The Musical*. Rather than renew her contract with Disney, Hudson decided to audition for *American Idol*, where she reached the final rounds before being eliminated in seventh place. After fulfilling her obligation to perform with the *American Idol: Season Three* tour during the summer of 2004, Hudson performed at charity events on Broadway and completed a concert tour throughout the Midwest.

During the summer of 2005, Hudson auditioned for *Dreamgirls*, a musical set in the Motown era that documented the rise and fall of a girl group. She beat out more than 780 competitors, including third-season *American Idol* winner Fantasia Barrino, to secure the role. Hudson's powerful performance of the song "And I Am Telling You I'm Not Going" brought audiences to their feet in movie theatres across

*Jennifer Hudson, 2007.* Alexandra Wyman—Wireimage.com/AP Images

the country. Aside from her Academy Award, she received a Golden Globe Award, a Screen Actors Guild Award, the Sammy Davis Jr. Award for entertainer of the year, and a British Academy of Film and Television Arts (BAFTA) Award. Hudson also appeared on the covers of many magazines, notably the March 2007 issue of *Vogue*, known as the annual "power issue." She broke a fashion

barrier as the most full-figured, curvaceous woman ever to have graced the magazine's cover.

In 2008 Hudson released her eponymous debut album and sang the national anthem at the Democratic National Convention at Barack Obama's request. That year she also appeared in the film sequel to the hit HBO show *Sex and the City* and in *The Secret Life of Bees*, alongside Queen Latifah. Despite widespread career success, Hudson's year took a tragic turn when her mother, brother, and nephew were found murdered in Chicago in October. She tearfully paid tribute to them in February 2009, when she accepted the Grammy Award for best rhythm and blues album. In May 2012, a jury returned a guilty verdict against the accused killer.

## CARRIE UNDERWOOD

Carrie Underwood (born March 10, 1983, Muskogee, Oklahoma, U.S.) grew up in Oklahoma, on her family's farm in Checotah. She started singing at a young age, initially at church and later in school plays and talent shows. In 2002 she entered Northeastern State University in Tahlequah, Oklahoma, with intentions to pursue a career in broadcast journalism. Two years later she interrupted her studies to audition for *American Idol*.

Underwood made the cut and ultimately won the competition after being chosen as the favourite by viewers. She received the top prize of a recording contract with 19 Recordings/Arista Records, and the resulting album, *Some Hearts* (2005), was a massive commercial success, selling some six million copies and cementing Underwood's status as one of *American Idol*'s most success-ful alumni. She supported the album with a 150-show tour in 2006, sharing bills with Kenny Chesney and Brad Paisley in addition to headlining her own dates. Underwood made time to return to school, however, and in 2006 she graduated magna cum laude with a B.A. in mass communications from Northeastern State University. That same year she won best new artist and best female country vocal performance at the Grammy Awards.

In April 2007 Underwood returned to *American Idol*, performing a cover of the Pretenders' "I'll Stand by You." Made available as a single on Apple's iTunes service, the song was down-loaded more than 300,000 times and became the first digital-only release to crack the Billboard Top Ten. At the 2007 Country Music Association Awards, Underwood repeated her win as female vocalist of the year and claimed single-of-the-year hon-ours for "Before He Cheats." In 2007 she also released her second album,

*Carnival Ride*, which sold more than half a million copies in its first week of release.

The following year Underwood was inducted as a member of the Grand Ole Opry, joining the ranks of top country music artists such as Garth Brooks, Trisha Yearwood, and Martina McBride. She collected her fourth Grammy Award in February 2009, taking home the trophy for best female country vocal performance—her third win in that category in four years. Two months later Underwood was named entertainer of the year by the Academy of Country Music, becoming the seventh woman to win the award in its four-decade history. In 2010 she won the Grammy Award for best country collaboration for "I Told You So," a cover version of a Randy Travis song that had originally appeared on *Carnival Ride* and that she re-recorded as a duet with Travis. She returned to the studio to record *Blown Away* (2012), an unapologeti-cally pop album that positioned her as the heir apparent to such cross-over giants as Shania Twain.

## SUSAN BOYLE

Susan Boyle (born April 1, 1961, Bangour Village Hospital, West Lothian, Scotland) grew up in Blackburn, a small Scottish industrial town, as the youngest of nine children. Because of complications during her birth, she was briefly deprived of oxygen, which left her with mild brain damage; in school she was diagnosed with learning disabilities, for which she was frequently teased and bullied. Boyle was drawn to music and singing as a young child, and at age 12 she began participating in musical productions at school. Her talent was quickly recognized by her teachers, who encouraged her to persist. After graduating from high school, Boyle worked briefly as a cook trainee at West Lothian College before beginning studies at the Edinburgh Acting School. She continued to cultivate her voice, singing in her church choir, at local karaoke bars, and at the Edinburgh Festival Fringe.

In 1995 Boyle unsuccessfully auditioned for the British TV talent show *My Kind of People*. Four years later her rendition of "Cry Me a River," which had been featured on a local charity CD, received positive reviews. She consequently exhausted her monetary savings to record a professional demo tape, which she mailed to record companies, radio and TV networks, and various talent competitions. Boyle's career ambitions were put on hold in 2000 after her sister died. She resumed with professional singing lessons in 2002 and subsequently produced several recordings for local performances and benefits, but she continued to receive only local fame.

Devastated by the death of her mother in 2007, Boyle completely withdrew from singing for nearly two years. In late 2008, however, she applied to audition for *Britain's Got Talent* to honour the memory of her mother, who had been a fan of the show and had encouraged her to become a contestant. In April 2009 Boyle appeared on an episode of the show, and her rendition of the song "I Dreamed a Dream" from the musical *Les Misérables* immediately silenced the cynicism of both the judges and the audience, earning her a standing ovation. Videos of Boyle's debut on the show (and a later appearance as a semifinalist) were viewed on the Internet by an estimated 100 million people worldwide; she placed second in the final competition. Her first studio album, *I Dreamed a Dream*, debuted at number one on the Billboard charts in November 2009 and was the second best-selling album of 2009, with more than 3.1 million copies sold. She released a second album, *The Gift*, in 2010. The following year *Someone to Watch Over Me* appeared. Boyle's autobiography, *The Woman I Was Born to Be*, was published in 2010.

# Conclusion

How, then, should rock's contribution to music history be judged? One way to answer this is to trace rock's influences on other music. Another is to attempt a kind of cultural audit. (What is the ratio of rock masterworks to rock dross?) But such approaches come up against the problem of definition. Rock does not so much influence other musics as colonize them, blurring musical boundaries. Any attempt to establish an objective rock canon is equally doomed to failure; rock is not this sort of autonomous, rule-bound aesthetic form.

Its cultural value must be approached from a different perspective. The question is not "How has rock influenced society?" but rather "How has it reflected society?" From the musician's point of view, for example, the most important change since the 1950s has been in the division of music-making labour. When Elvis Presley became a star, there were clear distinctions between the work of the performer, the writer, the arranger, the session musician, the record producer, and the sound engineer. By the time Public Enemy was recording, such distinctions had broken down from both ends: performers wrote, arranged, and produced their own material; engineers made as significant a musical contribution as anyone else to the creation of a recorded sound. Technological developments—multitrack tape recorders, amplifiers, synthesizers, and digital equipment—had changed the meaning of musical instruments; there was no longer a clear distinction between producing a sound and reproducing it.

From a listener's point of view, too, the distinction between music and noise changed dramatically in the second half of the 20th century. Music became ubiquitous, whether in public places (an accompaniment to every sort of activity), in the home (with a radio, CD player, or cassette player in every room), or in blurring the distinction between public and private use of music (a Walkman, boom box, or karaoke machine). The development of the compact disc only accelerated the process that makes music from any place and any time permanently available. Listening to music no longer refers to a special place or occasion but, rather, a special attention—a decision to focus on a given sound at a given moment.

Rock is the music that has directly addressed these new conditions and kept faith with the belief that music is a form of human conversation, even as it is mediated by television and radio and by filmmakers and advertisers. The rock commitment to access—to doing mass music for oneself—has survived despite the centralization of production and the ever-increasing costs of manufacture, promotion, and distribution. Rock remains the most democratic of mass media—the only one in which voices from the margins of society can still be heard out loud. Yet, at the beginning of the 21st century, rock and the music industry faced a new crisis. The development of digital technology meant that music could now be stored on easy-to-use digital files, which could in turn be transferred from personal computer to personal computer via the Internet. The resulting legal and corporate disputes about new digital formats such as MP3 and services such as Napster reflected both new commercial opportunities (musical rights holders had visions of making money every time a song was downloaded) and fears (that their songs would be exchanged without any money changing hands at all).

Beginning in late 1999, the Recording Industry Association of America, Bertelsmann AG, and some artists sued Napster, an Internet company whose "peer-to-peer" file-sharing program allowed users to download music for free. Artists lined up on either side of the issue. In the end Bertelsmann became the majority owner of Napster, eager to provide a fee-based service. But this was only the beginning of what became an ongoing process of both trying to prevent the free exchange of digital music (by extending copyright protection and pursuing both "illegal" Internet services and their users through the courts and by the use of different technologies of "digital rights management") and developing new paid downloading systems (such as Napster and iTunes). So far, and despite iTunes' commercial success, the record industry's attempt to halt the development of the Internet as the source of free music has been unsuccessful, and more farsighted entrepreneurs focused instead on the development of new ways to make money out of music rights.

While the issues here are new, the story line is not. Again, an emergent technology has meant new commercial opportunities being explored and developed by fledgling entrepreneurs before being absorbed and reordered by larger corporations, though these are now as likely to be telecommunications or computer companies as they are music companies. Even more striking is how much the new ways of using the Web have drawn on rock practices. The many file-sharing services that followed Napster have similarly involved a global network of home "tapers" and have drawn on the rock ideology of DIY, community, and anti-commerce. Networking sites such as Myspace and YouTube were quickly adopted by rock groups and rock fans whose use of the new promotional possibilities became a model for other entertainment sectors. However the various legal and economic issues are resolved, rock music will certainly be central to 21st-century ways of doing things. Rock, in short, not only reflects (and reflects on) social and cultural change; it is also a social force in its own right.

# Appendix

| EUROVISION SONG CONTEST | |
|---|---|
| **YEAR** | **SONG, SONGWRITER(S) (PERFORMER, COUNTRY)** |
| 1956 | "Refrain," Émile Gardaz, Géo Voumard (Lys Assia, Switzerland) |
| 1957 | "Net als toen," Willy van Hemert, Guus Jansen (Corry Brokken, Netherlands) |
| 1958 | "Dors mon amour," Pierre Delanoë, Hubert Giraud (André Claveau, France) |
| 1959 | "Een beetje," Willy van Hemert, Dick Schallies (Teddy Scholten, Netherlands) |
| 1960 | "Tom Pillibi," Pierre Cour, André Popp (Jacqueline Boyer, France) |
| 1961 | "Nous les amoureux," Jacques Datin, Maurice Vidalin (Jean-Claude Pascal, Luxembourg) |
| 1962 | "Un Premier amour," Rolande Valade, Claude Henri Vic (Isabelle Aubret, France) |
| 1963 | "Dansevise," Sejr Volmer-Sørensen, Otto Francker (Grethe and Jørgen Ingmann, Denmark) |
| 1964 | "Non ho l'età," Nicola Salerno (Gigliola Cinquetti, Italy) |
| 1965 | "Poupée de cire, poupée de son," Serge Gainsbourg (France Gall, Luxembourg) |
| 1966 | "Merci chérie," Udo Jürgens, Thomas Hörbiger (Udo Jürgens, Austria) |
| 1967 | "Puppet on a String," Bill Martin, Phil Coulter (Sandie Shaw, United Kingdom) |
| 1968 | "La, la, la," Ramón Arcusa, Manuel de la Calva (Massiel, Spain) |
| 1969 | "Vivo cantando," Aniano Alcalde, Maria José de Cerato (Salomé, Spain); "Boom Bang-a-Bang," Peter Warne, Alan Moorhouse (Lulu, United Kingdom); "De troubadour," Lenny Kuhr, David Hartsena (Lenny Kuhr, Netherlands); "Un Jour, un enfant," Eddy Marnay, Emile Stern (Frida Boccara, France) (four-way tie) |
| 1970 | "All Kinds of Everything," Derry Lindsay, Jackie Smith (Dana, Ireland) |

| EUROVISION SONG CONTEST | |
| --- | --- |
| **YEAR** | **SONG, SONGWRITER(S) (PERFORMER, COUNTRY)** |
| 1971 | "Un Banc, un arbre, une rue," Yves Dessca, Jean-Pierre Bourtayre (Séverine, Monaco) |
| 1972 | "Après toi," Klaus Munro, Yves Dessca, Mario Panas (Vicky Leandros, Luxembourg) |
| 1973 | "Tu te reconnaîtras," Vlinc Buggy, Claude Morgan (Anne-Marie David, Luxembourg) |
| 1974 | "Waterloo," Stikkan Anderson, Benny Andersson, Björn Ulvaeus (ABBA, Sweden) |
| 1975 | "Ding-a-Dong," Will Luikinga, Eddy Ouwens, Dick Bakker (Teach-In, Netherlands) |
| 1976 | "Save Your Kisses for Me," Tony Hiller, Lee Sheriden, Martin Lee (Brotherhood of Man, United Kingdom) |
| 1977 | "L'Oiseau et l'enfant," José Gracy, Jean-Paul Cara (Marie Myriam, France) |
| 1978 | "A-Ba-Ni-Bi," Ehud Manor, Nurit Hirsh (Izhar Cohen and the Alphabeta, Israel) |
| 1979 | "Hallelujah," Shimrit Orr, Kobi Oshrat (Gali Atari and Milk and Honey, Israel) |
| 1980 | "What's Another Year," Shay Healy (Johnny Logan, Ireland) |
| 1981 | "Making Your Mind Up," Andy Hill, John Danter (Bucks Fizz, United Kingdom) |
| 1982 | "Ein bisschen Frieden," Bernd Meinunger, Ralph Siegel (Nicole, West Germany) |
| 1983 | "Si la vie est cadeau," Alain Garcia, Jean-Pierre Millers (Corinne Hermès, Luxembourg) |
| 1984 | "Diggi-loo diggi-ley," Britt Lindeborg, Torgny Söderberg (Herrey's, Sweden) |
| 1985 | "La det swinge," Rolf Løvland (Bobbysocks, Norway) |
| 1986 | "J'aime la vie," Marino Atria, Jean-Pierre Furnémont, Angelo Crisci (Sandra Kim, Belgium) |
| 1987 | "Hold Me Now," Sean Sherrard (Johnny Logan, Ireland) |
| 1988 | "Ne partez pas sans moi," Nella Martinetti, Atilla Sereftug (Céline Dion, Switzerland) |
| 1989 | "Rock Me," Stevo Cvikich, Rajko Dujmich (Riva, Yugoslavia) |
| 1990 | "Insieme: 1992," Toto Cutugno (Toto Cutugno, Italy) |

| EUROVISION SONG CONTEST | |
|---|---|
| **YEAR** | **SONG, SONGWRITER(S) (PERFORMER, COUNTRY)** |
| 1991 | "Fångad av en stormvind," Stephan Berg (Carola, Sweden) |
| 1992 | "Why Me," Sean Sherrard (Linda Martin, Ireland) |
| 1993 | "In Your Eyes," Jimmy Walsh (Niamh Kavanagh, Ireland) |
| 1994 | "Rock 'n' Roll Kids," Brendan Graham (Paul Harrington and Charlie McGettigan, Ireland) |
| 1995 | "Nocturne," Petter Skavlan, Rolf Løvland (Secret Garden, Norway) |
| 1996 | "The Voice," Brendan Graham (Eimear Quinn, Ireland) |
| 1997 | "Love Shine a Light," Kimberley Rew (Katrina and the Waves, United Kingdom) |
| 1998 | "Diva," Yoav Ginay (Dana International, Israel) |
| 1999 | "Take Me to Your Heaven," Gert Lengstrand (Charlotte Nilsson, Sweden) |
| 2000 | "Fly on the Wings of Love," Jørgen Olsen (Olsen Brothers, Denmark) |
| 2001 | "Everybody," Maian-Anna Kärmas, Ivar Must (Tanel Padar, Dave Benton, and 2XL, Estonia) |
| 2002 | "I Wanna," Marija Naumova, Marats Samauskis (Marie N, Latvia) |
| 2003 | "Every Way That I Can," Demir Demirkan, Sertab Erener (Sertab Erener, Turkey) |
| 2004 | "Wild Dances," Ruslana Lyzhichko, Aleksandr Ksenofontov (Ruslana, Ukraine) |
| 2005 | "My Number One," Christos Dantis, Natalia Germanou (Helena Paparizou, Greece) |
| 2006 | "Hard Rock Hallelujah," LORDI (LORDI, Finland) |
| 2007 | "Molitva," Sasa Milosevic Mare (Marija Serifovic, Serbia) |
| 2008 | "Believe," Dima Bilan, Jim Beanz (Dima Bilan, Russia) |
| 2009 | "Fairytale," Alexander Rybak (Alexander Rybak, Norway) |
| 2010 | "Satellite," Julie Frost, John Gordon (Lena, Germany) |
| 2011 | "Running Scared," Stefan Örn, Sandra Bjurman, Iain Farquharson (Ell/Nikki, Azerbaijan) |
| 2012 | "Euphoria," Thomas G:son, Peter Boström (Loreen, Sweden) |

## ROCK AND ROLL HALL OF FAME

### NAME (YEAR OF INDUCTION)

| | |
|---|---|
| ABBA (2010) | David Bowie (1996) |
| AC/DC (2003) | Charles Brown[3] (1999) |
| Paul Ackerman[1] (1995) | James Brown (1986) |
| Aerosmith (2001) | Ruth Brown (1993) |
| Alice Cooper (2011) | Jackson Browne (2004) |
| The Allman Brothers Band (1995) | Buffalo Springfield (1997) |
| Herb Alpert and Jerry Moss[2] (2006) | Solomon Burke (2001) |
| The Animals (1994) | James Burton[4] (2001) |
| Louis Armstrong[3] (1990) | The Byrds (1991) |
| Chet Atkins[4] (2002) | Johnny Cash (1992) |
| LaVern Baker (1991) | Ray Charles (1986) |
| Hank Ballard (1990) | Leonard Chess[1] (1987) |
| The Band (1994) | Charlie Christian[3] (1990) |
| Dave Bartholomew[1] (1991) | Eric Clapton (2000) |
| Frank Barsalona[2] (2005) | Dick Clark[1] (1993) |
| Ralph Bass[1] (1991) | The Clash (2003) |
| The Beach Boys (1988) | Jimmy Cliff (2010) |
| Beastie Boys (2012) | The Coasters (1987) |
| The Beatles (1988) | Eddie Cochran (1987) |
| Jeff Beck (2009) | Leonard Cohen (2008) |
| The Bee Gees (1997) | Nat King Cole[3] (2000) |
| Benny Benjamin[4] (2003) | The Comets (2012) |
| Chuck Berry (1986) | Sam Cooke (1986) |
| Bill Black[4] (2009) | Elvis Costello and the Attractions (2003) |
| Otis Blackwell[1] (2010) | Floyd Cramer[4] (2003) |
| Black Sabbath (2006) | Cream (1993) |
| Chris Blackwell[1] (2001) | Creedence Clearwater Revival (1993) |
| Hal Blaine[4] (2000) | The Crickets (2012) |
| Bobby "Blue" Bland (1992) | Crosby, Stills and Nash (1997) |
| Blondie (2006) | Bobby Darin (1990) |
| The Blue Caps (2012) | The Dave Clark Five (2008) |
| Booker T. and the MG's (1992) | Clive Davis[1] (2000) |

| ROCK AND ROLL HALL OF FAME | |
|---|---|
| **NAME (YEAR OF INDUCTION)** | |
| Miles Davis (2006) | Marvin Gaye (1987) |
| The Dells (2004) | David Geffen[1] (2010) |
| Neil Diamond (2011) | Genesis (2010) |
| Bo Diddley (1987) | Gerry Goffin and Carole King[1] (1990) |
| Dion (1989) | Berry Gordy, Jr.[1] (1988) |
| Willie Dixon[3] (1994) | Bill Graham[1] (1992) |
| Dr. John (2011) | Grandmaster Flash and the Furious Five (2007) |
| Fats Domino (1986) | Grateful Dead (1994) |
| Tom Donahue[1] (1996) | Al Green (1995) |
| Donovan (2012) | Ellie Greenwich and Jeff Barry[1] (2010) |
| The Doors (1993) | Guns N' Roses (2012) |
| Steve Douglas[4] (2003) | Woody Guthrie[3] (1988) |
| Tom Dowd[4] (2003) | Buddy Guy (2005) |
| The Drifters (1988) | Bill Haley (1987) |
| Bob Dylan (1988) | John Hammond[2] (1986) |
| Earth, Wind and Fire (2000) | George Harrison (2004) |
| Duane Eddy (1994) | Isaac Hayes (2002) |
| Ahmet Ertegun[1] (1987) | The Jimi Hendrix Experience (1992) |
| Nesuhi Ertegun[2] (1991) | Billie Holiday[3] (2000) |
| The Everly Brothers (1986) | Holland, Dozier, and Holland[1] (1990) |
| The Famous Flames (2012) | The Hollies (2010) |
| Leo Fender[1] (1992) | Buddy Holly (1986) |
| The Flamingos (2001) | Jac Holzman[1] (2011) |
| Fleetwood Mac (1998) | John Lee Hooker (1991) |
| D.J. Fontana[4] (2009) | Howlin' Wolf[3] (1991) |
| The Four Seasons (1990) | The Impressions (1991) |
| The Four Tops (1990) | The Ink Spots[3] (1989) |
| Aretha Franklin (1987) | The Isley Brothers (1992) |
| Alan Freed[1] (1986) | Mahalia Jackson[3] (1997) |
| Milt Gabler[1] (1993) | Michael Jackson (2001) |
| Kenny Gamble and Leon Huff[1] (2008) | Wanda Jackson[3] (2009) |

## ROCK AND ROLL HALL OF FAME

### NAME (YEAR OF INDUCTION)

| | |
|---|---|
| The Jackson 5 (1997) | Lynyrd Skynyrd (2006) |
| James Jamerson[4] (2000) | Madonna (2008) |
| Elmore James[3] (1992) | The Mamas and the Papas (1998) |
| Etta James (1993) | Barry Mann and Cynthia Weil[1] (2010) |
| Jefferson Airplane (1996) | Bob Marley (1994) |
| Billy Joel (1999) | Martha and the Vandellas (1995) |
| Elton John (1994) | George Martin[1] (1999) |
| Little Willie John (1996) | Cosimo Matassa[4] (2012) |
| Glyn Johns[4] (2012) | Curtis Mayfield (1999) |
| Johnnie Johnson[4] (2001) | Paul McCartney (1999) |
| Robert Johnson[3] (1986) | Clyde McPhatter (1987) |
| Janis Joplin (1995) | John Mellencamp (2008) |
| Louis Jordan[3] (1987) | Metallica (2009) |
| B.B. King (1987) | The Midnighters (2012) |
| Freddie King[3] (2012) | The Miracles (2012) |
| King Curtis[4] (2000) | Joni Mitchell (1997) |
| The Kinks (1990) | Bill Monroe[3] (1997) |
| Don Kirshner[1] (2012) | The Moonglows (2000) |
| Gladys Knight and the Pips (1996) | Scotty Moore[4] (2000) |
| Leadbelly[3] (1988) | Van Morrison (1993) |
| Led Zeppelin (1995) | Jelly Roll Morton[3] (1998) |
| Brenda Lee (2002) | Syd Nathan[1] (1997) |
| Jerry Leiber and Mike Stoller[1] (1987) | Ricky Nelson (1987) |
| John Lennon (1994) | Laura Nyro (2012) |
| Jerry Lee Lewis (1986) | The O'Jays (2005) |
| Little Anthony and the Imperials (2009) | Spooner Oldham[4] (2009) |
| Little Richard (1986) | Roy Orbison (1987) |
| Little Walter (2008) | The Orioles[3] (1995) |
| Darlene Love (2011) | Mo Ostin[1] (2003) |
| The Lovin' Spoonful (2000) | Johnny Otis[1] (1994) |
| Frankie Lymon and the Teenagers (1993) | Earl Palmer[4] (2000) |

| ROCK AND ROLL HALL OF FAME | |
|---|---|
| NAME (YEAR OF INDUCTION) | |
| Parliament-Funkadelic (1997) | Leon Russell[4] (2011) |
| Les Paul[3] (1988) | Sam and Dave (1992) |
| Carl Perkins (1987) | Santana (1998) |
| Tom Petty and the Heartbreakers (2002) | Pete Seeger[3] (1996) |
| Sam Phillips[1] (1986) | Bob Seger (2004) |
| Wilson Pickett (1991) | The Sex Pistols (2006) |
| Pink Floyd (1996) | Del Shannon (1999) |
| Gene Pitney (2002) | The Shirelles (1996) |
| The Platters (1990) | Mort Shuman[1] (2010) |
| The Police (2003) | Paul Simon (2001) |
| Doc Pomus[1] (1992) | Simon & Garfunkel (1990) |
| Elvis Presley (1986) | Percy Sledge (2005) |
| The Pretenders (2005) | Sly and the Family Stone (1993) |
| Lloyd Price (1998) | The Small Faces/Faces (2012) |
| Prince (2004) | Bessie Smith[3] (1989) |
| Professor Longhair[3] (1992) | Patti Smith (2007) |
| Queen (2001) | The Soul Stirrers[3] (1989) |
| Ma Rainey[3] (1990) | Phil Spector[1] (1989) |
| Bonnie Raitt (2000) | Dusty Springfield (1999) |
| The Ramones (2002) | Bruce Springsteen (1999) |
| Red Hot Chili Peppers (2012) | The Staple Singers (1999) |
| Otis Redding (1989) | Steely Dan (2001) |
| Jimmy Reed (1991) | Jesse Stone[1] (2010) |
| R.E.M. (2007) | Seymour Stein[2] (2005) |
| The Righteous Brothers (2003) | Jim Stewart[1] (2002) |
| Smokey Robinson (1987) | Rod Stewart (1994) |
| Jimmie Rodgers[3] (1986) | The Stooges (2010) |
| The Rolling Stones (1989) | The Supremes (1988) |
| The Ronettes (2007) | Talking Heads (2002) |
| Run-D.M.C. (2009) | James Taylor (2000) |
| Art Rupe[1] (2011) | The Temptations (1989) |

| ROCK AND ROLL HALL OF FAME | |
|---|---|
| **NAME (YEAR OF INDUCTION)** | |
| Allen Toussaint[1] (1998) | Jann S. Wenner[2] (2004) |
| Traffic (2004) | Jerry Wexler[1] (1987) |
| Big Joe Turner (1987) | The Who (1990) |
| Ike and Tina Turner (1991) | Hank Williams[3] (1987) |
| U2 (2005) | Bob Wills and His Texas Playboys[3] (1999) |
| Ritchie Valens (2001) | Jackie Wilson (1987) |
| Van Halen (2007) | Bobby Womack (2009) |
| The Velvet Underground (1996) | Stevie Wonder (1989) |
| The Ventures (2008) | Jimmy Yancey[3] (1986) |
| Gene Vincent (1998) | The Yardbirds (1992) |
| Tom Waits (2011) | Neil Young (1995) |
| T-Bone Walker[3] (1987) | The (Young) Rascals (1997) |
| Dinah Washington[3] (1993) | Frank Zappa (1995) |
| Muddy Waters (1987) | ZZ Top (2004) |
| 1 Ahmet Ertegun Award (nonperformers).<br>2 Lifetime Achievement.<br>3 Early Influences.<br>4 Sideman. | |

# Glossary

**agitprop** Short for agitation-propaganda, a political strategy in which the techniques of both are used to influence and mobilize public opinion.

**anthem** A usually rousing popular song that typifies or is identified with a particular subculture, movement, or point of view.

**Auto-Tune** An audio processor that can alter the pitch of the human voice.

**baritone** (From Greek *barytonos*, "deep-sounding"), in vocal music, the most common category of male voice, between the bass and the tenor and with some characteristics of both.

**bombastic** Pompous, overblown.

**braggadocio** Boasting; cockiness.

**broadside** Volley of abuse or denunciation.

**cognoscenti** People who have expert knowledge in a subject; connoisseurs.

**conjunto** Kind of Mexican-American music that has been influenced by the music of German immigrants to Texas and that features the accordion in addition to Mexican elements.

**cover** The rerecorded version of a song or record.

**cow-punk** Musical sub-genre combining the elements of punk rock, country music, and the blues. Examples include Los Lobos and the Old '97s.

**crossover** A broadening of the popular appeal of an artist (as a musician) that is often the result of a change of the artist's medium or style; also, an artist or artistic work that has achieved a crossover.

**cumbia** Played on drums, flutes, and percussive instruments, Colombia's traditional cumbia music, which is popular throughout Central and South America, dates back to Colombia's colonial period.

**d'eux and d'elles** French words meaning from or about them. D'eux is the masculine form; d'elles is the feminine form.

**dissonant** Marked by or producing a harsh combination of sounds.

**dramedy** A comedy (as a film or television show) having dramatic moments.

**dream pop** Post-punk alternative rock subgenre known for its ethereal, breathy sound.

**dross** Discarded or useless material.

**elegy** Song or poem expressing sorrow or lamentation especially for one who is dead.

**eponymous** Named after a particular person or musical group; self-titled.

**ethnomusicologist** One who studies music that is outside the European art tradition.

**eulogy** Formal expression of praise of someone or something (as of the character and services of a deceased person).

**exurban** Region or settlement that lies outside a city and usually beyond its suburbs that often is inhabited chiefly by well-to-do families.

**falsetto** An artificially high singing voice.

**fashion-forward** Innovative and hip in clothing choices.

**goth rock** Rock music marked by dark and morbid lyrics.

**griot** A traditional West African troubadour-historian.

**hirsute** Hairy.

**Hopelandic** Invented "language" created by band Sigur Rós that is not really a language, but rather is one that allows the band's vocalist, Jón Bór Birgisson, to fill the sonic space where words would usually be sung.

**id** According to Austrian neurologist Sigmund Freud (1856 – 1939), there are three components of the human personality: id, ego, and superego. The id is the instinctual part of the personality and contains all the basic drives and emotions that come from the animal nature in humans.

**ingénue** Naïve girl or young woman.

**jury-rig** To erect, construct, or arrange in a makeshift fashion.

**laconic** Curt; terse; undemonstrative.

**manqué** Short of or frustrated in the fulfilment of one's aspirations or talents; a wannabe.

**mazurka** Polish folk dance for a circle of couples, characterized by stamping feet and clicking heels and traditionally danced to the music of bagpipes.

**Mercury Prize** Annual music prize awarded for the best album from the United Kingdom and Ireland.

**metronomic** Mechanically regular (as in tempo).

**moniker** Nickname.

**Neilsen SoundScan** Used throughout the United States and Canada, a system that allows subscribers to access data regarding music sales.

**paean** Tribute.

**pastiche** A creative work that adapts material or styles from a number of different sources to create a unique whole.

**patois** Dialect other than the standard or literary dialect.

**Pentecostal** Any of various Christian religious bodies that emphasize individual experiences of grace, spiritual gifts (such as speaking in tongues and faith healing), expressive worship, and evangelism.

**playa** Flat-floored bottom of an undrained desert basin that becomes at times a shallow lake.

**polka** Lively courtship dance of Bohemian folk origin characterized by three quick steps and a hop.

**posse** Entourage.

**Quebecois** French-speaking person from Quebec.

**ranchero** Also known as ranchera, a genre of traditional Mexican music originally performed by a single vocalist/guitarist.

**rave** Large overnight dance party featuring techno music and usually involving the taking of mind-altering drugs.

**reductio ad absurdum** Latin for "reduction to absurdity," in logic, a form of argument showing absurd consequences following the argument's denial, thus concluding that as the denial is untenable, the thesis must be sound.

**retronuevo** Combining elements of the past and the present. (*Nuevo* is Spanish for "new.")

**sea shanty** Song sung by sailors in rhythm with their work. Also knows as a sea chantey.

**secondary school** In Ireland, secondary school is essentially equivalent to middle (or junior high) school and high school combined.

**shoegaze** Louder, more aggressive style of dream pop.

**ska** Jamaica's first indigenous urban pop style.

**slacker** A person (especially a young person) who is perceived as being disaffected, apathetic, cynical, or lacking ambition.

**syncretic** Formed of two or more (often contradictory) beliefs.

**techno** Electronic dance music that first appeared in the U.S. in the 1980s and became globally popular in the '90s.

**theremin** Electronic musical instrument typically played by moving the right hand between two projecting electrodes with the left hand controlling dynamics and articulation.

**trip-hop** Genre of atmospheric down-tempo music influenced by movie soundtracks, 1970s funk, and cool jazz, and usually created using samples.

**Tropicália** Brazilian artistic move-ment of the late 1960s, the musical portion of which is characterized as blending Brazilian music, African rhythms, and rock and roll.

**upmarket** Upscale.

**waltz** Music for a waltz (a ballroom dance in ¾ time with strong accent on the first beat and a basic pattern of step-step-close).

**without portfolio** A politician without portfolio is one who operates without specific responsibilities or assignment.

**zaftig** Pleasingly plump.

# Bibliography

## MADONNA

Christopher Andersen, *Madonna, Unauthorized* (1991); and Mark Bego, *Madonna: Blonde Ambition* (1992), are biographies. Matthew Rettenmund, *Encyclopedia Madonnica* (1995), offers an irreverent but exhaustive treatment of the singer. J. Randy Taraborrelli, *Madonna: An Intimate Biography* (2002), glosses her music and film careers but explores her personal life in expansive detail.

## PRINCE

The most useful biography is Liz Jones, *Purple Reign: The Artist Formerly Known as Prince* (1998). Jon Bream, *Prince: Inside the Purple Reign* (1984), is an insightful study by a critic from Minneapolis who observed Prince's rise firsthand. Two other books illuminate his work and impact during the 1980s: Dave Hill, *Prince: A Pop Life* (1989); and John W. Duffy, *Prince: An Illustrated Biography* (1992). Robert Walser, "Prince as Queer Poststructuralist," *Popular Music and Society*, 18(2):79–89 (Summer 1994), is a more academic treatment of certain aspects of Prince's career. Jason Draper, *Prince: Chaos, Disorder, and Revolution* (2011), covers Prince's later career.

## U2

Bill Flanagan, *U2 at the End of the World* (1995), is an insightful, if frequently meandering, critical overview. Greg Garrett, *We Get to Carry Each Other: The Gospel According to U2* (2009), explores the band's spirituality and its influence on their work. U2 and Neil McCormick, *U2 by U2* (2009), utilizes firsthand accounts to present the most complete biography of the band.

## R.E.M.

Robert Christgau, *Christgau's Record Guide: The '80s* (1990), provides provocative discussions of R.E.M.'s albums from *Chronic Town* ("every so often a chaotic undertow suggests there's more to their romanticism than Spanish moss") to *Green*. Christgau struggles with the lack of literary specificity in the band's lyrics, promotes some understanding of their Southern origins, slightly underrates *Fables of the Reconstruction* while noting that the album "clinches it: their formal frame of reference is folk-rock," and uses the crucial word to explain R.E.M.'s appeal for a certain sort of rock-based fan and commentator: "reassuring." Patricia Romanowski, Holly George-Warren, and Jon Pareles (eds.), *The New Rolling Stone Encyclopedia of Rock & Roll*, revised and updated ed. (1995), pp. 826–827, presents a focused and informed narrative of the band's formation, development, and recording history through the *Monster* album. Mike Mills, "Our Town," in Clinton Heylin (ed.), *The Penguin Book of Rock & Roll Writing* (1992), pp. 401–408, is an essay about Athens written in 1985 by R.E.M.'s bassist. The first sentence—"When you mention 'the Athens scene' to anyone who's been here for four or five years, they get weird"—accurately establishes both the tone and ambition of the piece. Johnny Black, *Reveal: The Story of R.E.M.* (2004), uses firsthand accounts to relate the stories behind the band and some of its most memorable songs.

## ALTERNATIVE ROCK

Eric Weisbard, "Introduction: What Is Alternative Rock?," in Eric Weisbard and Craig Marks (eds.), *Spin Alternative Record Guide* (1995), pp. vii–xii, discusses bands before, during, and after the alternative moment, with special emphasis on marginal and college-era practitioners; the essay also emphasizes "alternative sensibilities." Alan Cross, *The Alternative Music Almanac* (1995); and Pat Blashill and Michael Lavine, *Noise from the Underground* (1996), cover the history of alternative music. Michael Azerrad, *Our Band Could Be Your Life: Scenes from the American Indie Underground 1981–1991* (2001), surveys the significant bands of the postpunk and early alternative rock era. Jim Walsh, *The Replacements: All Over but the Shouting: An Oral History* (2007), relates the story of one of the genre's seminal bands. Sara Marcus, *Girls to the Front: The True Story of the Riot Grrrl Revolution* (2010), chronicles the growth of the riot grrrl movement in the Pacific Northwest.

## NIRVANA AND GRUNGE

Michael Azerrad, *Come As You Are: The Story of Nirvana* (1993), includes a discography. Justin Henderson, *Grunge Seattle* (2010) explores the Seattle scene and profiles the personalities that gave rise to the grunge movement. Greg Prato, *Grunge Is Dead: The Oral History of Seattle Rock Music* (2009) features more than 100 interviews with formative grunge artists and people who were involved with the scene.

## WILCO

Greg Kot, *Wilco: Learning How to Die* (2004); and Dan Nadel and Peter Buchanan-Smith (eds.), *The Wilco Book* (2004), provide comprehensive coverage of the band up to 2004.

## HIP-HOP

David Toop, *Rap Attack 3: African Rap to Global Hip Hop* (1999), is probably the book most successful at revealing hip-hop's debts to earlier forms of African American popular music. In answer to the question of whether hip-hop lyrics are a form of poetry, Lawrence A. Stanley (ed.), *Rap: The Lyrics* (1992), allows readers to make up their own minds by presenting the writings of hip-hop's greatest lyricists. Tricia Rose, *Black Noise: Rap Music and Black Culture in Contemporary America* (1994), argues that technology, urban sociology, race politics, and feminism have intersected in hip-hop to foment a hotbed of postmodern artistry and controversy. Nelson George, *Hip Hop America* (1998), presents a serious fan's view of the long road

hip-hop took from street fests to mainstream market profitability and semirespectability. Dan Charnas, *The Big Payback: The History of the Business of Hip-Hop* (2011), examines the corporate history of hip-hop, from the earliest amateur releases to the rise of entrepreneurs such as Diddy and Jay-Z. Havelock Nelson and Michael A. Gonzales, *Bring the Noise: A Guide to Rap Music and Hip-Hop Culture* (1991), is a detailed introduction to the history of rap and a guide to the best recordings. Alan Light (ed.), *The* Vibe *History of Hip Hop* (1999), explores the full scope of hip-hop's origins and expansion with contributions from more than 50 writers; Jeff Chang, *Can't Stop, Won't Stop: A History of the Hip-Hop Generation* (2005), examines the sociocultural and musical history of the genre; Murray Forman and Mark Anthony Neal (eds.), *That's the Joint!: The Hip-Hop Studies Reader* (2004), is a wide-ranging anthology of writings from both the academic and popular press; Sacha Jenkins, Elliott Wilson, Chairman Mao, Gabriel Alvarez, and Brent Rollins, *Ego Trip's Book of Rap Lists* (1999), is humorous and opinionated but dense with information and true to the spirit of the culture.

## HOUSE

Matthew Collin, *Altered State: The Story of Ecstasy Culture and Acid*

*House* (1997), is an authoritative history of British house and rave culture that focuses on the drug MDMA: its influence on the music, its illegality and dangers, and its diffusion from a late 1980s criminal subculture into the mainstream of 1990s British life. Simon Reynolds, "The End of Music," in his *Blissed Out: The Raptures of Rock* (1990), pp. 167–186, celebrates house music for its psychedelic, avant-garde qualities and as posthumanist black pop music that breaks with the concept of soul, and his *Generation Ecstasy: Into the World of Techno and Rave Culture* (1998), a critical history of house and techno from 1980 to the late 1990s, deals with recreational drug culture and the sociological ramifications of the rave scene, with more emphasis on the music itself than *Altered State*. Steve Redhead (ed.), *Rave Off: Politics and Deviance in Contemporary Youth Culture* (1993), includes two standout essays: Antonio Melechi, "The Ecstasy of Disappearance," pp. 29–40, which uses the historical origins of Britain's acid house scene in the nightclubs of the Mediterranean vacation island Ibiza as the basis for a theory of rave culture as a form of "internal tourism;" and Hillegonda Rietveld, "Living the Dream," pp. 41–78. Sarah Thornton, *Club Cultures: Music, Media, and Subcultural Capital* (1995), a sociological study of British

club and rave culture using the Pierre Bourdieu-inspired notions of "subcultural capital," explores the struggles of underground scenes to avoid being co-opted by the mainstream; while the analysis of the media panic over British acid house is provocative, the music itself is neglected. Chris Kempster (compiler and ed.), *History of House* (1996), a collection of articles from the musician's magazine *The Mix*, concentrates on the working methods of leading producers and house music's technical underpinnings.

## TECHNO

David Toop, *Ocean of Sound: Aether Talk, Ambient Sound, and Imaginary Worlds* (1995), is a loosely structured but provocative and often poetic exploration of the tangled roots of ambient music, discussing the work of many prime movers in electronica, the home-listening offshoot of techno. Steve Redhead, Derek Wynne, and Justin O'Connor (eds.), *The Clubcultures Reader: Readings in Popular Cultural Studies* (1997), compiles useful articles written by music journalists and academics from the cultural studies field on all aspects of club and rave culture. Matthew Collin, *Altered State: The Story of Ecstasy Culture and Acid House* (1997), is an authoritative history of British rave culture from acid house to jungle focusing on the drug ecstasy: its influence on the music's development and its diffusion from late 1980s criminal subcultures into the mainstream of British life in the 1990s. Simon Reynolds, *Generation Ecstasy: Into the World of Techno and Rave Culture* (1998), a critical history of techno and offshoots such as jungle, gabba, electronica, and trance, deals with recreational drug culture and the rave scene's sociological ramifications but emphasizes the music itself more than *Altered State* does.

# INDUSTRIAL MUSIC

*Industrial Culture Handbook* (1983) contains articles about industrial obsessions such as warfare, crime, and gore films, as well as interviews with industrial musicians including Throbbing Gristle, SPK, and Cabaret Voltaire and extensive discographies, bibliographies, and filmographies. Dave Thompson, *The Industrial Revolution* (1992) is an indispensible treatment of the genre.

# Index